CW00801355

DISASTERS AT SEA

Disasters at Sea

TITANIC TO EXXON VALDEZ

Captain Richard A. Cahill

Century
London Sydney Auckland Johannesburg

Published in Great Britain in 1990 by Century
An imprint of Random Century Ltd
20 Vauxhall Bridge Road, London SW1V 2SA

Century Hutchinson Australia (Pty) Ltd
20 Alfred Street, Milsons Point, Sydney, NSW 2061, Australia

Century Hutchinson New Zealand Ltd
PO Box 40–086, 32–34 View Road, Glenfield, Auckland 10, New Zealand

Century Hutchinson South Africa (Pty) Ltd
PO Box 337, Bergvlei 2012, South Africa

Set in 11pt Linotron Baskerville

Printed and bound in Great Britain by
Mackays of Chatham, Chatham, Kent

British Library Cataloguing in Publication data

Cahill, Richard A.
Disasters at sea.
1. Shipwrecks, history
I. Title
910.45

ISBN 0-7126-3814-8

Unsaid

'She's your command, skipper,' the company says to me,
For better or worse, you're the boss of this hearse
As soon as she puts to sea.

Use your own judgement, skipper – hold her well off the coast
Keep a true log – heave to in the fog
Safety first is our boast.'

Slave to a berth and tradition, I listen and bow my head,
But the orders I hear with my inner ear
Are the ones that are left unsaid.

'The hooker's insured, skipper – get her out and in.
Our sailing dates and cargo rates
Mean twelve knots – thick or thin.

From here to there is our motto. To hell with the wind and the tide.
You make these joints by cuttin' the points –
Not by playing 'em wide.

So use your own judgement, skipper, but think of the penalty.
There's better captains than you on the beach
We know where they are – they'd be easy to reach,'
The company whispers to me.

(From *The Street and the Sea*, a collection of verse
by James A. Quinby)

Contents

Acknowledgements

I have benefited from the help and advice of a large number of people in writing this book. I would like first of all to thank Rear-Admiral Thomas A. King, former superintendent of the US Merchant Marine Academy at Kings Point, who contributed the foreword. Rear-Admiral Paul Krinsky, the current superintendent, provided assistance in a variety of ways. Mr George Billy, the librarian at Kings Point, and his staff were particularly helpful in my research, as was Mrs Rayama Feldman, the director of the Maritime Research and Development Center.

Mr Mark Greenwood at the Marine Library of the UK Department of Transport at Sunley House in London provided much valuable assistance in my search for materials. Mr Julian Parker, the secretary of the Nautical Institute in London, allowed me to borrow materials from the institute's files. Mr Douglas Foy, former deputy secretary of the institute, provided generous assistance in research. The Nautical Institute and Safety at Sea International lent photographs.

Mr Michael Grey, the former editor of *Fairplay*, offered suggestions and much helpful comment in my search for answers to obscure questions. Captain A. N. Cockcroft lent me books and periodicals containing much useful information. Others who provided assistance are Captain D. J. F. Bruce of Liberian Services, Dr Paul Mayo of the Department of Naval Architecture and Ocean Engineering at the University of Glasgow, and Captain E. J. Kempton, former master of the *Montcalm* who read the section on the *Lakonia* and let me borrow his files on that incident.

The Bundesministerium Fur Verkehr of Hamburg generously responded to my questions pertaining to the sinking of *Pamir* and provided me with much material on that casualty. Captain Chris Allport read the entire manuscript and offered many helpful comments and suggestions, as did Captain John Denham. Captain Frank

Seitz provided invaluable assistance in my efforts to make sense of what happened to *Exxon Valdez*. Captain Owen Clancy also vetted the manuscript. My brother Dan P. Cahill contributed valuable technical comment. I also benefited greatly from the literary criticism and advice of Dr Nancy K. Shields. Finally, I wish to acknowledge the generous assistance, advice and constructive criticism offered by R. J. Holubowicz who read each version of every chapter.

Captain Richard A. Cahill

Author's Note

For those readers who are interested in some of the more technical aspects of the subject I have included such matter in appendixes.

For ease of presentation I have ignored the fact that women are appearing in increasing numbers on the bridges of ships and in the engine room. Where I have used the masculine pronoun readers are invited to add the feminine.

Expressions of time are, in most places, expressed in naval fashion, i.e., 0800 is 8:00 am, 2000 is 8:00 pm.

Foreword

The relationship of the skilled, professional mariner with both the natural elements (the complexity and unpredictability of which are legend) and his new and more technologically demanding ships, must be of continuing concern for those with responsibilities for transportation by sea. Man remains the final decision maker affecting lives, property and, now, an increasing potential for damage to our environment. Disasters at sea can still be best avoided when the decision making is in the hands of the truly competent mariner.

Captain Richard A. Cahill has, following his graduation from the United States Merchant Marine Academy, spent a lifetime at sea, from deck officer to shipmaster, and he represents the highest quality of professional mariner. In this book Captain Cahill minutely dissects and discusses a series of frightful maritime disasters that span three quarters of a century. Whether a mariner or simply a general reader interested in well-told stories and carefully crafted analysis of past newsworthy happenings, the reader's attention will be captivated by the material and the manner of Captain Cahill's lively and authoritative account.

Captain Cahill has made his point. In an age of systems, one maritime 'system' remains essential: that of the human being in command, his subordinates, and the relationship between the two. One can only conclude that while we aim for the highest standards of design, construction and equipment, reinforced by every intention to safely manage our modern ships, nevertheless, if we do not also direct equal attention towards ensuring true professionalism in on-board operation and command of those ships, the tragic history that Captain Cahill has documented is bound to repeat itself.

Thomas A. King
Rear-Admiral, U. S. M. S. (ret.),
Kings Point, N.Y.
1 June 1990

Introduction

Accounts of shipwrecks and other marine disasters exercise a fascination that is all but universal. Disasters at sea are rich in examples of heroism and cowardice, superhuman skill and determination, appalling ineptness or feckless indifference and, on occasion, even criminal negligence if not more sinister behaviour. The name that inevitably springs to mind whenever disasters at sea are mentioned is *Titanic*. An accident such as the one that claimed *Titanic* is unique; while many lesser ships have been lost in collisions with icebergs, the loss of White Star's flagship was memorable not merely because it hit a berg, but because of the events that preceded and followed the disaster. No other ship calamity of modern times has ever captured the imagination of the public to the same extent. *Princess Victoria*, *Flying Enterprise*, *Morro Castle*, *Dara*, *Lakonia*, *Andrea Doria*, *Torrey Canyon* and *Amoco Cadiz* are other ships whose misfortunes briefly dominated the front pages of the newspapers. More recently the capsizing of the *Herald of Free Enterprise* and the stranding of *Exxon Valdez* have filled our television screens. By and large the loss of a ship merits only passing notice unless large numbers of people are lost, injured or disadvantaged and what usually claims the attention of the media is the event itself; only occasionally are the causes probed and even where an official investigation is held it is rare that the probing goes so deep as to reach the root cause of the tragedy.

Safety has never ranked very high in the scale of priorities of those who own ships. Over two centuries ago Samuel Johnson observed: 'No man will be a sailor who has contrivance enough to get himself into a jail; for being in a ship is being in a jail, with the chance of being drowned.' He went on to say: 'A man in jail has more room, better food and commonly better company'[1], an indication of how hazardous and uninviting the mariner's occupation was viewed to be in his day. The peril inherent in the seafarer's trade has existed from the time man first ventured forth to test his skill and luck in his unequal contest with Neptune. While great ship tragedies such as befell *Titanic* forced shipowners to search for means to mitigate the risks for those who travel by sea, the attitude prevalent in Samuel Johnson's time has not greatly changed.

Although it was not uncommon in the days of sail for those who risked their capital in maritime ventures also to hazard their lives in command of the ships they owned, the recognition that one need not risk all in pursuit of gain was made more appealing by the introduction of the practice of marine insurance. By the time Johnson had arrived on the scene marine underwriting was already well established in London. Although it was not the intent of marine insurers to encourage shipowners to ignore considerations of safety in the operation of ships, that has often been its effect. If the validity of White Star Line's insurance had been called into question through failure to provide enough lifeboats for all of *Titanic*'s people, the cost of the additional equipment would hardly have been a dominant consideration in arriving at the decision of how many boats *Titanic* should carry. In the most recent large scale marine disaster, the capsizing of *The Herald of Free Enterprise*, the cavalier attitude of the management of the operating company towards elementary safe operating procedures strongly reinforces the view that safety continues to take a back seat to operational expediency.

The chief officer of that unfortunate vessel was subject to brutal criticism for his failure to verify personally that the bow doors of the ferry were closed before the ship left her berth. The court of inquiry noted in passing that in a recent move to cut operating costs the management had reduced the complement of deck officers. Under the old manning scale another officer had the responsibility for the closing of the bow doors of the ferry. With the elimination of this officer these duties fell on the chief mate, whose normal station when the vessel left her berth was on the bridge. Obviously he could not perform both duties simultaneously, so operational expediency led to the neglect of this added duty.[2] As a consequence almost 200 lives were lost.

In the major portion of the cases investigated in this study the lack of interest displayed by the owners (and those who act for them) in matters of safety is manifest. The question thus arises, can the owners of ships be trusted to operate them in a manner compatible with the public interest? Experience suggests that the answer to this question is often no. This is not to say that all or even most of those who hire others to take the risks inherent in the seafarer's profession are indifferent or callous. Safety, however, almost always costs money, and funds thus spent can rarely show a result that can be readily identified as a contribution to revenue.[3] It is thus an uncommon owner who will freely commit resources to something so unlikely to yield a tangible return.

The traditional maritime powers have laws that require adherence to higher standards of operation than many owners would otherwise freely follow. This adds to their operating costs, and places them at a commercial disadvantage with rivals subject to less stringent regulation. Many such owners have been driven into bankruptcy. Others have chosen to improve their competitive position by 'flagging out', a term used to denote a shift of registry to a flag of convenience. Numerous commentators have attempted to equate flag of convenience shipping with sub-standard operation, but it is not that simple.[4] Some of the major oil companies have had flag of convenience fleets, mainly under the Liberian flag, for a number of years, and these ships are usually manned and managed at the highest level. So one cannot simply or even generally categorize an operation by flag. Even under traditional flags there can be vast differences in standards.

One can say, however, that the ships of some nations, on average, demonstrate substantially higher standards of operation than others, and these standards are reflected in the casualty rates over a period of years. These nations are almost without exception countries which have a substantial maritime tradition. They are the northern European countries including the United Kingdom and France, the United States and Japan.[5]

The seafaring traditions of what were until recently the major maritime powers are firmly rooted in the days of sail, when the risks were so daunting that what we would now regard as commendable caution might then have been seen as timidity. But the modern version of this tradition is based on prudence, and it probably stems in large part from the public reaction to the circumstances of the loss of *Titanic*. In the years since it has been clearly defined in a host of court decisions, most particularly those in the United Kingdom. So impelling is this stress on prudence that one can almost say that no seaman can be regarded as competent who is not also prudent.

Prudence cannot be defined as just caution, though it certainly partakes of it, but rather its essence is the ability to accurately assess risk and govern one's conduct accordingly. That comes with experience gained in one's early years when serving with seamen steeped in this tradition. There can be no safe operation of ships without this prudence, and the casualty figures suggest that it is less likely to be found among those seafarers who lack the advantage of this tradition.

Though many of the old liner companies in the major maritime nations staunchly uphold these traditions it is the practitioners that are its true custodians.[6] The exemplar of this tradition is the master. Unfortunately, those responsible for command appointments today are subject to increasingly competitive pressures that often seem incompatible with prudence. Under such circumstances these pressures are likely to be transmitted from shore to ship resulting in a degradation of traditional attitudes and practices.

Technology *may* sooner or later make our maritime traditions irrelevant, but until such time as that is an accomplished fact the course of wisdom is to take whatever action is necessary to preserve this national or transnational heritage. Our economic prosperity is dependent upon the efficiency of ocean transport. If one equates cheapness with efficiency then one can perhaps view the current shipping trends with equanimity. But if safety is an essential ingredient of the equation then we cannot be so sanguine.

I

The Loss of *Titanic*

Perhaps the single greatest factor contributing to marine disasters is the assumption that considerations of safety need only concern the owner and builder to the extent that restriction is thrust on each of them by existing regulations and law. Anyone with the money to build a ship, or the powers of persuasion to convince a bank to lend it, is free to take what liberties his imagination may suggest in its design as long as he complies with existing requirements of classification societies and legal regulations dictated by experience. In so far as the vessels he plans do not depart too radically from already proven designs the risks normally encountered are acceptable. But where new ground is broken the codes of building conduct are commonly inadequate. Nowhere was this more so than in the design and building of *Titanic*.

Without doubt the loss of the White Star liner *Titanic* was the most dramatic marine disaster of modern times. It has been the subject of books, movies, and television programmes, as well as countless articles in periodicals and newspapers and endless speculation. Such being the case one might well think that further investigation of the subject could yield little of further worth, but because of its pre-eminence in the annals of disasters at sea a review of the circumstances surrounding this tragedy should not be amiss and, if nothing else, it sets the scene admirably for the accounts of disasters which follow.

Though alongside today's marine behemoths *Titanic* would seem of no great size she was by the standards of her time rightly considered huge. She measured 882.5 feet from stem to stern with a beam of 92 feet and had a loaded summer draught of 35 feet. The ULCC (ultra large crude carrier) *Seawise Giant*, built in 1979 with a length overall of 1513 feet, beam of 226 feet and a deep draft of almost 100 feet

5

would clearly dwarf *Titanic*, but that is not to say that this ill-fated liner was of mean dimensions: from her loaded waterline to the top of her masts she was as tall as an eleven-storey building and as long as two football fields. A more realistic comparison would be with more modern passenger liners such as *Queen Mary* and *Queen Elizabeth*. They had an internal cubic capacity (measured in gross tons of 100 cubic feet to the ton) of something over 80,000 compared to *Titanic*'s, which was in the region of 46,000. The most significant comparison for our purposes is the number of passengers and crew each carried. The *Queen Elizabeth* could accommodate a total of 3653 passengers and crew while *Titanic* had a capacity of just under 3400.

White Star, her owners, were pioneers in the transatlantic passenger trade, though this is not to say that they had decades of experience in the design and operation of such vessels. Indeed, the contrary was the case as vessels of this class and size were a very recent innovation. Competition for this prestigious and lucrative business, however, had spurred the major competitors in the trade, Cunard, North German (Norddeutscher) Lloyd, and the French Line to commission and build increasingly larger and faster vessels. Just before the turn of the century, little more than a decade before the launching of *Titanic*, the largest vessel afloat was the 14,000 ton *Kaiser Wilhelm der Grosse* built by North German Lloyd in 1897. On her maiden voyage she set a disputed record of 21.39 knots for a crossing. Cunard's *Lucania* had averaged 21.8 knots on a passage almost three years before. There was a dispute, however, over the award of the Blue Riband. Was it given for the fastest average time or the shortest time of crossing? Three trips later the German liner settled the argument with an eastbound passage of 22.35 knots, which remained a record until the Cunard four-stackers *Mauritania* and *Lusitania* appeared on the scene a decade later.

This acceleration in the design and building of such large vessels had stretched the skill of naval architects to a point where instinct was perhaps a more reliable guide than the empirical principles of their profession. They encountered similar problems to those faced by the naval architects of recent times when the closing of the Suez Canal and the onset of the oil embargo tempted shipowners and operators to break new ground in the commissioning and building of the VLCC (very large crude carrier), ULCC and other specialized and outsize vessels.

Since about the turn of the century the emphasis was on speed, but the size of the three vessels planned by White Star was such that current design technology was pushed to its economical limits. It was the intention of J. Bruce Ismay, the managing director of the company, to build vessels capable of operating at a competitive speed, but to concentrate on luxury as a means of attracting the famous and wealthy. In 1902 the American magnate J. Pierpont Morgan had caused consternation and chagrin in official British maritime circles by his acquisition of a controlling interest in White Star through the agency of his International Mercantile Marine Company (IMM), which had previously taken over the Belgian Red Star Line and several of the largest United States shipping companies. Though Ismay and his friends had initially opposed Morgan's takeover it soon became apparent that Morgan was not a threat to Ismay's position. Indeed, Ismay became president and managing director in 1904.[1]

At the Senate hearings conducted into the *Titanic* disaster vice-president Phillip A. S. Franklin, of the New York branch of the IMM, testified that the International Mercantile Marine Company (capital about $100 million) owned or controlled the International Navigation Company (Ltd.) of England. The IMM owned the shares of the Oceanic Steam Navigation Company, which in turn owned the White Star ships. He went on to say that *Titanic* was built at a cost of just over £1.5 million, of which only two thirds was insured. The balance of cover was carried by White Star.[2]

One night in 1907, not long after the new Cunarders had entered service, Ismay was a guest of Lord W. J. Pirrie, the guiding genius of the renowned Belfast shipbuilders Harland & Wolff. After the meal they sat down over coffee and cigars to discuss White Star's response to Cunard's sleek new ocean greyhounds. They decided then to build three vessels of nearly 45,000 gross tons with a service speed of about 22 knots. This would enable them to compete respectably though not surpass the speed of their competitor's vessels, but would instead through the lavishness of their appointments and gastronomic excellence outdistance their rivals in pursuit of comfort and luxury.

The ships contemplated were of such proportions that existing facilities for their employment were inadequate, and there was initial resistance from those on the New York end to plans to provide a suitable berth. That opposition collapsed when port authorities at Boston offered an alternative, and there was even talk of a terminal at Montauk Point on the tip of Long Island. A more co-operative attitude was evident in Britain where White Star had shifted the passenger operation from Liverpool, which had long been the principal port of call for transatlantic liners flying the British flag, to Southampton which was just across the Channel from Cherbourg and provided a convenient embarkation point for travellers from the Continent. Officials in Southampton were eager to comply with Ismay's wishes and work began immediately to lengthen a berth.

Olympic, the first of White Star's giants, was laid down in 1908 and commissioned in the summer of the next year. As the commodore of White Star Captain Edward J. Smith, popularly known as 'E. J.', took command. *Titanic* was nearing completion at an adjoining berth. *Olympic* was billed as the safest ship afloat. She was designed with a system of watertight subdivision and electrically operated watertight doors that made her seemingly unsinkable. She could sustain flooding of any two adjacent watertight compartments and remain afloat and upright. Since damage of this kind would ordinarily only be inflicted by collision with another vessel, there were likely to be few occasions when damage would extend beyond two adjacent compartments. The claim that the liner was unsinkable, and the confidence, if not complacence, it inspired was plausible but unfortunate in light of subsequent events. Prior trials with a smaller pilot class of vessel had convinced Ismay and his builders that triple expansion reciprocating engines, driving triple screws through steam generated by twenty-nine separate boilers in six boiler rooms would provide the most efficient means of propulsion. Unfortunately the machinery arrangement allowed for astern power only through the two outboard engines, and there was some feeling later that this might have contributed to the accident which proved fatal to *Titanic*.

Olympic performed flawlessly on her maiden voyage, much to the delight of Bruce Ismay and Thomas Andrews, the managing director of Harland and Wolff. There was no doubt some disappointment in that she was considerably underbooked, but the luxury of her accommodation and public rooms excited critical acclaim on both sides of the Atlantic. Ismay wrote: 'Everything on board ship worked most satisfactorily, and the passengers were loud in their praises of the accommodation and table. The machinery worked excellently and there was no hitch of any kind in connection with same.' She offered standards of opulence, comfort and safety unmatched by any

8

of her competitors, and both Ismay and J. Pierpont Morgan were more than pleased with their fine new vessel.

The decoration of the public rooms varied widely, ranging from Jacobean English and Georgian to that of Louis XV and Louis XVI. She offered the most spacious public rooms afloat as well as a Turkish bath, racquet court, gymnasium and a large swimming pool. Unfortunately her sailing coincided with the preparations for the coronation of George V, so the event did not attract the publicity it would otherwise have generated. Although the weather was not altogether ideal the maiden voyage was otherwise uneventful, although it threatened to be marred by a tug boat strike in New York. Fortunately that didn't materialize and spared Captain Smith the unenviable job of trying to berth his huge vessel at pier 59 North River unaided. Given the formidable nature of that task it is likely that the passengers would have disembarked at an anchorage, which would have been an inauspicious beginning for so promising an enterprise.

On her succeeding voyages *Olympic* continued to perform at a high standard, but as she left Southampton three months later and proceeded towards Spithead Channel she was overtaken by the cruiser *Hawke* on a converging course in the vicinity of Bramble Bank. What happened next was a matter of dispute.[3] *Hawke*'s bow took a sudden sheer to starboard and before her swing was checked she struck *Olympic* on her port quarter opening a gash of about 40 feet in her hull. *Hawke* suffered even graver damage and there was fear she might sink. The flooding was fortunately brought quickly under control and *Hawke* limped back to her berth at Portsmouth. White Star's contention that the warship was to blame at first prevailed, but after an acrimonious legal wrangle the court of appeal held the liner at fault. Had Captain Smith enjoyed less than the complete confidence of Bruce Ismay this expensive incident might have accelerated his retirement, but it did nothing to lower White Star's confidence in him or the design of their vessel. Smith was in fact due to retire, but Ismay prevailed on him to take *Titanic* on her maiden voyage.

Captain Edward J. Smith was nearing his sixtieth birthday. A native of Staffordshire he now lived with his wife and young daughter on the edge of the New Forest outside Southampton. After serving an apprenticeship with Gibson & Co. of Liverpool he joined White Star in 1880. He had commanded most of the White Star liners of recent years on their maiden voyages, and he planned to retire at the

9

completion of that of *Titanic*. He had spent thirty-eight years at sea of which the last twenty-five had been in command. He was an inspiring figure, admired and respected by his crew and all who knew him. Second Officer Charles Lightoller in later years characterized him as 'a man any officer would give his ears to sail under. Broad, bluff, hearty, you would think at first sight, "Here's a typical western ocean captain, and I bet he's got a voice like a fog horn." But,' continued Lightoller, 'he had a pleasant, quiet voice and an invariable smile – a voice he rarely raised above conversational level, although when he barked an order it made a man come to himself with a bump. He was one of the ablest and most experienced of the Atlantic skippers.'[4] (The author had the privilege early in his career of serving as chief officer with Captain Smith's nephew, Captain Robert A. Smith, a consummate seaman who enjoyed a distinguished career with the United States Lines Company commanding several of their largest passenger liners. Lightoller's description of *Titanic*'s master could also have been used for his nephew.)

Captain Smith was a natural leader with a calm demeanour and ready smile. His personality radiated authority, tact, good humour and confidence. Lightoller also said of him: 'I had been with him many years, on and off, in the mail boats, *Majestic* mainly, and it was an education to see him conn his ship up through the intricate channels entering New York at full speed. One particularly bad corner, known as Southwest Spit, used to make us fairly flush with pride as he swung her round, judging his distances to a nicety; she heeling over to the helm with only a matter of feet to spare between each end of the ship and the banks.'

'Though I believe he's an awful stickler for discipline,' Sixth Officer James Moody told his sister, 'he's popular with everybody.'[5] He had commanded seventeen White Star ships during his distinguished career, and Ismay said of him, 'He was a man in whom we had entire and absolute confidence.'[6]

As one would expect, the officers who served 'E. J.' were the pick of the White Star fleet. The chief officer, Henry Tighe Wilde, had been Smith's chief officer in *Olympic*. A tall, powerfully built man of thirty-eight he had originally turned down the appointment to *Titanic*. He had settled in on her sister ship and as 'E. J.' planned to retire after the maiden voyage he preferred to stay where he was. William McMaster Murdoch was therefore given the berth initially, but Smith wanted Wilde for this last triumphant voyage. It was not a question of dissatisfaction with Murdoch, who was a splendid officer, but Wilde had served as chief officer in *Olympic* since her launching and as she was temporarily laid up for a voyage Wilde was transferred.[7] Murdoch, who was equally experienced and slightly older, must have felt some resentment at this 'demotion'. He was a cool, impassive Scot of the soundest judgement and presence of mind. He was ripe for command and wanted it. But he could hardly kick up a fuss over this temporary setback so he stoically swallowed his disappointment. The most colourful of the lot was Charles Herbert Lightoller who had also been forced to step back. He was known as a 'hard case' and would have fit easily into one of Conrad's novels. His sister was inclined to worry about his lack of reverence for danger, but he laughed at her anxiety. 'Don't you bother,' he reassured her, 'the sea is not wet enough to drown me. I'll never be drowned.'[8] Such confidence could not be denied, nor was it.

The heady advances made in design and construction led those responsible for them to make unwarranted and mistaken claims. The earlier assumptions about the 'unsinkability' of *Olympic* were, of course, carried over to *Titanic*, which perhaps encouraged the designers to ignore and discount considerations of safety to which they might otherwise have given closer attention. The Welin davits installed in *Titanic* permitted nesting of the lifeboats in such a way that a number sufficient for all the passengers and crew could have been carried without difficulty. That was originally contemplated, but Ismay apparently decided against it.[9]

If *Titanic* were truly unsinkable why go to unneeded expense and trouble to provide the lifeboats and rafts that prudence would dictate for a less advanced vessel? The regulations of the day took no direct account of the number of passengers a ship was designed to carry, and simply prescribed the number of lifeboats on the basis of a formula based on gross tonnage. *Titanic*, as *Olympic* before her, had a mere twenty lifeboats with a capacity for only 1178 people.

This overconfidence in *Titanic*'s capabilities and capacity was quite likely communicated to those chosen to sail her. There is no question but that Captain Smith and his officers were fine seamen of outstanding ability, but they were probably caught up in the enthusiasm of their employer Bruce Ismay, and of the builder, Thomas Andrews, for the superlative vessel shortly to be entrusted to their care. Given Ismay's dislike of contradiction it is somewhat understandable if they were inhibited from expressing reservations or doubts as regards the equipment and outfitting of this ocean queen, even in the unlikely event that they entertained any. It would have been considered an unheard-of presumption in any event for an employee, even one so highly regarded as Captain Smith, to have ventured uninvited into a preserve traditionally viewed as the exclusive domain of the owner.

Ismay had meanwhile been busy planning a number of alterations in the design of his new flagship to make her even more luxurious. Among the changes were an enclosed promenade deck and an expansion of the capacity of the first class saloon, which could now seat 500 passengers at one sitting. As an added attraction for the rich and powerful a restaurant, the Café Parisien, was to stay open round the clock catering to those whose whims and style of life found the scheduled dining routine of the saloon inconvenient. The passenger capacity had also been slightly increased to 2516, which brought the gross tonnage up to 46,329.

In the week that *Titanic* spent at Southampton preparing for her first voyage the Department of Trade's chief inspector Captain Clarke made no concessions to expediency. He insisted on personally sighting everything within his brief. So meticulous was he in his attentions that Lightoller later remarked, 'He [Captain Clarke] would not accept anyone's word as sufficient and got heartily cursed as a consequence.'[10] It was not his concern, however, to question matters of policy that determined the number of the ship's lifeboats. More-over, it almost certainly never occurred to him to do so, and while perhaps the matter might have crossed the mind of Captain Smith and one or two of his senior officers it was not, as already remarked, one they would confidently consider broaching.

Once again fate conspired to cheat White Star of the publicity normally accorded the maiden sailing of such a magnificent vessel.[11] Britain was in the throes of a national coal strike and so the press treated the sailing of *Titanic* as a matter of secondary importance. The coal strike also made it difficult to meet the bunkering require-ments for the big liner. With a bit of ingenuity this and other obstacles were overcome and about noon on 10 April 1912 a long blast on *Titanic*'s whistle signalled her imminent departure.

Again the passenger list, although glittering, was disappointingly short. Only a little more than half of the 2566 berths were taken up. Any faint premonitions of doom would, however, have been hard to detect in the atmosphere of anticipation and gaiety attending the sailing of this superb ship. The more likely reason for the shortfall in bookings was that *Olympic* had sailed less than a week before.

Both Ismay and Andrews were among the passengers for *Titanic*'s maiden voyage as they had been for that of *Olympic*. J. Pierpont Morgan was also one of the scheduled passengers, but he cancelled at the last minute. So too did Lord Pirrie who was ill. Nor were they the only ones. The American ambassador to Paris could not go because his successor was delayed, but others had less concrete reasons for cancellation. Henry Clay Frick, an associate of Andrew Carnegie, and Norman Craig, an MP and well-known barrister were two of a number who decided not to make the trip at the last minute. There was apparently a certain prejudice against maiden voyages at that time, and there is good reason to regard them with some suspicion.[12] The passenger list, none the less, included a spectacular array of some of the most famous of the day. John Jacob Astor, Benjamin Guggenheim, Mr and Mrs George Widener, the Countess of Rothes, Sir Cosmo and Lady Duff Gordon, Mr and Mrs Washington Dodge, Mr and Mrs Rothschild, Mr and Mrs Arthur Ryerson and their children, Mr and Mrs Isidor Straus, and John B. Thayer, managing director of the Pennsylvania Railroad, were a few of the prominent and wealthy on board.

As the big liner eased out of her berth and slowly moved down Southampton Water towards the Solent and the sea beyond two of her competitors in the berth just ahead, the American Line's *New York* and White Star's *Oceanic*, were almost drawn in her wake. The displacement of water by *Titanic*'s huge hull caused a surge that actually tore the *New York* from her moorings and could have caused damage that might have aborted this fateful voyage, but quick work by Captain Smith enabled one of the attending tugs to check *New York*'s swing into the river and nudge her safely back into her berth. *Oceanic* theatened to follow her example but her mooring lines held fast thus sparing *Titanic* further embarrassment. The wife of the American impresario H. B. Harris observed the narrow escape from *Titanic*'s deck, and as the big ship drew away, a stranger standing by her side turned to her and said, 'This is a bad omen,' and after a pause asked, 'Do you love life?' When she acknowledged that she did he replied, 'Then get off this ship at Cherbourg if we get that far. That's what I'm going to do.' Mrs Harris laughed and expressed her confidence by referring to the almost universally held belief in the liner's unsinkability. But she never saw the stranger again during the remainder of the voyage.[13]

The foreboding voiced by the mysterious passenger to Mrs Harris at Southampton was apparently shared by others. Chief Officer Wilde had written to his sister expressing his unease. 'I still don't like this ship . . . I have a queer feeling about it.' A young fireman, John Coffey, shared his apprehension and expessed it in action. He deserted at Queenstown (now Cork) in Ireland, but he signed on the *Mauritania* a few days later suggesting it wasn't the sea but the ship that frightened him.[14]

About seven o'clock in the evening after leaving Southampton the glittering White Star flagship anchored at Cherbourg to take on several hundred continental passengers. From there she steamed on to Queenstown to pick up the remainder, who mostly travelled steerage. At 2 p.m. on the 11th, *Titanic* departed with 1316 passengers and 891 crew and headed out into the grey Atlantic. Her massive engines were soon brought up to sea speed, and at about five that afternoon Fastnet lighthouse was abeam to starboard. *Titanic* steamed towards her icy rendezvous.

Reports of icebergs began coming in right from the start, though the first ones were to the north of *Titanic*'s intended track. The weather was ideal and the speed of the new liner increased with each passing day. Though there was never any intention to try for a record, a fast passage on the maiden voyage would receive much more publicity than on a later one. The extent of Ismay's direct influence over the operation of the ship can be inferred from the meeting he had with Chief Engineer Bell while the ship was in Queenstown. He had enquired about the quantity of bunkers aboard with a view to driving the ship 'at full speed' on the last two days if the weather was suitable.[15] *Titanic* was not due in New York until early Wednesday morning, but it now appeared there was a possibility of arriving Tuesday evening. Though Ismay had earlier declared there was no point in pushing the ship the possibility of an early arrival was too enticing to ignore. Extra boilers were lit and steam pressure increased as *Titanic* approached the area where ice was reported off the Grand Banks.

Sunday, the 12th, was traditionally the day for boat drill aboard White Star ships, but Smith postponed it, possibly in misguided deference to the managing director and the many illustrious passengers aboard. Had Ismay the dedication to safety that White Star's policy instructions to masters spelled out in seemingly unequivocal detail, 'E. J.' would hardly have allowed – or acquiesced in – either this imprudent increase of speed into an area of known danger or the cancellation of the boat drill.

Sunday was also the day for Captain's inspection, and as that colourful ceremony caused no inconvenience to passengers the master, accompanied by his department heads, proceeded from stem to stern and deck to deck along several miles of passageways. That duty over, Captain Smith made his way up to the main dining room to conduct Sunday church services. He was an impressive figure in his blue uniform with four gold stripes on each sleeve, reading prayers from White Star's special prayer book in a sonorous voice. From there he proceeded to the bridge where he presided over the navigational ritual of taking the sun's meridian altitude, the final step in establishing the vessel's noon position. The vessel had made a day's run of 546 miles, and the increasing throb of the engines gave promise of exceeding even that promising figure during the final two days.

While the master was making his inspection another ship, *Caronia*, was reporting ice at latitude 42° between longitude 49° to 51° west. Shortly before 2 p.m. that afternoon *Baltic* warned of the same in 41°51′ north and 40°52′ west. At almost the same time another, *Amerika*, reported bergs in 41°21′ north and 55°8′ west. Around supper time *Californian* confirmed these earlier reports, and several hours later *Mesaba* sent a similar warning. All of these reports showed ice nearly in the path of the huge liner. Unfortunately not all of these messages reached the bridge. None the less, Captain Smith and his officers clearly knew there was a distinct possibility, even likelihood, of encountering ice during the night. The lookouts were even specifically warned to keep a sharp watch for bergs, yet no one seemed particularly concerned about this possibility. No extra lookouts were posted. No special instructions were given to the engineers to standby for possible emergency manoeuvres, and the advisability of slowing the vessel to allow more time to react should a berg be sighted ahead does not appear to have been considered. This is hardly surprising since that would have run counter to the hope for a higher average speed on the morrow. Captain Smith must have known the risk he was taking, but this marvellous vessel he commanded was on her first voyage while he was on his last. Many of the first class passengers aboard had made more than a single crossing on vessels of which he was master, and indeed most of them were aboard *Titanic* because he commanded it, in such esteem and affection was he held.

The transatlantic steamship passenger trade was highly competitive and during the span of a half century or so of its evolvement it had become customary to press on in spite of ice, at least in clear weather. During the early decades in which this practice became confirmed the speed of the vessels involved was little more than 10 knots. At such speeds it was not unreasonable to expect that a berg ahead could be sighted and safely avoided, and so the practice and custom that was to lead Captain Smith and his ship to its doom became fixed. As the speed of ships crept upwards the practice became less justifiable, and as it approached and passed 20 knots it can be seen in retrospect as so hazardous as to exceed the limits of prudent seamanship. Yet who was to draw the line, and say that a practice established at speeds half of that of the newest liners was no longer valid? At the US Senate inquiry held shortly following the disaster a parade of distinguished masters of transatlantic liners unhesitatingly testified that they would have done as Captain Smith had done.

To have slowed his ship under the circumstances would have suggested a degree of timidity most out of keeping with his character.[16] He was not known as a vain man and his position had not turned his head, but he had an understandable pride in his reputation and he did not want to sound a sour note on his last voyage before retirement. So *Titanic* plunged ahead at full sea speed. The risk was accepted and there was no need to lose sleep about it.

That evening the Wideners gave a dinner party in the restaurant at which Captain Smith was one of the guests. All around were the rich and famous and 'E. J.' was probably reluctant to leave these congenial surroundings, but the new liner was approaching the ice area and duty called. Shortly before nine he excused himself and made his way to the bridge where he had a brief chat with Second Officer Lightoller. The weather, which is of such importance in a seaman's life, was a natural topic of discussion and the master remarked on the cold and then the wind, or rather the lack of it. Normally that would be welcomed, but under the circumstances it was somewhat worrying: the breaking of the sea against the base of a berg is often one of the first things seen on a dark night, but in the dead calm prevailing that helpful aid to discovery would be missing. As Captain Smith's eyesight became accustomed to the darkness he remarked that 'It seems quite clear,' and Lightoller agreed. Under the circumstances haze was a distinct possibility and danger, and the master observed that if the visibility became impaired in the slightest, speed would have to be reduced. With that comment he turned to go to his cabin, saying, 'If it becomes at all doubtful let me know at once; I'll be just inside.'[17]

Chief Radio Operator John George Phillips had had a hectic day. He and his assistant, Harold Bride, had been deluged by messages from the celebrated and wealthy, and he was well aware that complaints from any of these customers could not be brushed aside. He was working the station at Cape Race, and when the Leyland Line's *Californian* attempted to interrupt with a message about icebergs he brusquely told her operator to shut up. They knew all about the ice. Hadn't there been five warnings already earlier in the day, including one from the same ship?

Phillips, who had just celebrated his twenty-fifth birthday the day before, had had little rest during the previous twenty-four hours as he and Bride had been repairing a faulty piece of equipment. It had thus been agreed between them that Bride would relieve him at midnight rather than the normal end of his watch at 0200. As Bride entered the radio shack from his adjacent sleeping quarters he asked how things were going. Phillips said he had been busy working Cape Race, and almost as an afterthought he remarked that he had felt a jolt not long before as if the ship had struck something. He thought *Titanic* might have to turn back due to damage that she may have suffered.

Both the young men – Bride was only twenty-two – were highly regarded by their employer the Marconi Marine Company (see appendix 1), founded by the Italian physicist Guglielmo Marconi less than a decade before. Both were dedicated enthusiasts of their trade, as were most of the operators in the infancy of wireless telegraphy, but this youthful enthusiasm, stimulated by the heady glamour of their employment, was unfortunately not balanced by the seasoned judgement that ordinarily only comes with years of experience. Phillips had just recently joined the Marconi training school in Liverpool in 1906 and after passing the postmaster-general's examination top of the class he spent three years at the company's high-power transmitting station at Clifden in the west of Ireland before taking up employment aboard some of the biggest liners of the day. Bride had less than a year at sea. Radio operators then and even now wear two 'hats': they serve the ship, but they also serve the company that owns and services the radio station aboard the vessel. This ordinarily produces no conflict of any significance, but aboard the big passenger liners of the past the real 'business' was the traffic between passenger and shore. It also formed an essential part of the service offered by the owners of the vessel, so there was enormous pressure to cater to the insistent and influential with potential neglect of ship's traffic.

When First Officer Murdoch relieved Second Officer Lightoller at about ten o'clock that evening the sky was cloudless as well as moonless, but the sea was calm and the sky ablaze with stars. *Titanic* sliced through the inky night at 22.5 knots, and though there was not a breath of air the ship's movement created an apparent wind equal to a fresh breeze, or force 5 on the Beaufort scale. The temperature hovered on the freezing point and the lookouts in the crow's nest on the foremast just forward and twenty feet above the bridge were bitterly cold and looking forward to a relief at midnight.

Able seaman Frederick Fleet, along with his watch partner Reginald Lee, was one of six lookouts who split the three watches. He had spent the last four of his six years at sea on White Star liners before joining *Titanic* in Belfast several months before. Fleet had been cautioned by the first officer when he came on duty to keep a sharp eye out for icebergs, and as he peered intently into the dark night he perhaps wished he had a pair of binoculars to aid in that task.[18] That deficiency had been discovered after the vessel departed Southampton and First Officer Murdoch had made a mental note to rectify it when the ship reached New York.

As the watch neared its end Fleet looked forward to his relief and a hot cup of cocoa below, but he didn't allow those comforting thoughts to interfere with his duty. Suddenly a smudge about the size of his hand loomed on the horizon dead ahead. As he strained his eyes to make sure his imagination wasn't tricking him the object rapidly grew in size and distinctness. Now convinced that one of the icebergs he had been warned to look for was directly in *Titanic*'s path he gave three quick rings on the bell on the mast and reached for the phone, another recent innovation. The sharp ring of the phone was promptly answered by the junor watch officer, Sixth Officer Moody, who moved briskly to lift it from its cradle on the after bulkhead of the wheelhouse: 'What do you see?'

'Iceberg dead ahead,' was Fleet's anxious answer.

Moody instantly relayed this alarming news to Murdoch on the bridge wing whose reaction was calm but immediate. On seeing the ominous shadow looming dead ahead out of the darkness he shouted to Quartermaster Hitchens to put the helm hard to starboard (a holdover from sailing ship days: to starboard the helm meant the rudder would go to the left), as he lunged for the engine order telegraph and rang full astern. Then he pulled the switch that caused the electrically operated watertight doors to close. No more than a minute had passed since he had received Fleet's warning, but to the two seamen in the crow's nest it must have seemed like an eternity.

As *Titanic* hurtled towards the sheer grey wall of ice that now loomed ahead Fleet and his mate Lee watched in horror. When the helm is put over on a ship the size of *Titanic* several seconds will elapse before the effect of the rudder action causes the vessel's head to begin to swing. Though the ship's heading changes in these first few moments after the application of helm, her path through the water does not. Before entering her turn she will 'skid' through the water for a considerable distance, which in the case of *Titanic* was probably about a ship's length. Before she entered her turn the bow of *Titanic* struck the underwater base of the berg.

Although considerable ice was later discovered on her fore deck the force of the blow was scarcely felt throughout much of the ship. Some of those in the immediate vicinity were thrown from their bunks by the violence of the shock. Most of those elsewhere described the blow as resembling the impact of a wave or a slight vibration, but certainly nothing to occasion alarm, although Phillips thought the jolt that he had felt might have damaged the ship. Some indeed felt nothing, and Quartermaster George Rowe standing watch on the after docking bridge thought the bump was similar to that experienced when a vessel lands on a dock wall while berthing. It was some time before he learned that the ship itself had suffered fatal damage.

Captain Smith was in his quarters just abaft the wheelhouse, and like almost all experienced ship masters he was ultrasensitive to any noise or movement of his vessel. Feeling the jolt and hearing the grating noise of the berg as it slid down the vessel's side he dashed into the wheelhouse. 'What was that Mr Murdoch?'

'We have struck ice,' answered the first officer. 'I was going to port round it, but it was too close. I put the engines astern, and could do no more.'[19]

It was said later that had the engines not been reversed the vessel might have responded earlier to her helm and so perhaps narrowly avoiding a collision with the berg. The centre-line propeller was not capable of being reversed, and as it had the greatest influence upon the rudder the most effective action would have been to leave all engines going ahead. Even had the watch engineers been expecting a 'bell' (a manoeuvring order) they would have been unable to respond quickly enough to have made any significant difference. As they were not, it is almost certain that the ship would have collided with the berg before they were actually able to apply astern power.

A seemingly more telling criticism was that, if First Officer Murdoch had not put the helm over but met the berg head on, the damage, though serious, would not have been fatal, as it would probably have merely crumpled the fore peak and perhaps have resulted in the flooding of the number one hold.[20] However, it is all very well to reach that conclusion after the fact, but the instinctive reaction of most seamen would be that of Murdoch's: to try to avoid collision by helm action.

When the wreck was recently discovered it was reported that the damage to the hull of *Titanic* consisted of a series of small fractures and sheared rivet heads instead of the more extensive damage originally reported. Subsequent investigation, however, indicates that the bow of *Titanic* is embedded so deeply in the ocean floor that the damage inflicted by the iceberg cannot be inspected.[21] In the event the first five watertight compartments were opened to the sea, and the damage extended some several feet aft of the bulkhead between the fifth compartment and the number five boiler room, which was the sixth compartment (the boiler rooms were numbered forward of the engine room, which was aft of the boiler rooms). *Titanic* was constructed to a two-compartment standard, which meant that she was capable of surviving flooding of a minimum of any two adjacent compartments without submerging adjacent watertight bulkheads. Beyond that point there was danger of water in a flooded compartment spilling over into an adjacent compartment and causing progressive flooding. In fact vessels are often capable of surviving more than this theoretical limit, depending upon their condition of loading, the distribution of bunkers and the nature of the flooding (see appendix 2). In *Titanic*'s case the builder and designer, Thomas Andrews, calculated that had the damage extended no further than the fourth compartment she would have been able to remain afloat, providing the bulkhead between the fourth and fifth compartments remained intact. The fact that the damage extended several feet into the sixth compartment made it obvious she was doomed. Once the flooding reached its natural limit in the damaged compartments the water would overflow into the next compartment astern, and then progressively into those compartments aft until all reserve buoyancy was lost and the vessel plunged to the bottom.

One can well imagine the anguish and despair felt by Captain Smith as well as Mr Andrews. Only a few short hours ago the captain was being fêted and admired by a glittering array of famous and distinguished passengers. The maiden voyage of *Titanic* was to be the spectacular finale to a celebrated career, after which Captain Smith was looking forward to a well-earned retirement. Now all was in ruins.

Only six years before when he had assumed command of *Adriatic* on her maiden voyage he had said: 'I cannot imagine any condition which would cause a ship to founder. I cannot conceive of any vital disaster happening to this vessel. Modern shipbuilding has gone beyond that.'[22] If he had felt that confident in the survival capability of that earlier and less perfect vessel, his belief in the invulnerability of this pinnacle of the shipbuilder's art must have been beyond question. This confidence had perhaps led him to ignore his seaman's instinct when the reports of ice on his track reached him earlier in the day. The likelihood of encountering a solitary berg directly on the path in the middle of the broad reaches of the north Atlantic was so remote that it could be safely ignored, he must have reasoned. His officers and crew were as fine as could be found, and it was altogether reasonable to expect that in the improbable event of an encounter their diligence and prompt reaction would at worst result in a near miss. The visibility was excellent and a berg must surely be distinguishable with its vast shining white bulk at a distance of at least a mile, which would allow ample time and room to avoid it. Even if the impossible did occur and they struck a berg the damage could be quickly contained by the marvellous expedient of those amazing electrically operated watertight doors. The respected technical journal *Shipbuilder* had pointed out, in a special edition devoted to *Titanic*'s construction, that not only did she have an unprecedented number of watertight compartments but that 'The captain can, by simply moving an electric switch, instantly close the watertight doors throughout and make the vessel practically unsinkable.'[23] This was not merely a bit of advertising propaganda but the considered opinion of one of the most reputable journals in the field. When Captain Rostron (the master of *Carpathia*) testified before the Senate hearing into the disaster he volunteered the statement that, 'The ships are built nowadays to be practically unsinkable, and each ship is supposed to be a lifeboat in itself. The boats are merely supposed to be put on as a standby. The ships are supposed to be built, and the naval architects say they are, unsinkable under certain conditions. What the exact conditions are, I do not know, as to whether it is with alternate compartments full, or what it may be. . . .'[24]

Captain Smith's confidence in this 'door of last resort', was expressed in his first words to Mr Murdoch after learning of the accident. 'Close the emergency doors.' Murdoch's response, 'The doors are already closed', may have momentarily allayed the apprehension felt by *Titanic*'s master when he felt the initial jolt, but his confidence in the invulnerability of his splendid ship to any accident began to be eroded soon after the first reports began coming in.

The reversal of the engines had soon brought *Titanic* to a halt and the engines were stopped while the extent of the damage was ascertained. The ear as well as the other organs of the senses soon learns to filter out what might be called background noises, such as that made by the constant and uniform throb of ship's engines, so as to remain alert for other more important signals. The sudden stilling of such background noise is almost as vivid a sensual warning as an abrupt thud or shock, and it was that which alerted most of the passengers and crew to *Titanic*'s altered circumstances.

After first determining that all had been done that could be done in the first few moments following the collision Smith took a quick look aft to see if the iceberg was still in sight and then quietly took charge. He sent one of the junior watch officers, Fourth Officer Joseph Boxhall, below to make a quick survey of the extent of the damage and report back. The initial report was encouraging, no apparent damage could be found. But he had not gone far enough down into the ship. The master was more sceptical and told him to find the carpenter and get him to sound the holds. As Boxhall started down the ladder to the bridge wing he met the carpenter coming up. His news was more accurate and ominous. 'She's making water fast,' he blurted out. Hard on his heels was the postal clerk Iago Smith whose place of business was far down in the number one hold, which he confirmed was 'filling rapidly'.

Next to appear on the scene was Bruce Ismay who had played such a controversial and ambivalent role since the vessel's departure. Walter Lord, in his book *A Night to Remember*, described him as a sort of super-captain, revelling in his role as the one with final authority in this glittering enterprise. After the decision to abandon ship was taken he attempted to interfere in the conduct of that operation until given a dressing down by Fifth Officer Harold Lowe, an outspoken Welshman. Ismay knew of at least one of the ice warnings that had been received: Captain Smith had handed him the one from *Baltic* as he was sitting down to lunch. Lord described Ismay as a man 'who liked to remind people who he was.'[25] However, when the chips were down Ismay reverted to his role as a passenger and, as the last boats were being launched, he seated himself in the bows of one of the collapsibles. He was later pilloried by the press for not having gone down with the ship, yet he was more to be pitied than censored.

Captain Smith now sent for Thomas Andrews, the builder, who knew the vessel from the keel up, and together they made their own inspection to get a clear idea of the extent of the damage. Back on the bridge Andrews made some quick calculations and then gave Smith the grim news – his ship was doomed; there was no way she could survive the damage she had sustained and he gave her at most a couple of hours afloat.

The captain now made his way back to the radio shack and told Chief Operator Phillips to send out a call for assistance. The North German Lloyd steamer *Frankfurt* replied almost at once, at eighteen minutes past midnight, then the Canadian Pacific's *Mount Temple*, the *Virginian* and the Russian tramp *Birma*. Closest of all, it seemed, was the Cunarder *Carpathia*, but her single operator was off watch and there was no auto-alarm (see appendix 3) to alert him. Fortunately Harold Cottam, *Carpathia*'s wireless operator, was in a helpful mood. He had earlier been working Cape Cod and had heard that station calling *Titanic*. Before he turned in he gave his colleague Phillips a courtesy call, 'Did he know of the traffic for him at Cape Cod?'

Phillips's response brought him bolt upright: 'Come at once. We have struck a berg. It's a CQD. Position 41°46′N, 50°14′W.'[26]

Cottam at first was too shocked to digest fully what he had heard, and he asked Phillips whether he should inform his captain. Receiving an affirmative he rushed down to tell *Carpathia*'s first officer and together they gave the alarming news to the master of the vessel, Arthur H. Rostron. Although Rostron had been at sea for twenty-seven years his command experience was marginal, but he recognized the gravity of the situation instantly and lost no time in turning his ship north towards the scene of the disaster. *Titanic* was apparently 58 miles to the north and west[27] on a bearing of 308 degrees and Captain Rostron informed his chief engineer to squeeze every last bit of steam out of his boilers in order to reach the stricken liner as soon as possible. Meanwhile Rostron had given instructions to his chief officer, chief engineer, chief steward, purser and the ship's surgeon to make every preparation for the hundreds of distressed survivors he hoped shortly to pluck from the sea.

Carpathia's normal cruising speed was about 14 knots, but Chief Engineer Johnstone realizing what was at stake did everything possible to see that every ounce of steam pressure available was used for propulsion. The steam normally used for heating and hot water for domestic use was cut off, while the watch below was rousted out to lend a hand in stoking the boilers. Everyone not needed for a more essential task grabbed a shovel to feed the fire boxes. With the rising steam pressure the throb of the engines quickened. As the limit the old boilers could hold was approached *Carpathia*'s speed exceeded anything witnessed since her sea trials. No one aboard had ever seen her pressed so hard.

In the vessel's wireless shack Harold Cottam could no longer raise *Titanic*. He heard her desperate traffic with *Olympic* much further away but he was unable now to communicate directly, his set was too weak. At 0150 came a last plea: 'The engine room is full up to the boilers', then silence.[28]

On *Carpathia*'s bridge Captain Rostron was deep in thought. Had everything been done that could be done? He went over the points one by one but he could think of nothing he had overlooked, and now could only wait. Extra lookouts had been posted, the chief officer had the ship's boats ready and nets rigged for picking up survivors. At his side stood Second Officer James Bisset peering through binoculars for a glimpse of lifeboats, or icebergs. Suddenly Rostron saw the glare of a green flare half a point to port (a compass point is equal to eleven and one quarter degrees). It seemed a long way off, and high out of the water. It was only 0240, perhaps *Titanic*'s position had been out.

Then a few minutes later the second mate saw another flash of light two points to port. It was no flare but a reflection from a berg. Other bergs now loomed out of the darkness, and Rostron's elation was checked by the sobering recollection that *Carpathia* was also at risk. Other flares were now sighted, along with other bergs. At 0330 he calculated he was within a few miles of *Titanic*'s reported position, but there was no sign of the ship or her lifeboats. At 0350 he rang 'standby' on the engine room telegraph and at 0400, 'stop'. By his calculations *Carpathia* was on the spot. Moments later another green light flared up almost ahead. He could make out the dim outline of a lifeboat. As Captain Rostron rang 'slow ahead' and manoeuvred his vessel to starboard to pick up the boat on his port side a berg loomed up directly in his path and he had to swing hard to port. Other boats now hove into view and Captain Rostron and his crew set about the task of plucking them from a sea now seen to be cluttered with bergs and smaller ice. By 0830 the last of the survivors were aboard, including a shattered Bruce Ismay who would accept no nourishment and wanted only to be left alone. (He came in for some harsh criticism in the weeks to come, and within a year he gave up his post with White Star. He had bought an estate in the west of Ireland during the British inquiry and though he maintained a house in Mayfair until his death in 1937 he spent more and more time in Ireland.) Captain Rostron at first attempted to involve Ismay in some of the decisions attendant to the disposition of the passengers, but Second Officer Lightoller later testified that 'I may say at that time Mr Ismay did not seem to me to be in a mental condition to decide anything. I tried my utmost to rouse Mr Ismay, for he was obsessed with the idea, and kept repeating, that he ought to have gone down with the ship because he found out that women had gone down. I told him there was no such reason; I told him a very great deal; I tried to get that idea out of his head but he was taken with it; and I know the doctor [*Carpathia*'s] tried too; but we had difficulty in arousing Mr Ismay, purely owing to that, wholly and solely, that women had gone down in the boat and he had not.'[29] A more charitable view was taken by the court of inquiry which pointed out that 'Had he [Ismay] not jumped in he would merely have added one more life, his own, to the number of those lost.'[30]

When the final count was made it was found that *Carpathia* had

rescued 705 survivors out of some 2200 aboard when *Titanic* departed
from Queenstown. Among those missing were Thomas Andrews, her
builder, and Captain Edward Smith, her master. Various conflicting
stories were told about *Titanic*'s gallant but tragic master, but none
could be substantiated. Suffice to say, he went down with his ship
and it is unlikely he wanted to be numbered among those who
survived.

At the Senate hearings Captain Rostron was asked his opinion
about the course and speed of the White Star liner, and he replied
that they were quite proper.[31] When vice-president Phillip A. S.
Franklin of White Star was questioned about the company's navigational policies he referred to White Star's rule 101:

> Commanders must distinctly understand that the issue of these
> regulations does not in any way relieve them from the
> responsibility for the safe and efficient navigation of their
> respective vessels, and they are also enjoined to remember that
> they must run no risk which might by any possibility result in an
> accident to their ship. It is to be hoped that they will ever bear in
> mind that the safety of the lives and property entrusted to their
> care is the ruling principle that should govern them in the
> navigation of their vessels and that no supposed gaining of
> expedition or saving of time on voyage is to be purchased at the
> risk of accidents. The company desires to maintain for its vessels a
> reputation for safety and looks only for such speed on the various
> voyages as is consistent with safe and prudent navigation.
> Commanders are reminded that the steamers are to a great extent
> uninsured and that their only livelihood, as well as the company's,
> depends upon immunity from accident. No precaution which
> ensures safe navigation is to be considered excessive.[32]

Notwithstanding these seemingly explicit instructions it was the
common practice of Captain Smith to maintain full speed under
conditions similar to those facing him on the night of the tragedy.
The testimony of a large number of experienced and respected
masters of vessels in the trade confirmed that this was an accepted
practice,[33] and none could be found to criticize his conduct. The
Board of Inquiry took the view that Captain Smith was guilty of
nothing more than a mistake.

> He made a mistake, a very grievous mistake, but one in which, in
> face of the practice and past experience, negligence cannot be said

to have had any part; and in the absence of negligence it is . . . impossible to fix Captain Smith with blame. It is, however, to be hoped that the last has been heard of the practice and that for the future it will be abandoned for what we now know to be more prudent and wiser measures. What was a mistake in the case of the *Titanic* would without doubt be negligence in any similar case in the future.[34]

But whatever happened on that cold, clear night off the Grand Banks, the public outcry both in the United States and in the United Kingdom demanded that a culprit be identified. Captain Smith would at first glance seem the most likely candidate since he was steaming at full speed in a known area of ice, but while he was certainly guilty of following a misconceived practice the subsequent investigations showed that he was only following the 'ordinary practice of seamen', and he was moreover a very distinguished and sympathetic character who met a gallant end.

J. Bruce Ismay who had the misfortune to survive the affair was briefly considered by the press and some public officials as a fitting candidate for scapegoat. One of the most scathing indictments was penned by the eminent naval historian, Rear-Admiral A. T. Mahan, who wrote, 'I hold that under the conditions, so long as there was a soul that could be saved, the obligation lay upon Mr Ismay that that one person and not he should have been in the boat.'[35] He was savaged and lampooned by the American press, and to a lesser extent by the British. But the more staid journals urged suspension of judgement, and *Shipping World*, which reflected the opinions of the shipping industry in Britain, felt he had nothing to answer for. After all, it would seem that if he was guilty of anything it would be bad judgement in choosing to sail on the doomed liner. His guilt, however, was of a more subtle nature, and it stemmed from the owner/servant relationship that had earlier led Samuel Plimsoll to a lifetime of protest.

Few of Ismay's colleagues approved of his private behaviour and his reputation was now in tatters, but his conduct as a shipowner had to be defended, otherwise they all stood condemned. Fortunately there was a very likely candidate ready at hand to which the attention of the press could be directed and concentrated: Captain Stanley Lord, the master of the *Californian*.

*

27

Captain Lord had very sensibly stopped his vessel for the night when he encountered field ice some dozen miles or so to the north of *Titanic*'s track. We will recall that his radio operator attempted to warn *Titanic* of the ice in her path not long before she struck the berg, but had been told to shut up because she was interfering with the commercial traffic from Cape Race. The watch officer of the *Californian* later saw eight white rockets to the south at the approximate time that the liner's rockets were fired, but Captain Lord who was dozing in the chart room did not take the trouble to investigate.

The pros and cons of that issue have been argued vehemently ever since, but the recent discovery of the wreck of *Titanic* indicates that the reported position was in error.[36] Be that as it may the question is irrelevant as concerns the apportioning of blame for the sinking of *Titanic*. The question of whether or not Captain Lord could or could not have saved those on *Titanic* after she had struck the berg did, however, afforded those on the board of inquiry a splendid opportunity for deflecting the criticism away from the real culprit towards a tangential target.

The American press had already chosen Captain Lord to fill the part of scapegoat, so it was a simple matter for the British board of inquiry to pick up and exploit that lead. Unlike the *Titanic*'s master, Captain Lord was not a popular man; he was reportedly arrogant and autocratic, and governed his men by fear. It was unlikely that his conduct would be defended with the same tenacity as Lightoller demonstrated when Captain Smith's conduct came under attack. And so it proved. By insinuation, innuendo, and outright accusation where it seemed warranted, Lord was made to shoulder a large portion of the blame for the deaths of those who perished when *Titanic* sank. Thus there was less need to pursue others responsible with vigour.

It can in retrospect hardly be contested that Captain Smith was reckless in pressing on at full speed on a moonless night into an area of known danger. However, when this point was put to Charles Lightoller by Mr Thomas Scanlon, the counsel for the National Sailors' and Firemens' Union, he replied, 'Then all I can say is that recklessness applies to practically every commander and every ship crossing the north Atlantic.'[37] And no matter how hard he was pressed Lightoller would not admit that the chances taken were reckless. However, when the father of one of those lost, Thomas

Ryan, brought suit for damages the charge was gross negligence, and that charge was accepted by the court as proven.[38]

It is hard to believe that Captain E. J. Smith was a reckless or grossly negligent man, and by logical extension, that the same was true of all those other north Atlantic masters alluded to by Lightoller; yet Smith stood convicted of that charge. Why then was his conduct so uncharacteristic in this respect? The company policy as set out above was unequivocally against taking such risks as resulted in the loss of *Titanic*. The answer was then and is still today that owners are against recklessness as long as it does not put them at a competitive disadvantage. An editorial in the *Nautical Magazine* during the inquiry had revealed the true state of affairs.

> Masters in the Atlantic service would be only too thankful if this caution [the White Star policy statement given above] were the recognized procedure in the trade; but it is not. Of course Captain Smith has the blame put on him, but we seamen know perfectly well how the case stood and we should fancy that Lord Mersey with his long experience in the Law Courts must have had a shrewd suspicion as to the real state of things. But Captain Smith must be blamed, in our opinion most unjustly; he had enough responsibilities on his shoulders without the added burden of Mr Ismay's presence, and every one of us would sooner have our owner's room than his company, particularly upon a first voyage. There is enough secret pressure put upon masters to keep up speed and make passages as it is, and the presence of an autocrat on board does not tend to ease that pressure. No master would go at full speed if expecting to meet with ice unless he were obliged. . . .'[39]

Joseph Conrad was equally outspoken, and in addressing those who

> . . . know how much the merchant service, ships and men, has been to me, will understand my indignation that those men of whom (speaking in no sentimental phrase, but in the very truth of feeling) I can't even now think of as otherwise than as brothers, have been put by their commercial employers in the impossibility to perform their plain duty; and that from motives which I shall not enumerate here, but whose intrinsic unworthiness is plainly revealed by the greatness of that disaster. Some of them have perished. To die for commerce is hard enough, but to go under

29

that sea, we have been trained to combat, with a sense of failure in the supreme duty of one's calling is indeed a bitter fate. Thus they are gone, and the responsibility remains with the living who will have no difficulty replacing them by others, just as good, at the same wage. . . .[40]

If these company regulations were meant to be strictly enforced the speed of the vessel would hardly have been allowed to build up as the most hazardous leg of the passage was approached. Would 'E. J.' have handed Ismay the ice report received from *Baltic* revealing that the path ahead was strewn with bergs? It is ironic that such great play was made of the 'unsinkability' and hence ultrasafety of *Titanic* while at the same time such elemental disregard for safety was shown in other critical aspects. Lightoller later commented, '. . . when one had known, full well, and for many years, the ever present possibility of just such a disaster, I think in the end the B. O. T. [Board of Trade] and White Star won.'[41]

Of the other two White Star liners of *Titanic*'s class, *Olympic* went on to a distinguished career in the First World War as a troop carrier. The third, which had not yet been named when *Titanic* began her fateful voyage, was christened *Britannic* and served as a hospital ship in the Mediterranean. On 21 November 1916 she struck a mine in the Adriatic which caused damage similar to that which sank *Titanic* though with a less tragic result.[42]

2

The Ro-Ro: An Unsafe Design

It may seem curious to the uninitiated observer that fifty years after the sinking of the 'unsinkable' *Titanic* a pronounced trend had gathered headway towards the construction of vessels much less resistant to flooding than had been *Titanic*. The claims about *Titanic*'s 'unsinkability' had been based upon an increased standard of longitudinal subdivision. She had fifteen watertight bulkheads in a length of 882 feet, which enabled her to sustain flooding of any two adjacent compartments without sinking. In fact she could have flooded her first four compartments and remained afloat, so she more than fulfilled the requirements for safety in that respect. Standards of compartmentation have indeed risen even higher since that famous casualty, but they are only applicable to certain types of passenger vessels.

One would think that those who insure ships would be very particular about their safety features and ability to withstand the potential dangers of fire and collision. The classification societies (see appendix 4) that have grown up to meet demands for increased safety standards have laid down quite rigorous requirements in certain respects, but it is the view of underwriters and the classification societies who are their customers that the responsibility for safety belongs to the shipowner. The underwriter's function is limited to providing insurance against the risks of the venture. Unfortunately, safety regulations are almost always outdated. They are a reaction to hazards that have manifested themselves in casualties of sufficient importance to generate a public response. The ingenuity of shipowners and builders in devising ways to circumvent and avoid restrictions in the design and construction of vessels is notorious. The development of the ro-ro, or roll-on, roll-off vessel is a graphic illustration of this fact.

*

During the Second World War the needs and requirements of amphibious warfare dictated the development of vessels that could quickly and easily land cargoes and troops on to open beaches. Numerous craft, of which the LST (landing ship tank) was typical, were subsequently designed to meet this demand. These vessels had doors in the bow that opened and a ramp behind them that was lowered to enable vehicles such as tanks and trucks to drive in and out of the single hold. This provided a simplicity of cargo movement that could hardly escape the notice of commercial traders and those who catered to them. Matters of safety and seaworthiness were not primary considerations in the development of these vessels. War is a high-risk undertaking and hazards that in peacetime might be deemed inadmissible are accepted as a matter of course.

In the years immediately following the war a number of these craft were acquired by commercial operators and used for inter-island trade in the Caribbean and Far East as well as Europe and the Persian Gulf. In the short haul trades in which they were initially used they did not pose an unacceptable risk from an underwriting standpoint so their use in this context increased and grew to be recognized. They were obviously ill-suited to the transatlantic trade. None the less, the United States Military Sea Transportation Service introduced the USNS *Comet* (one of the first ships designed specifically for roll-on, roll-off use) into service in 1958 and the commercial development of the ro-ro soon followed.[1] Ferries were a natural employment for this sort of ship since the widespread acquisition of automobiles by individuals created a ready market for a service that could allow a traveller and car to resume their journey almost as soon as the vessel docked.

The problem concerning watertight subdivision in these vessels had been neatly sidestepped by simply making the weather deck (the highest continuous watertight deck), at which watertight bulkheads must terminate, the platform on which the vehicles were carried. Owners and builders had an example ready at hand to follow: that of the shelter deck vessel. The development of the shelter deck vessel had followed from the way in which tonnage (on which assessment of canal dues was based) was calculated at the Panama Canal. In conventional freight vessels before the war shipowners had seized on the expedient of lowering the gross tonnage of their ships by simply cutting 'tonnage openings' in the upper 'tween deck bulkheads and making the deck below the main or weather deck. Provision was made for securing the 'tween deck hatch openings with tarpaulins, thereby *theoretically* meeting the requirements for watertightness prescribed by existing regulations.

These 'shelter deck' ships, as they were known, were therefore supposed to have these 'tween deck hatches secured before loading was resumed in the upper 'tween decks. However, such practice would normally mean that cargo operations would be disrupted while the ship's crew secured these openings. As that would entail added stevedoring costs, and as it was not uncommon to conduct cargo operations around the clock, this disruption could occur in the middle of the night. To keep the crew standing by for such an eventuality was an expense the chief officer, who was responsible for the operation, would not willingly incur. The common practice was to ignore this precaution since as long as the vessel remained intact the neglect of this precaution would make no difference. Occasionally a casualty – usually a collision – would occur, resulting in the loss of such a vessel. But even where a ship had a collision she would not necessarily be lost unless she also happened to be loaded to her marks at the time – which was unlikely. Under such circumstances this unsafe practice came to be widely accepted, in fact some did not realize the hazard they exposed themselves to by following it, and in practice the vessels were usually operated no differently than those constructed to a safer pattern.

The average ro-ro was, and usually still is, a shelter deck vessel. The main deck is the platform on which the structure rests that encloses most of the vessel's cargo (vehicle) carrying space. This deck will often extend without obstruction for almost the entire length of the ship. There will be scuppers and drains to carry away water which might leak in through deck openings or stern or bow doors, but they are often inadequate to cope with a large and sudden ingress of water when a door fails, such as happened with the *Princess Victoria*, as will be seen presently. In such case sudden flooding of this deck will set up large 'free-surface' moments resulting in a large list. (Free surface is the term given to the destabilizing effect of loose water in an enclosed space.) Tanks or double bottoms in which fuel or water are usually carried are divided longitudinally into port and starboard tanks to restrict the free surface, since it is apparent that the greater the breadth of a compartment the greater the freedom the liquid has to run from side to side. The resulting list may well be followed by a sudden shift of some of the vessel's cargo or the entry

33

of more water as other deck openings become submerged. Within a matter of minutes this may cause the capsizing of the ship, as happened in the case of the *European Gateway* described at the end of this chapter.

Conventional standards of watertight subdivision ensure that when a vessel is subject to internal flooding she will have sufficient stability to resist capsizing unless the damage exceeds the standard to which she is required to conform. Because her main deck is also her weather deck there will be no danger of a large accumulation of water on the main deck. The same is not true of ro-ros, nor is it true of some types of bulk carriers and other specialized vessels. With a ro-ro a collision is almost certain to rupture the hull both above and below the main deck and, as the hull extends above the main deck there will be a sudden inflow of water into this more or less enclosed space, setting up the free surface heeling moments mentioned above and, potentially, resulting in the kind of casualties this chapter will now go on to examine in detail.

The *Princess Victoria*

The storm that lashed the north coast of Scotland on the early morning of 30 January 1953 had already claimed several victims as the then British Railways ferry *Princess Victoria* prepared to sail from Stranraer for the port of Larne some 16 miles to the northeast of Belfast. The 7000 ton motor vessel *Clan MacQuarrie* had been driven on to the rocks approximately 10 miles from the Butt of Lewis to the west of Pentland Firth just before midnight the day before. A Fleetwood trawler, the *Michael Griffith*, had disappeared about 9 miles south of Barra Head early on the morning *Princess Victoria* sailed.

Princess Victoria had been built in 1947 and was one of a new class of ships designed to carry vehicles as well as passengers and cargo on the short passage between northwest Scotland and Northern Ireland. The cars and cargo were loaded through an opening in the stern. This arrangement allowed rapid loading and discharging of the vehicles, but the opening through which the cars were loaded had only steel doors to close it. As there was no provision to make this aperture watertight the vessel was vulnerable to flooding, though scuppers in the vehicle deck were ordinarily adequate to accommodate any water that entered.

Captain James Ferguson, her master, had served his apprenticeship in ocean-going vessels and had sailed offshore until he had obtained a master mariner's certificate. Since returning to his native home he had served as master of cross-channel passenger ships for almost twenty years. This had been interrupted only by the Second World War when he and his vessel entered naval service as a mine-layer and troop landing ship. He was both liked and respected by those who served under him, and *Princess Victoria* was known as a happy ship. He had two grown sons, a comfortable home, and a loving wife to whom he returned each evening after his ship had completed her daily round trip. It was an ideal life for a short-sea sailor, and one that suited Captain Ferguson to a tee.

As he strode up the gangway on this boisterous January morning he no doubt knew of the gale force winds out of the northwest, but because of the natural shelter of Stranraer harbour its force was not fully felt. The mooring lines had been doubled because of the gale warnings but the passenger ferry lay comfortably at her moorings. The longshoremen had been stacking the pallets of cargo in the after end of the car deck as she was carrying no vehicles on this passage. The crew, most of whom were natives of the port, were arriving aboard and fell into the routine duties of preparing to take *Princess Victoria* to sea. Gales were a familiar part of their service and this one seemed little different from dozens of others they had faced. They served a tried and trusted master, who was every inch a seaman, backed by officers who knew their jobs and could be trusted to carry out their duties without fuss. The stewards had relatively little to do as out of the more than 1500 passenger berths available only 125 had been taken up.

The chief officer, Mr Duckels, though an Englishman, had served long enough in the service to be regarded by the local men almost as a native. He was a tall, well turned-out, cheerful man and the threatening weather did not dull his spirits as he went about the vessel that blustery morning. It certainly did not occur to him or to those under him to question the wisdom of taking the ship to sea. She had often been through as bad or worse. So promptly at 0745 her mooring lines were cast off and she was backed out of her berth.

The radio officer, David Broadfoot, was not the vessel's regular operator but was only relieving. His permanent billet was in another vessel in the same service. As the ferry was manoeuvred around to a northerly heading Broadfoot sent out the routine departure message

35

to the Portpatrick wireless station. The operator there acknowledged it and informed him that they were in for a battering as the wind was out of the north-northwest at 65 knots and increasing.

The course up Loch Ryan is about 340° and this put the wind and sea almost dead ahead. Even before *Princess Victoria* had cleared Milleur Point on the northeast tip of the peninsula to the west the ferry was making heavy weather of it. The bow of the sturdy vessel dug deeply into the churning seas and as the water broke over her bow the vessel shuddered as the stern lifted the screws out of the water. Normally Captain Ferguson would have hauled to port to round Corsewall Point, but he wisely chose to keep on to the north and get well clear of the lee shore before attempting to come around to the west.

The tide was setting out of the loch as *Princess Victoria* sailed, but with the wind and sea out of the north this factor perhaps seemed almost irrelevant. Whether Captain Ferguson did give much thought to this or not cannot now be said, but this together with the shelving sea bed combined to create a short, steep, confused sea that imparted a violent and unpredictable motion to the ferry. Visibility was now becoming restricted in heavy snow squalls though it was still sufficient for a shepherd tending his flock on a hill to the east to see *Princess Victoria* plunging and twisting in the violent seas.

It is unclear exactly what transpired in the next few hours as all of the officers and most of the crew were lost with the ship. As near as can be determined from the testimony of those who survived, it appears that Captain Ferguson decided that the violence of the sea and wind was more than he reckoned for and he intended to take his vessel back to Stranraer. The ferry was perhaps 4 miles to the north of Milleur Point at this time and as he attempted to bring her around in the tumultuous seas the steel doors on the stern were battered by a succession of heavy seas, finally forcing them open. The water flooded into the car deck dislodging the cargo stowed there and causing *Princess Victoria* to take a starboard list. A seaman, hearing the surge of the water, opened a door leading into the space and seeing what had happened rushed to the bridge to report it. Captain Ferguson sent the second officer, Mr White, aft with half a dozen seamen to try to resecure the doors as he sought shelter for the vessel in Loch Ryan. The second officer soon reported that nothing could be done as one of the doors had been distorted, thus preventing it closing. The master therefore stepped up his efforts to bring his vessel around head to the sea and back her into the loch.

This would have been an impossible feat with an ordinary ship but *Princess Victoria* was fitted with a bow rudder, but Captain Ferguson felt this daunting task of seamanship was worth a try. The carpenter and a couple of seamen were sent forward to disengage the locking bolt that held the rudder. With green seas breaking over the bow this was dangerous work and Captain Ferguson soon realized that he could not ask his men to continue in what appeared to be an almost hopeless and possibly fatal endeavour. With the abandonment of this last-ditch venture Captain Ferguson realized that *Princess Victoria* needed assistance and at 0946 he told David Broadfoot to send out an urgent signal for help: 'HOVE TO OFF MOUTH OF LOCH RYAN. VESSEL NOT UNDER COMMAND. URGENT ASSISTANCE OF TUG REQUIRED.'[3]

Ironically two salvage tugs, had been laying at Stranraer until a few days before. Now they were sheltering at Douglas on the Isle of Man some 50 miles to the south. Another tug, the *Salveda*, was about 20 miles from the reported position, but not immediately realizing the gravity of the situation, did not respond until after 1100, and when she did reach the reported position she found nothing.[4]

Unable to reach the shelter of Loch Ryan Captain Ferguson decided to try to gain the open sea and possibly reach the shelter of the Irish coast some 25 miles to the southwest. He caused word to be passed to seamen and stewards that the vessel would be subjected to heavy rolling in the next few hours, and he spoke to the passengers over the public address system offering them reassurance. Although there was obvious concern there was no panic. Lifebelts were distributed and the stewards showed the passengers how to don them, but that was seen as little more than a formality. *Princess Victoria* was, after all, British built and manned. The master was a first class seaman, and while the passage would no doubt be uncomfortable no one suggested that this sturdy ferry would not complete it. The crew meanwhile went quietly and methodically about the task of seeing that the boats and liferafts were ready for use.[5]

Down below in the engine room the danger to the vessel was more apparent. The water from the car deck was overflowing the sills of doors that were not designed to be watertight[6] and the water was already ankle deep. The pumps were working flat out to stem the water's rise but it seemed to be slowly creeping up. The list of the

37

vessel was also increasing. However, as long as the engines could be kept turning over, the ship could be brought to safety under the skilful management of Captain Ferguson. While he still believed his vessel could be saved he was only too aware of the gravity of his situation, and shortly after the initial call for help had been sent out Captain Ferguson directed David Broadfoot to send out an SOS. This was at 1031 and it was followed two minutes later with the details: 'FROM PRINCESS VICTORIA: FOUR MILES N.W. OF CORSEWALL. CAR DECK FLOODED. HEAVY LIST TO STARBOARD. REQUIRE IMMEDIATE ASSIST-ANCE. SHIP NOT UNDER COMMAND.'[7]

The operator on duty at the wireless station at Portpatrick, Mr Ross, had known David Broadfoot for years, and though at first he could hardly credit that this ship he knew so well was in danger of sinking he reacted with alacrity to the alarming news. He first tried to take a radio bearing of the stricken vessel while the other operator on watch who manned the radio telephone sent a message on the teleprinter to inform the coast guards. A messenger was next dis-patched to find the station superintendent, Mr McGregor. A call was then sent out by both Morse and radio telephone to alert all shipping in the area.

The coast guard station at Portpatrick had been notified by telephone and the lifeboat *Jeannie Speirs* was made ready for launching. The commanding officer of the naval base at Rothsea Bay had already been informed, and the destroyer HMS *Contest* was preparing to get underway and anticipated reaching the scene around 1400.

Shortly after eleven the *Jeannie Speirs* headed out of Portpatrick and turned north into the raging Irish Sea. Unfortunately, though, *Princess Victoria*'s distress message had been misinterpreted. The misunder-standing was understandable: vessels in distress are not normally capable of maintaining headway, and the coast guard had assumed that the ship was drifting out of control before the wind. It probably made little difference, as the chances of the lifeboat finding *Princess Victoria* in such weather conditions were, at best, remote, but it illustrates the further problems the rescuers faced. The wind-driven spume and increasing snow squalls not only made it more difficult for those trying to find the ferry, but made it almost impossible for those on *Princess Victoria* to fix the ship's position. The list had increased to over 30 degrees rendering her radar useless, and that combined with the violent motion of the vessel did the same to her radio direction finder (RDF) as well as her echo sounder.

Normally the Irish Sea was alive with shipping and there would have been numerous ships and smaller craft responding to the distess call of *Princess Victoria*. On this wild day, however, the vessels scheduled to sail – other than *Princess Victoria* – had chosen to stay inside. Only HMS *Contest* and the Portpatrick lifeboat dared brave the heavy seas to search for the battered ferry. Unfortunately they were headed for a position she had already left. Up to this point it had been assumed that *Princess Victoria* was drifting south under the influence of the northerly wind. RDF bearings of the distress signals taken at Portpatrick placed the ferry on a line to the northwest of Portpatrick. Bearings from other stations, however, suggested that *Pincess Victoria* might be considerably further to the west and closer to the Irish coast. The fact that these bearings did not give a good 'cut' and were furthermore taken over the land – which usually causes distortion – caused them to be discounted. Those evaluating the bearings had assumed that the ferry was drifting while in fact she had been continuing on under her own power for the past four hours.[8]

An hour earlier the *Jeannie Speirs* had arrived at a position one mile south of North Cairn in the supposed vicinity of the stricken vessel but could find no trace of her. This was at first attributed to the poor visibility in the driving snow and spume, but RDF bearings from Seaforth radio also indicated that *Princess Victoria* was much further to the west. Then at 1308 when the ferry again repeated her SOS she added that her engines were now stopped. The implications of this did not at first sink in and at 1315 Broadfoot signalled that preparations were being made to abandon ship as *Princess Victoria* was now on her beam ends. Then at 1347 came a startling message: 'PRINCESS VICTORIA TO SOS [Portpatrick radio] – CAPTAIN SAYS HE CAN SEE . . . LIGHTHOUSE . . . OPELTND . . . OFF ENTRANCE BELFAST LOUGH. SORRY FOR MORSE.'[9]

It was at once clear why the *Jeannie Speirs* had been unable to find *Princess Victoria*: she was some 13 miles southwest of where they had thought she was! In spite of the shock Portpatrick radio immediately asked: 'Is it Copeland?' (one of a small group of islands off the mouth of Belfast Lough). 'Yes,' came the answer. Unfortunately visibility was then obscured by a snow squall, preventing a bearing, but at 1406 Broadfoot gave an estimated position of 5 miles east of Copeland Island. Four minutes later he repeated the message, and then silence.

The astounding news that the sinking ship was not off Corsewall Point but at the mouth of Belfast Lough caused an immediate reaction. The lifeboat crew at Donaghadee off Copeland Island had been summoned at 1322 when Portpatrick radio had first begun to suspect that *Princess Victoria* might be further westward than had hitherto been believed. At 1340 the boat was launched. As she passed out of the harbour she learned over her radio telephone that *Princess Victoria* had just reported sighting the Irish coast. Unfortunately the position given placed the beleaguered ship five miles due east of Mew Island, which was several miles to the south of her true position. The visibility was down to 50 yards in the driving snow and wind-driven spray, and when the lifeboat reached the reported position she found nothing. *Princess Victoria* had in fact by now sunk and the survivors were struggling in the raging seas several miles to the north.

The news that *Princess Victoria* was within sight of the Irish coast had also been heard by three coasting vessels sheltering in Belfast Lough. They had not thought it prudent before to venture further in the weather raging outside, but on receipt of this news they immediately picked up their anchors and joined the search. The coastal freighter *Orchy* was in ballast and her master had earlier stuck his nose outside and, not liking what he saw, returned to seek a sheltered anchorage. A small tanker, *Pass of Drumochter*, had previously decided to take on ballast at anchor and await improvement in the weather before proceeding, while another coastal vessel carrying 800 cattle, the *Lairds Moor*, was also waiting for the storm to pass.

When Portpatrick radio sent out a CQ informing all vessels of *Princess Victoria*'s position and plight the masters of these three tiny ships did not hesitate to abandon the safety of their anchorage to join in the rescue attempt. They established contact by radio telephone and agreed to co-ordinate their efforts by proceeding in tandem. The *Lairds Moor* and *Orchy* both had radar and they took up positions on each side of the tanker as they put out to try to find the doomed ferry, which by now had slipped beneath the waves.

It was never accurately determined just where *Princess Victoria* sank, but shortly before 1300 Seaforth radio, in the Mersey, had obtained a bearing which, when crossed with another taken by Portpatrick radio, gave a position about eight miles north of the position later given by *Princess Victoria*. The Isle of Man lay between the Seaforth bearing and the ship so it was assumed at the time that this had distorted it. Although it was unlikely that the bearings had established the precise position of the ferry it should have been obvious that the true position of the hapless vessel was well to the west of where it had been previously assumed. In retrospect it should have been realized that it would have been almost impossible for an accurate bearing to have been obtained from a vessel on her beam ends, and the search area should have been broadened because of these uncertainties. Still, it would be unfair to criticize decisions made under such adverse conditions.

It seems quite incredible that *Princess Victoria* could have continued to make headway with such a heavy list and with water steadily rising in her engine room, and so it must have seemed to those directing the search ashore – which explains why they were so reluctant to believe she had done so. It is a tribute to the doggedness and courage of her engineers that they stayed at their perilous posts as had those on *Titanic* so many years ago.

For almost an hour before she finally sank she had been nearly on her beam ends, yet, in spite of this, Captain Ferguson had almost succeeded in bringing his disabled vessel into the safety of Belfast Lough. To have come so close and yet have failed must have been a bitter disappointment to this splendid seaman, and when his engines finally failed within sight of the Irish coast he was faced with an agonizing decision. Even in her extremity the ferry seemed as if she might stay afloat long enough for the rescue vessels to reach her, and to give the order to abandon ship under such dire circumstances was undoubtedly the most difficult decision he had ever been called on to make. No one was eager to leave the ship. On shore the wind was clocked at over 80 miles an hour. David Broadfoot had contacted HMS *Contest* to see if they had *Princess Victoria* in sight, but they did not and were themselves making very heavy weather of it.

The chief engineer had struggled up from below with the despairing news that the engines were now useless. Rockets were fired in the vain hope that one of the vessels searching might see them. The extreme list had long since made the lifeboats unmanageable but the port boats were released in the hope they might float clear as the vessel went under. The starboard boats were so close to the water that it was both a very tricky and hazardous operation to get them clear. The order to abandon ship was given just after 1400, and as the signal was made on the whistle passengers and crew began to scramble aboard the starboard boats. The number four boat, filled mainly with women and children and a few seamen to man it, was launched successfully, but as it drifted astern a sea lifted it under the counter and spilled its occupants into the water. The number two boat furthest forward just managed to float clear but it contained only six men. As the vessel rolled over the number six boat was catapulted over to the starboard side and most of those saved scrambled aboard.[10] A few managed to reach rafts that floated free. *Princess Victoria* had still not given up and floated bottom up, and some of the passengers and crew had managed to seek momentary refuge there. The hulk was obviously settling, however, and those standing on it had no alternative but to try to reach one of the rafts drifting nearby.

The destroyer *Contest* had now arrived at the reported scene of *Princess Victoria*'s sinking but it was soon obvious that there was something wrong. There were no survivors, no wreckage, nothing. *Contest* turned south assuming that the ferry had drifted in that direction under the influence of the wind. The Donaghadee lifeboat sighted the destroyer through the snow squalls and turned to follow her. The *Jeannie Speirs* had already been following for some time in the belief that *Contest* had more complete information of the location of the wreck. Two aircraft from the search and rescue station at Aldegrove arrived to join in the search but it seemed that *Princess Victoria* had disappeared without a trace.

Meanwhile the three small vessels that had put out from their anchorage in Belfast Lough were continuing their sweep to the north. The *Orchy*, being in ballast and more vulnerable to the effects of the wind, had taken the more northward station so as to keep well clear of the Copelands. They were on a southeasterly heading and at about 1445 the *Orchy*'s mate caught a glimpse of something almost ahead. It was a lifeboat, and then another. Beyond were capsized lifeboats, liferafts and people struggling in the water. A call was quickly made over the radio telephone urging others engaged in the search to steer for *Orchy*'s position.

Other vessels quickly converged on the scene but the task of plucking the survivors from the turbulent sea was no easy undertaking. Some were snared with boat hooks only to be found dead when brought aboard. Even in relatively calm weather picking people up from liferafts and boats can prove difficult, and when these people are half drowned and tossed about in a raging sea it can prove almost impossible. In the end only forty-one of the one hundred and seventy-four men, women and children aboard were rescued.[11]

At the formal investigation convened two months later it came to light that only a little more than a year previously the same doors had been damaged off Larne allowing the car deck to be flooded. It had been noted at the time that the drainage was inadequate but nothing had been done.[12] When the marine superintendent of British Railways (Scottish Region) testified he attempted to deflect the criticism directed towards British Railways, which had caused the president of the court, Mr John Campbell, to characterize the management as 'flabby'.[13]

The marine superintendent asserted that the weather was altogether exceptional creating conditions that could not reasonably be foreseen, and he appeared to be discounting the effect that inadequate drainage might have on the seaworthiness and safety of the vessel. This was in contradiction to the testimony of competent eyewitnesses and was rejected by the court. When it was suggested that *Princess Victoria* was in fact unseaworthy due to the vulnerability of the stern door and the inadequacy of the car deck scuppers to provide proper drainage, he fell back on the fact that surveyors for both Lloyd's Register of Shipping and the Ministry of Transport had approved the vessel for the service in which she was engaged.

What was at issue here, though it was ignored, was the basic design of the vessel and whether that design itself was unseaworthy. The vessel had a large enclosed cargo space which if flooded would create such an area of free surface as to compromise the vessel's stability. To compensate adequately for that defect would have necessitated freeing ports of such size as to have made the cargo space unsuitable in heavy weather for the carriage of cargo or vehicles. This reveals a major flaw in the vessel's design in respect to its safety. This flaw identified, there is the further disquieting fact that neither owner, designer nor the approving authorities had an adequate appreciation (or if they did, they ignored it) of the necessity to compensate for this inherent weakness in design by provision of construction features to alleviate it as near as practically possible.[14]

The vessel had on an earlier occasion suffered similar damage, though with a less serious result, and then too the responsible company officials failed to treat the matter with the attention it deserved. In examination of a discussion between Captain Morrow, an assistant manager of British Railways, and the master of *Princess Victoria* in August 1952, relative to the need for larger scuppers the court noted:

> It is most important to note how Captain Morrow treated this suggestion. He made a joke of it and referred to the inconvenience suffered by ladies with 'fancy shoes and nylon stockings'. Capt. Morrow states that the master was interested in draining the spaces at the side of the engine casing, and that he, the master, thought that larger scuppers would fit the bill, that at the same time the enlarging of one or two on either side of the ship's side in that space would not do any harm. Again no action was taken, and the matter was postponed until the passenger survey in 1953.[15]

It is significant that though the court held that the 'Loss of the *Princess Victoria* was caused by the default of the owners (the British Transport Commission) and the managers'[16], the 'builders and Lloyd's Register of Shipping should be absolved from any responsibility for the loss of the ship'.[17] The language of the court seems equivocal, as does its decision. The 'default' of the owners did, after all, consist in the final analysis of building a vessel of intrinsically unseaworthy design, but the implications of such a far-reaching conclusion seems to have escaped their notice.

It would perhaps be unfair to suggest that the builders were in any way responsible for such a design flaw, yet had they erred in almost any other matter of design they could have been held accountable. The responsibility of the classification society (in this case Lloyd's) whose rules and regulations proscribe and prescribe what may and may not be done in the construction of a vessel is perhaps an issue closer to the heart of the matter. The very reason for a classification society is to ensure that vessels are built to standards and rules that enable them to meet the natural hazards of the sea with a reasonable degree of confidence. Unfortunately these rules and regulations are based upon past experience, and when a vessel is proposed that radically departs in design from those on which the rules are based some unpleasant and occasionally horrific results can be expected.

Finally, when vessels are designed, those who too often have the last say are those whose interest and responsibility lies largely, if not solely, in the carriage of cargo. As long as what they want does not conflict with the rules, speculative objections relating to safety considerations may and often do receive short shrift. This is understandable and justifiable – up to a point. Without freight the only place for a ship is the bone-yard, but in the irresistible drive to maximize freight revenues some voice of caution about the possible risks of a proposed design or practice should be heard and heeded. In the traditional 'old-line' companies there was usually someone high in the hierarchy to supply that voice; but even in the best of them the risk of not venturing what a competitor might resulted in many a questionable practice. The number of lifeboats carried by *Titanic* and the accepted practice of maintaining full speed at night in known areas of icebergs, are but two examples. In the current situation, where there is no long tradition or extensive background of experience it seems unlikely that considerations of safety will carry much weight so long as there is no specific prohibition of a contemplated risk, or the inhibition of an exorbitant insurance premium.

Zenobia

The *Zenobia* was the first of three ro-ro vessels built in the Kockums shipyard at Malmo for the Nordo Shipping Company of Sweden. The keels were laid down in late 1978 and *Zenobia* went into service in September of the following year. The ships were designed for the company's liner trade between Greece and Syria, but they were also built to operate on the Great Lakes of North America which necessitated a limitation on their width because of the locks on the lakes. The ships were a little over 540 feet in length, the breadth was 75.5 feet, and they had a gross tonnage of 8920. They were designed to operate in either of two roles: strictly cargo ships, or as cargo/passenger vessels. In the latter case, and on the voyage in question, up to 175 passengers could be, and were carried, being generally the drivers of the trucks carried as cargo. The trucks, or lorries, were loaded through the stern-ramp and stowed by lashing in the large open decks between the double hulls or skegs through which the propeller shafts ran. The bridge and accommodation was forward of the cargo spaces. Twin diesel engines gave the ship a top speed of 21 knots though the service speed was several knots lower, and the twin rudders made the vessel extremely manoeuvrable. So sharply could she turn in fact that it imparted a considerable heeling moment at full speed, and it was necessary to restrict the rudder angle under such conditions.

Because of the manner of their construction these ships had very critical stability requirements. They were normally quite tender, which means that they heeled or listed very readily, and if the strictest attention was not given to the loading of the cargo and distribution of weights aboard, the ship could become unstable. The problem had, moreover, been aggravated during the construction of the vessel when alterations were made to increase the ship's deadweight capacity, which raised the centre of gravity thereby decreasing the vessel's stability. Although the loading and stability manuals furnished by the builders described the problems and stability requirements in detail it appears that neither the master nor the deck officers of *Zenobia* fully appreciated all the implications of the unique stability problems of the vessel.

The owners and builders of the ships were of course aware of these problems and special two-week courses had been arranged for deck and engineer officers to acquaint them with their new vessels. Practical demonstrations of the equipment and systems of the ships were also arranged, but only about half the officers in fact participated. In view of later events it seems clear that the company underestimated the seriousness of the problem facing them in the operation of these vessels. While ship's officers – and particularly masters – have, or should have, sufficient grasp of the principles of ship stability to cope with problems that might arise in the normal course of ship operation, the reality is that this understanding is far too often quite rudimentary in nature; when faced with involved and somewhat sophisticated stability considerations such understanding may be found wanting.[18]

A preview, so to speak, of the problems that would finally result in the loss of the vessel occurred during mid February in 1980 on a voyage from Patras, Greece to Tartous, Syria. After passing the Kythere Strait *Zenobia* encountered storm force winds and heavy seas. The ship was on a course of 104° making about 16 knots with the wind and sea broad on the port bow when, at about 0100, two freak seas in succession struck the vessel. The first caused her to heel about 35 degrees to starboard and when she had begun to roll back, the second struck her when the angle of inclination was still about 20 degrees causing her to lurch heavily in the same direction to about 40 degrees where she stayed.

The heavy rolling had snapped the lashings on about forty of the trucks causing them to shift. The vessel was immediately hove to bow on to the sea, and transfer of fuel and ballast brought the ship back to an even keel. The truck drivers aboard had had quite enough of this and their threatening behaviour forced the master to put into the nearby port of Volos.

The subsequent investigation into this potentially disastrous incident was apparently somewhat superficial. In any event the conclusions that should have led to recommendations to prevent a recurrence of such a situation were not reached. A shift of cargo will ordinarily cause a list due to the off-centre weight, but when a list on the order of 40 degrees results, and the weight of the cargo shifted is of no exceptional magnitude, questions must – or should – arise about the stability characteristics of the vessel as well as the loading practices that affect it. However, this was not done and the stage was set for a more serious and disastrous denouement.

It is significant that all of the officers, including the master, assigned to *Zenobia* were not only relatively new to the vessel but to that class of vessel. Indeed, the most senior officers were new to the company, none of them having as much as a year of service. The master had joined Nordo five months before and had been in *Zenobia* for only half that time. He had served at sea for sixteen years, part of which time he had been in the Swedish navy. The chief officer had been going to sea for thirteen years, but had only joined the company seven months before and had been aboard *Zenobia* for only a month. The chief engineer had been at sea for eight years of which a little over three months had been with Nordo and in *Zenobia*, and only half of that time in the position of chief engineer. The other deck officers and engineers had comparably brief experience in the vessel. From what happened both before and after the vessel took the initial dangerous list it appears that the level of organization and awareness of the vessel's critical characteristics was not high.

On departure from Koper, Yugoslavia the crew consisted of thirty persons of whom twelve were the Yugoslav catering crew. There were 121 passengers: the drivers of the lorries carried as cargo. When the ship departed shortly after midnight on 30 May 1980 bound for

47

Tartous there were 135 vehicles aboard, most of them trucks, weighing just over 3900 tons. There was also about 600 tons of water ballast, three quarters of it in the wing tanks, and there was an equal amount of fuel. The master later declared that the vessel was ready for sea and seaworthy, though in light of subsequent events it seems that the vessel had less than the required stability for her displacement, which would have rendered her unseaworthy.

After departure the vessel proceeded down the Yugoslav coast, through the Greek islands and north of Crete, until shortly after midnight on 2 June she had reached a position about 10 miles south of Cape Dolos on the island of Cyprus. The wind was light from the west and the sea was very slight. The senior second mate had just taken over the watch and with him on the bridge was the lookout and one of the passengers. The second mate undertook to demonstrate the operation of the auto-pilot to the passenger. The auto-pilot was of an advanced type and could be controlled manually by means of a joy stick. When the second mate engaged the joy stick he put the rudders over a degree to each side, first to port and then to starboard. Whether or not the steering mechanism malfunctioned at this point or whether the second mate did something that caused it to do so is not known, but the ship began to take a pronounced sheer to starboard. To counteract that he laid the joy stick over to port. The ship, however, continued to sheer to starboard whereupon the second mate shifted to normal hand steering and put the helm to port, though whether the rudders did in fact go to port is not known because the rudder angle indicator light had been turned down and was not visible.

As her turn to starboard accelerated *Zenobia* began to heel to port, and she did so very quickly coming to rest within about three seconds at an angle of about 40 degrees. The list was so extreme that it lifted the propeller on the starboard side out of the water, which began to race until stopped by the overspeed trip on the governor. The port screw was stopped by the engine staff.

This alarming development brought the captain racing to the bridge followed closely by the other officers. He quickly gave orders to have the boats prepared for launching and the passengers were instructed to make ready to abandon ship. The chief engineer and his staff were told to stand by to ballast the starboard wing tanks in an attempt to counteract the list. As they made their way below they discovered that because of the extreme list, water from the seawater intake used to cool the engines was pouring through one of its vent pipes into the cargo spaces instead of back into the sea through the overboard discharge. From the cargo deck the water was spilling into the engine room through the lift shaft for the engine room elevator. All their efforts for the next half hour or so were spent in plugging the vent pipe. Before they finished the water level on the port side of the engine room was estimated by the chief engineer to be about 10–13 feet with a similar level in the port shaft tunnel.

They then tried to ballast the number six wing tank but found they could not do so because the intake located on the starboard side was now above sea level due to the list. Efforts were then made to shift ballast from the number five wing tanks (anti-heeling tanks) from port to starboard but that too failed. Attempts to shift fuel oil from port to starboard were also frustrated because the oil was cold and could only be pumped with great difficulty and very slowly. Finally fire hoses were rigged to fill the starboard wing tanks from the deck, but the intake for the fire pump was also out of the water. The list had also been somewhat aggravated by cargo shifting as well as the flooding in the cargo spaces and engine room. Fortunately the weather was fine and the vessel's drift was negligible, being only about a tenth of a knot to the east.

At about 0030 the master broadcast a Mayday signal over the VHF set which was picked up by Haifa radio and the German container ship *Ville de Levant* about an hour's steaming time away. It was also heard by a Russian cargo ship at anchor in Limassol Roads which started to weigh anchor and proceed to the scene.

At 0110 assistance from the tug *Onisillos* belonging to the port authority at Limassol was requested, and the *Ville de Levant* arrived about 0130. The job of ferrying the passengers and catering crew from *Zenobia* to the German ship began not long thereafter using *Zenobia*'s boats. When the Russian ship arrived about fifteen minutes later one of her boats was used to assist in the transfer. This operation was completed around 0330 and the passengers and excess crew were taken to Limassol by the German vessel. A helicopter had meanwhile been dispatched but was not used because no one had been injured.

The tug arrived about 0730 and her master at first refused to tie up alongside *Zenobia* because of her heavy list. The wind had started to pick up a little and the increasing sea made it difficult to moor safely alongside. Nevertheless, the tug captain was eventually prevailed upon to pass a fire hose through the side port on the starboard side used for embarking pilots, so that water could be pumped into the starboard wing tanks. The hose parted due to the surging of the tug before anything could be accomplished and the tug master persuaded *Zenobia*'s captain to let him tow the disabled ship to Lanarca about 15 miles away where the tanks could be filled in the sheltered waters of the bay.

The towing hawser was accordingly made fast on the bow of *Zenobia* and the tow got underway at approximately 0900. The trip was made without difficulty at a speed of about two knots and *Zenobia* was anchored in about some twenty fathoms with seven shots of cable in the water on her port anchor. The master wanted to begin pumping water from the tug as soon as possible but the port authorities refused. After some discussion it was decided to use a tug from Lanarca and let *Onisillos* return to Limassol. The local tug, *Mercantonio Brigadino*, was supposed to be alongside by 0500 the following morning.

During the night an owner's representative accompanied by a salvage expert hired by the hull insurers arrived and they, together with the master, began to plan the operation. An inspection was made at 0600 and the list was estimated still to be 40 degrees. About an hour later the diesel generator supplying electricity failed due to cooling problems, and attempts to use other pumps and machinery aboard the vessel continued to be frustrated by the heavy list.

The *Mercantonio Brigadino* arrived alongside while these efforts were in progress. Filling of the number four starboard wing tank had meanwhile begun, but proceeded very slowly, however, because of the great height the water had to be pumped through and the limited capacity of the tug's pumps. This continued throughout the day but no appreciable reduction in the list was observed. During the morning it had also been discovered that more water was flowing into the cargo decks through vent pipes for the seawater intakes on the port side and some of it was flowing down the lift trunk to the engine room. The pipes were plugged but not before an appreciable amount of water was added to what had accumulated there already. Some seepage was also noticed around the port stern-ramp. Pumps in the forward pump room were started to try to reduce the water level in the engine room using the emergency generator, but these efforts were hindered by the evaporation of cooling water causing the generator to overheat. At about 1900 two more hoses from the tug were hooked up but that did not increase the rate of ballasting to any great extent.

During that day the Greek salvage tug *Vernicos Dimitrios* had been engaged to assist in the operation but was at first prevented from doing so by a court order obtained by the Cyprus Port Authority on behalf of a salvage claim for the towing services of the *Onisillos*. That problem was eventually sorted out and just before midnight the *Vernicos Dimitrios* moored alongside and began to hook up hoses for ballasting of the number three and four starboard wing tanks. The salvage tug began pumping about 0130 on the morning of 5 June. At about the same time the emergency generator failed for the last time due to overheating, forestalling any further attempts to pump out the water in the engine room.

By 0600 the number four wing tank was filled, which reduced the list to 32 degrees. Unfortunately the valve connecting the wing tanks was in the open position, as it was supposed to be when the tanks are empty, and it was not closed when the ballasting began. That allowed water to flow into the port tank and then through the vent into the 'tween deck. This interrupted the ballasting for about three hours until the source of the leakage could be established. At about the same time ballasting of the starboard anti-heeling tank was begun. By 1230 the list had only been reduced to about 30 degrees.

Ballasting of the wing tanks on the starboard side continued throughout the day. During the afternoon the number five and six double bottom tanks began to be filled, and the filling of the remaining starboard wing tanks and double bottom tanks continued through the night and into the following day with an attendant steady decrease in the list. By 1100 on the 6th the vessel had been restored to an even keel. Not long after the task of removing the water in the engine room and cargo decks was tackled by means of emergency pumps.

There was apparently a degree of confidence now that the ship's problems had seemingly been solved and the engine crew began to restore the ship's main engines and auxiliary machinery to working order. However, shortly thereafter, *Zenobia* began to list again slightly to port, suggesting that the vessel was not out of danger; although the list at the beginning was so slight that it would have been scarcely noticed. At 1230 the salvage tug suspended her operations and left.

During the afternoon a number of electric motors that had been damaged by the flooding were taken ashore for repair. The port side port, or pilot gate, was opened to put them in a boat and was left open. Full electric power had by now been restored and the water in the engine room and cargo spaces began to be pumped out. Most of it was gone by 2300 and the ship was again on an even keel, but it was only a short time after that the ship took a list to starboard of between two and three degrees. To counteract this development, ballast was pumped into the port trim tank aft.

All throughout these efforts to restore the ship to an even keel there seems to have been no strict account kept of the effect of the ballasting on the vessel's stability, and at the very least the effects of free surface were ignored. Although some of the tanks were filled it is unlikely that they were pressed up, or filled completely, and while the free surface in any one of these tanks – other than double bottom tanks – was not individually great, in sum it was appreciable. Whenever a vessel takes a list because of insufficient stability the measures adopted to right the ship must be such as to increase the stability, and not simply to counteract the list by ballasting or shifting fuel and water. This fundamental principle was apparently ignored here, and as *Zenobia* was slowly brought to an upright position by counter-ballasting, her stability, or metacentric height (GM), must have been perilously close to zero (see appendix 5). Her tendency to assume a list for no apparent reason after she had been righted was an indication of this, and when she suddenly listed in the opposite direction about 2320 this was an ominous indication of her precarious situation.

As ballast was pumped in the port trim tank to counteract the starboard list *Zenobia* slowly came upright, but shortly before midnight she suddenly flopped to port to an angle of about 10 degrees. She hesitated there momentarily but the list continued to increase slowly until it reached about 20 degrees. The master had meanwhile gone to the bridge when this happened and someone called from below to say that water was flowing in from the open pilot gate on the port side. When the ship had flopped the engineers had left the engine room and found the pilot gate open and water flowing into the 'tween deck. They attempted to close it but the inflow of water and a pilot ladder rigged in the opening frustrated their attempt. The list increased as the water poured in, and finally at 0020 the order was given to abandon ship and the crew boarded the tug *Mercantonio Brigadino*. The master asked the tug captain to tow *Zenobia* into shallower water, but he refused saying that such a decision could only be taken by the supreme court of Cyprus.[19]

An attempt to reach the port authorities over VHF radio was unsuccessful and the tug proceeded into the harbour at full speed where permission to tow the ship into shallower water was given at 0108. There was now no power on the vessel to pick up the anchor and there was no equipment available to cut the anchor cable. There was a cutting unit aboard the *Vernicos Dimitrios*, however, and that was transferred to the harbour tug about 0145. When the tug arrived about ten minutes later at the spot where *Zenobia* had been anchored there was only some debris floating on the water. *Zenobia* now rested on her side some twenty fathoms below.

At the investigation carried out by the Swedish Maritime Investigation Commission several of the ship's officers testified that the stability of the *Zenobia* had been a constant source of worry to them. They complained that not only did they lack control over the loading of the vessel, and hence her stability, but the weights of the trucks and trailers loaded were only known approximately, so calculation of the ship's stability could not be carried out with the precision her delicate condition demanded.[20]

The quick turn-around time of ro-ro and container ships has resulted in far-reaching and sometimes disturbing changes in traditional attitudes and practices regarding the loading and stowage of cargo aboard such ships. It is perhaps misleading to use the word 'traditional' in such a context since these vessels are so radically different from conventional dry cargo carriers that the traditions associated with the latter cannot always be easily applied to the former. The responsiblity for the stowage of cargo formerly held by the chief officer under the master has now largely been taken from him. He has none the less remained saddled with the responsibility to see that the stowage is proper and stability adequate. However, without any direct control over the cargo operations, he is usually forced to rely on those ashore who control this operation that they will do it in a manner that will meet with his approval. Unfortunately, that is not always the case.

Prior to the advent of these radically new cargo carrying systems the desire of the stevedore to load the ship in the most expeditious and economical manner was often in conflict with the responsibility of the chief officer to see that it was safely stowed. That led to continual compromises, but the chief officer could not fulfil his responsibilities if he made concessions that might jeopardize the safety of the vessel or its cargo. Under the new system this balance between the interests of safety and economy has been undermined if not destroyed. The man ashore now has responsibility for both safety and economy, and the sometimes nebulous considerations of safety are occasionally compromised by the pressing and more immediate necessities of economy. As safety is often a question of avoiding risks that may be more or less remote, a gamble that these risks will fail to materialize can often pay off. Such risks a conscientious ship's officer will not entertain, if for no other reason than that his life may be held in the balance. Others, for whom the dispatch of the vessel is the overriding concern, may tend to overlook these considerations that formerly dictated the stowage of the cargo.

Most of these new vessels are not so marginally stable as was *Zenobia*, and even with such a sensitive ship a gamble with her stability is unlikely to lead to disaster or even to trouble. Had the second mate not fiddled with the auto-pilot *Zenobia* would most likely have reached her destination without incident, even though she made the passage with less than the required stability. Even after she acquired the list that necessitated her deviation to Lanarca she would probably have survived the mismanagement of the efforts to right her had the reasonable precaution of closing the pilot gate been taken. But the mistakes were made, so the 'gamble' was lost. It was only fortunate that the vessel went down without any of her crew or passengers.

European Gateway–Speedlink Vanguard

The *European Gateway* was a 4263 gross ton ro-ro motor vessel built in Bremerhaven in 1975 and lengthened in 1980. The vessel was owned by the Monarch Steamship Company Ltd., but was operated by the Atlantic Steam Navigation Company Ltd. Both of these companies were subsidiaries of European Ferries Plc, which operates ferries under the name of 'Townsend-Thoresen'. She was 441 feet in length overall with accommodation for 300 passengers and thirty-six crew. On the night of the collision, however, she fortunately had only thirty-four passengers, all of whom were drivers of vehicles she was carrying. *European Gateway* had two trailer decks that were accessed by both bow and stern doors, and she was built to a one-compartment standard with fifteen watertight bulkheads, four of which were penetrated by manually operated watertight doors. The main deck, at which these bulkheads terminated, was the lower trailer deck, which was only about six feet above the waterline to which the vessel was loaded. It was calculated that a list of 10 degrees was necessary to submerge the main deck and that at 12 degrees the vessel would capsize. It was further calculated that had the number two and three watertight doors not been open *European Gateway* would not have listed as much as 10 degrees.

Speedlink Vanguard is a ro-ro rail cargo ship built in 1973 at Scheepswerven in Holland and lengthened in 1977. She was approximately 473 feet in length with a main and upper rail deck accessed through stern doors. She was owned by Northern Coasters Ltd., and was under demise charter to Sealink UK Ltd., which meant that the latter were her effective owners.

European Gateway had left her berth in Felixstowe at about 2230 and then proceeded down the channel bound for sea. Though there was a strong west-southwesterly wind blowing the visibility was good. *Speedlink Vanguard* was inbound from Zeebrugge and her master, Captain J. Bolton was aware of *European Gateway*'s departure from Felixstowe and sighted her well before the two vessels were due to meet somewhere in the vicinity of the Cork Spit buoy.

Normally the ships would have met in the channel and passed port to port. As the master of the outbound ferry, Captain H. H. McGibney passed the Pitching Ground about a mile from the Cork Spit buoy he decided to pass outside the dredged channel at the buoy. He estimated at this time that he would pass ahead of *Speedlink Vanguard* by about a mile and he duly informed Harwich harbour of his intentions. He made no attempt to communicate this information directly to *Speedlink Vanguard*, as he assumed that as all vessels underway in the channel were required to monitor the VHF the inbound vessel would hear and understand the transmission. Unfortunately the watch officer of *Speedlink Vanguard* had just stepped into the chart room at this time and the master was on the bridge wing and out of earshot. The quartermaster at the wheel did hear the message but failed to realize its significance and said nothing.

Captain McGibney later testified that in such a situation where there was inbound traffic he would leave the channel in order to avoid meeting another ship, but the practice was not universal and indeed Captain Bolton was unaware of it. He hence fully expected *European Gateway* to alter course to starboard as the vessels approached the Cork Spit buoy where the channel changed direction from 331° (outbound) to 270°.

On passing the Number Three buoy Captain Bolton altered course to starboard to 280° to give *European Gateway* more room, but as the distance closed to less than a mile and *European Gateway* continued to stand on, Captain Bolton ordered hard right wheel and sounded one blast on the whistle in accordance with the rules. When the distance had closed to about half a mile it became apparent that collision was imminent and Captain Bolton ordered the engines full astern.

Captain McGibney had meanwhile expected *Speedlink Vanguard* to alter to port to follow the channel and did not immediately appreciate that the other vessel had altered to starboard. When he did it was too late and though he ordered the helm put hard to starboard *Speedlink Vanguard* struck his ship on the starboard side just forward of midships in the way of the generator room.

Speedlink Vanguard had been making 14.5 knots but the reversal of her engines had reduced her way to about 6 knots at the time of the collision. Those in the engine room of *European Gateway* felt a 'bump of no great severity', but saw a wall of water about three feet high pouring through the watertight door that separated the generator room from the main engine room. The starboard generator was knocked out almost immediately and the port about ten seconds later. This cut off the fuel injection pumps leaving the vessel with only emergency power. The chief engineer, Mr Lynagh, ordered the evacuation of the engine room and, after confirming that everyone was out of the flooded space, he intended to try to close the watertight doors from a remote control station located in the upper vehicle deck. While making his way there he encountered the second engineer, Mr Wilson, and ordered him to close the doors while he reported to the master on the bridge. The *European Gateway* had by this time developed a list of about 10 degrees to starboard.

Wilson succeeded in closing the number three door and was in the process of closing the number two door when he was almost struck by a large trestle which shifted as the ship continued to list. The *European Gateway* had by now taken the ground and was heeling rapidly making it increasingly difficult to stand. The vehicles were straining at their lashings and capsizing seemed imminent. Under such adverse circumstances it was obvious that nothing more could be done and the second engineer abandoned his efforts. Water was now flooding into the main vehicle deck.

The bow of *Speedlink Vanguard* at first remained embedded in the side of *European Gateway*, but the momentum of the latter, at the point of collision, caused *Speedlink Vanguard* to pivot to starboard and she broke free in a shower of sparks. The *European Gateway* took a list to starboard almost at once. Captain McGibney immediately ordered the radio officer, Mr Sibley, to inform Harwich harbour control of the collision by VHF, but that order had already been anticipated. He instructed the second officer, Mr Wood, to sound the general alarm and then to telephone the purser and have him muster the passengers in the saloon. He tried to contact the engine room to order the watertight doors closed but could not get through. He then gave the order to lower the lifeboats to the embarkation deck. The public address system had failed and efforts to use portable VHF sets instead were also unsuccessful.

The purser, Mr Cartwright, had meanwhile instructed the passengers to don warm clothing and lifejackets which they would find in their cabins. This led to some confusion as the lifejackets were ordinarily stowed elsewhere. The crew were now having difficulty in lowering the boats on the starboard side due to the increasing list. The falls of one of the boats jammed and another which they succeeded in lowering to the level of the embarkation deck was then – due to the list – too far outboard for it to be in reach. Most of the passengers had assembled in the vicinity of this boat and some of them were now inclined to jump overboard but were dissuaded by Captain McGibney who had taken charge.

Word of the disaster had quickly spread round the harbour and the response was immediate. The pilot launch *Valour* was in the process of putting a pilot aboard the inbound *Dona Futura*, and the coxswain, Mr Lee, made for the scene as did the *Dona Futura*. The Harwich and Walton lifeboats followed shortly thereafter as did a number of tugs and other vessels. Mr Lee in the *Valour*, after several attempts, was able to push the number three boat alongside *European Gateway* in which position passengers and crew were able to use it as a gangway from which to make their way to the pilot launch. Twenty-eight men in all were rescued in this fashion. The number one boat with four men aboard was overturned and one man was lost, the rest being rescued by the pilot launch. This rescue operation by Mr Lee and his men was accomplished under threat of being trapped under *European Gateway* should she capsize before the operation could be completed, and they displayed great courage and determination.

On the port side the list soon made it impossible to launch any boats, but some of the crew, under the direction of the chief officer, Mr Samples, succeeded in launching a liferaft into which a number of crewmen and passengers were able to escape. Unfortunately, as the vessel's list increased the ladder was lifted too far out of the water to reach the raft and the painter which secured the raft alongside tautened and threatened to capsize the raft. The occupants were forced to jump into the sea and five of these either drowned or succumbed to hypothermia.[21]

The remainder of those finally rescued found refuge on the hull of *European Gateway* as she settled on her side in thirty feet of water. The chief officer, recognizing that the vessel could not completely sink in the depth of water in which she had settled advised those in the immediate vicinity to stay with the ship, and they were taken off by the pilot boat *Patrol* and the tug *Alfred*. In spite of the confusion and the difficult conditions the court considered it remarkable that only six men were lost. The loss of life might have been much higher except for the skill and determination of the rescuers, including some of the officers and crew of the stricken vessel.

The court devoted a great deal of time and attention to the actions and decisions that brought this casualty about, but in the final analysis it is quite clear that had the masters of the two vessels been in direct communication by VHF as they approached their meeting place near the Cork Spit buoy there would have been no collision. Unfortunately, the Department of Trade in their wisdom had published a merchant shipping notice in May 1978 warning mariners of the dangers of using VHF in such a manner. The effect of this was to discourage mariners in UK waters from availing themselves of this valuable aid to navigation. This matter has been discussed elsewhere and need not detain us here,[22] but a question of more immediate interest is that pertaining to the practice of keeping watertight doors open in confined waters.

A number of theories were considered and rejected by the various experts involved as to why *European Gateway* listed to the point where the main vehicle deck was subjected to flooding. Stability calculations for vessels of this type in a damaged condition are based upon a supposition of symmetric flooding. It was concluded, however, that *European Gateway* must have suffered transient asymmetric flooding immediately following the collision to have caused her to list beyond the point of no return, which is calculated in this case to be 12 degrees.[23]

In accounts of collisions it is occasionally remarked that the vessel takes an initial list following the collision but, as the flooding progresses, the list decreases and perhaps disappears. Where the vessel involved has no enclosed deck above the main deck this transient asymmetrical flooding is of no consequence and so the assumption that flooding following collisions is symmetrical is a tenable one. In the case of a vessel such as *European Gateway* this is not necessarily the case.

Calculations submitted at the investigation showed that if the watertight doors had been closed *European Gateway* would not have heeled beyond the point of no return and would have righted herself.[24] The debate then centred around whether the watertight doors should have been closed, given the operational practicalities of *European Gateway* and similar vessels. The governing conditions were spelled out in the Merchant Shipping Regulations of 1980, based upon the SOLAS (Safety of Life at Sea) convention of 1974, which stated that 'every watertight door . . . shall be kept closed while the ship is at sea except when it is required to be open for the working of the ship'.[25] The latter part of the phrase was understandably the source of much contentious discussion.

Given the construction of *European Gateway* and many other similar vessels, a very strong and possibly conclusive argument can be made for leaving the watertight doors open, at least in good visibility. In arriving at its conclusion the court turned to examine the 'current practice' and found that except for the Belgian RMT Line, which operates cross-channel ferries, the current practice was in line with that followed by *European Gateway*, in the same way as *Titanic* followed current practice in proceeding at full speed at night in a sea area where icebergs might be encountered. What was not discussed was the desirability of allowing ships to be so constructed as to make it necessary to allow watertight doors to be kept open in areas and conditions where by all other criteria it was beyond dispute that they should be closed.

The problem that this case and others in this book illustrate so forcibly is that vessel safety appears to be at best a secondary consideration as far as many shipowners are concerned, and the same holds true with those who design and build their vessels. Indeed, at a seminar on ship safety held at the University of Glasgow, sponsored by their Department of Naval Architecture and Ocean Engineering in June 1983, a prominent member of the British shipbuilding community, Marshall Meek, in his address frankly stated that 'there seems to be no real pressure from the parties involved in building or operating ships for greater safety'.[26] Vessels are understandably built with commercial considerations foremost, and safety requirements are rarely considered beyond what the regulations spell out. As has been pointed out before, with tried and tested designs and classes this rarely causes problems because regulations have come into being over the years that deal more or less adequately with flaws in the original design. It is when new types of vessels are conceived and built, however, that flaws in their design can easily go unrecognized until a casualty provides a demonstation.

Unfortunately by the time the flaw is revealed the design may have been widely adopted (as has been the case with ro-ro vessels) thereby creating a vested interest in doing as little as possible to tamper with the flawed design.[27] Considerable pressures are brought to bear on regulatory bodies to compromise and adopt questionable 'solutions' to the problem. Until fairly recently this laissez-faire approach caused no great public inconvenience or damage, and while the victims may have been less than happy with the results it has long been accepted that mariners know, or should know, the hazards of their profession as well as its potential consequences.

Casualties to passenger ships, however, are capable of generating a degree of public concern that can result in real and often very expensive solutions, though not infrequently the measures adopted are expedient reactions of a 'covering your tracks' kind. The French response to the *Amoco Cadiz* catastrophe, related in a later chapter, was at least in part of this nature. The fact that allowing such huge tankers, with such a monstrous potential for damage to the environment, to operate under the anarchic and archaic conditions of an earlier stage in ocean transport, did in itself all but guarantee that such a disaster would occur, was all but overlooked. One of the more recent examples of the 'covering your tracks' phenomenon is that of the capsizing of *The Herald of Free Enterprise*.

60

The Herald of Free Enterprise

The disaster in 1987 in Zeebrugge which occurred, with the loss of nearly 200 lives, when the ro-ro ferry *The Herald of Free Enterprise* capsized on leaving port only confirmed what knowledgeable seafarers, surveyors, naval architects, shipbuilders and shipowners have known for years. These ships are inherently unseaworthy. It remains to be seen whether economic considerations will again prevail over considerations of safety. But no matter how skilful the seamen sailing such a ship, no matter how well designed and constructed, as long as the basic design remains unaltered so that free surface can envelop the major portion of the interior of the ship if her watertight integrity is compromised, such vessels will continue to provide a vehicle for further preventable disasters.

In reading the account of the formal investigation into the capsizing of *The Herald of Free Enterprise* one is left with the distinct impression that one of the most serious flaws in the management structure of Townsend-Thoresen was the lack of a man with command experience in a senior management position ashore. It is extremely difficult if not impossible for someone without command experience to fully understand and appreciate the problems and concerns of the master.

The masters of the *Spirit* class vessels, of which *The Herald of Free Enterprise* was one, had long been uneasy about the vulnerability of their vessels to flooding through the bow doors. On several occasions vessels had sailed with their bow doors open. Over three years before *The Herald of Free Enterprise* met her end a sister ship, *The Pride of Free Enterprise*, sailed from Dover with both bow and stern doors open because the assistant bosun had fallen asleep and failed to carry out his duty.[28] A year later the master of that vessel promulgated a circular advising all deck officers and relevant ratings:

> Twice since going on the Zeebrugge run, this ship has sailed with the stern or bow doors open. No doubt this is caused by job/rank changes from the Calais run; however, all those named persons must see that the system is worked to make sure this dangerous situation does not occur. Give it your utmost attention.[29]

In June of the following year one of the *Pride*'s masters wrote a memorandum to the managing director of the fleet suggesting that indicator lights be installed so that masters on the bridge would have a means of knowing that these doors were shut. This suggestion was circulated among the various marine managers for comment. The deputy chief superintendent replied: 'Do they need an indicator to tell them whether the deck storekeeper is awake and sober? My goodness!' The replies of the others were no more sympathetic and the idea was rejected.[30]

None the less, the masters continued to press the matter and in October 1986 the deputy chief superintendent replied to a memorandum on the matter sent to him by the senior master in the service:

Bow and stern door remote indication
. . . I concur in part with Mr King's penultimate paragraph that the project is unnecessary and not the real answer to the problem. In short, if the bow and stern doors are left open, then the person responsible for closing them should be disciplined. If it is still considered that some modification is required then a simple logic system, e.g., if the clam doors are open and the inner watertight doors closed then the door insecure alarm operates. The stern door on the other hand is visible from the vehicle deck at all times, therefore the problem should not arise. So in conclusion, the bridge indication is a 'no go'.[31]

Justice Sheen commented that, 'Enough has been said to make it clear that by the autumn of 1986 the shore staff of the company were well aware of the possibility that one of their ships would sail with her stern or bow doors open.'[32] The solution offered was to discipline the person responsible. 188 people lost their lives as a direct result of this decision by the management. Justice Sheen concluded by remarking that, 'This topic has been discussed at length because it illustrates the attitude of the marine department to suggestions made by the masters.'

Needless to say the indicators have now been installed and a number of other specific recommendations of the court designed to prevent a recurrence of this accident have been adopted.[33] The fundamental reason for the casualty, none the less, remains. The vessels, including two new ones introduced into service in 1988, remain as vulnerable as ever to capsizing should the vehicle deck be flooded. P&O, the parent company who understandably replaced the tarnished colours of Townsend-Thoresen with their own, have, however, seemingly done all that can reasonably be expected to make their ships safe under the circumstances.

Unlike the casualty involving *European Gateway* the P&O ferries now keep their watertight doors closed at sea, except one opening on to the engine control room. This can be closed either from the bridge or the control room so it seems likely that the flooding could be confined to the damaged compartments. Under such circumstances the vehicle deck should remain above the waterline. If, however, there is a sea of any size running it is quite likely that some water would make its way into the vehicle deck, and if adequate measures were not taken to immediately contain and remove it, stability could be eroded with potentially disastrous results. It is extremely unlikely, however, that this would happen with such rapidity that the vessel would capsize before lifeboats and liferafts could be launched and passengers and crew evacuated if needed.

The vessels are operated at a very high standard and on a recent trip on *The Pride of Bruges* (formerly *The Pride of Free Enterprise*) the author was very favourably impressed with the competence of the master and his watch officers. Although they operate in an area where the risk of collision is perhaps as great as any in the world the level of vigilance is correspondingly high. The vessels are highly manoeuvrable and handled with such prudence and skill as to minimize the risk of collision. Closed circuit television monitors enable the master to see if the bow and stern doors are in fact closed. A high capacity ballast pump has been installed so that the forward ballast tank can be quickly emptied, enabling the vessel to avoid sailing by the head. Short of major and perhaps impractical structural changes in these ships it appears that P&O have done all that can reasonably be expected to make their ferries as safe as possible. What the public is entitled to assume is that any ferries built in the future will be so designed and constructed that they will no longer be vulnerable to fatal flooding of the vehicle decks.

Concern about ro-ro safety is no new thing. As long ago as 1980 maritime authorities in Russia, France and Norway were voicing fears about the lack of watertight subdivision in such vessels, though the UK Department of Trade expressed confidence in the design and many others in IMO (International Maritime Organization) shared that complacency.[34]

In the investigations into these casualties there were occasional passing references to the inherent defects of ro-ro vessels, but so advantageous is this design from the standpoint of cargo carriage that no serious consideration is given to questioning the concept itself.

Admittedly the seamen who man these vessels represent a small minority of those affected by this mode of transport. It can be argued that the principle of the 'greater good of the greater number' dictates that the undeniable advantages of ro-ro ocean transportation in lowering its costs far outweigh the equally undeniable risks to which the seamen who sail them are subject. After all, it can be said, no seaman is forced to go to sea in these ships.

Whatever the moral validity of that argument, it would be a rash shipowner indeed who would attempt to uphold it when it comes to the carriage of passengers rather than freight. Until *The Herald of Free Enterprise* capsized the loss of life in the relatively few ro-ro passenger ferry casualties had been rather modest. Regrettably it does not seem that the conclusions reached by the court of inquiry into this disaster will bring about any fundamental change. The disintegration of the space shuttle *Challenger* before a television audience of millions brought to light the disturbing disregard of safety considerations whenever economic forces are allowed free rein in coming to decisions. The history of ocean transport suggests that not even such a dramatic exposure of design or operating defects will put things right.

3

Foundering

The Oxford English dictionary definition of foundering is 'to fill with water and sink'. The reason why vessels fill with water, however, are various, but usually some element of human error, oversight, or acceptance of an excessive risk is found in the circumstantial chain of events leading to the loss. A ship's hull cracks in heavy weather causing flooding, loss of stability and further flooding until all reserve buoyancy is lost and the vessel sinks. Other ships in the same storm survive. Why did this one not? The hull may have been weakened by wastage, rendering it vulnerable to stress. The cargo may have been improperly stowed causing excessive strain as the vessel labours in a seaway. A flaw in the design or construction of the ship may have made it susceptible to stress. Improper stowage or securing of cargo may result in shifting causing a heavy list thereby allowing water to enter through deck openings. Inadequate maintenance and repairs may likewise compromise the watertightness of a ship. In some cases the inexperience and/or ineptitude of the master and his crew are responsible. All of these factors lead to avoidable risks, but putting things right usually entails an expenditure of money the owner may be reluctant to make.

In the days when sail was the sole means of propulsion, ships were often driven on to a rocky shore by violent winds and seas through no lack of skill by captain and crew or indifference of owner to her seaworthiness. Marine insurance evolved out of such circumstances to offer financial protection against such whimsical 'acts of God'. Marine insurance policies still contain clauses referring to 'acts of God', but claims made under that cover today can usually be traced to human foibles. Illustrations of this will be seen in the cases that follow.

Flying Enterprise

One of the most publicized sea sagas of modern times concerned a small American cargo ship that lay almost on her beam ends for close to two weeks with a split hull and shifted cargo, before finally sinking almost within sight of her port of refuge. Although most people today might not recognize the name *Flying Enterprise* that gallant little ship and her intrepid captain caught the imagination of the world during the first days of the new year of 1952.

Flying Enterprise was one of a number of C-1 class cargo ships constructed during the Second World War. She had been built as the *Cape Kumukaki* in 1944, and in many ways the 'Cape' ships were the most comfortable though smallest of the 'C' type vessels built for the US government and later sold to private operators at the end of hostilities. The 396-foot vessel of 6711 gross tons was equipped with steam turbine engines of 4000 horsepower that drove her at a speed of 14 knots. The crusty Danish maritime maverick Hans Isbrandtsen acquired her in 1947 for a little over $900,000 and she formed one of his fleet of twelve cargo vessels trading round the world. He had first come to public attention in the late forties when his ships, defying the blockade imposed by the Nationalist Chinese on mainland Communist China, were subjected to strafing and bombing attacks as they sailed into such ports as Tsingtao and Shanghai. He came in for some less welcome publicity when one of his captains shot and killed a cabin steward he claimed was insubordinate and threatening – even though the man wore handcuffs when shot.

Isbrandtsen, though a staunch American patriot as were many nationalized US citizens, was none the less proud of his Danish blood, and favoured seamen from his native land to command his ships. Henrik Kurt Carlsen, who now lived in Woodbridge, New Jersey with his wife and two daughters, was typical of those Hans Isbrandtsen chose as masters of his ships. Carlsen had grown up in Denmark in the town of Elsinore and played as a boy in the halls of Hamlet's castle with the keeper's son. He had gone to sea at the age of fifteen and made ten voyages in square-riggers while he learned his trade. His mother, who still lived in Denmark, later described him as 'a wonderful boy, but obstinate'. The world would come to be familiar with just how obstinate Kurt Carlsen could be.

Like many of his compatriots who followed the sea, Carlsen was abroad when the Germans occupied his country. He took up employment on American ships not long after and became a citizen during the War. He was, not unnaturally, attracted to the ships operated by his fellow countryman, Hans J. Isbrandtsen. After obtaining a licence as second mate the dark, stocky young Dane gained rapid promotion aboard the Isbrandtsen ships. He was given his first command in 1947 at the age of thirty-three and had been master of the *Flying Enterprise* for three years when that ship sailed for New York from the German port of Hamburg on 21 December 1951. Carlsen was one of ten Isbrandtsen masters allowed to fly his 'own flag', an honour granted after a master 'showed his stuff'. Carlsen's pennant was black with his name in large gold letters and jagged gold streaks of lightning in each corner.

Flying Enterprise began loading her cargo in Rotterdam where some 1200 tons of pig iron was stowed in two of the ship's five holds; 762 tons in number two hold and 408 in number four. The pigs, or ingots, were about an inch thick, six inches wide and eighteen inches long. A variety of other items were loaded there and later in Hamburg, including some Volkswagens, 850 tons of coffee, some mail and money from a Swiss bank – which later became the source of some speculation. The pig iron, which no doubt seemed by far the most uninteresting of the articles stowed in the ship's holds, was to prove to be of vastly more significance than more glamorous items such as rare paintings, which also formed part of the cargo.

The stowage of the pig iron in the number two hold was in pyramid form, reaching a height of about eight feet in the square, or middle of the hold, and tapering off to nothing at the sides. In number four hold the pigs were levelled off. No explanation was offered why it was not felt necessary to level off the stowage in the number two hold, but a matter of even greater importance was that the pigs were not secured in any way. It was later said that this was the normal practice and so no blame could be attached to the ship for the stowage. It would, of course, have been not only very costly but very awkward to have tommed the cargo down because of the depth of the holds, but it would have been practical to have done this had the pigs been stowed in the lower 'tween decks, which were substantially shallower. (Tomming is accomplished by laying down a floor of dunnage, rough flat planks, over the stowage and then securing it by means of heavy timbers wedged vertically between this floor and the underside of the deck above.)

An old rule of thumb for stowage of cargo, however, is to put two thirds in the holds and one third in the 'tween decks. This practice will usually ensure that the vessel has adequate stability. It may in fact be *more* than adequate, creating excessive stability, resulting in a stiff ship, which means that the vessel's motion in a seaway will be quick and jerky, causing undesirable stress and strain on the cargo and the ship. There is, none the less, a tendency among seamen who have not made themselves thoroughly conversant with all the subtleties of stability and stowage to follow this rule of thumb to be on the side of safety. It was this consideration that may have influenced those aboard *Flying Enterprise*.

Christmas aboard a cargo ship is ordinarily a staid if not grim affair. Although there are usually ample decorations, and the cooks and stewards go to great pains to provide a traditional Christmas meal, the absence of one's family results in an atmosphere not entirely conducive to the Christmas spirit. Occasionally recourse will be made to another kind of 'spirits' to enliven the mood, but that is not a recommended practice in a vessel proceeding down the English Channel, first beset by fog and then buffeted by gales. It would have been remarkable if a tot or two were not consumed aboard Kurt Carlsen's ship during the holidays, but there was never a suggestion that this was one of the problems that began to beset *Flying Enterprise* as she cleared Land's End. There were several women and a few children among the ten passengers embarked at Hamburg, and they may have helped in a small way to warm the atmosphere in the ship's dining saloon on Christmas Day. But as the fog gave way to gales on Christmas Eve tension rather than conviviality was a more likely product of the day. The storm that was blowing up was perhaps no more severe than countless others that sweep across the Western Ocean every winter, but it was sufficiently fierce to close all the ports on the south coast of England and cause fifteen ships to come to grief before it blew itself out.

On 26 December *Flying Enterprise* had reached a position about 400 miles west of Bishop Rock, but her chances of making any appreciable progress forward during the next day or two seemed slender, with hurricane force winds out of the northwest and forty-foot seas. As these North Atlantic rollers pummelled and buffeted the half-loaded ship Carlsen decided to heave to until the worst passed. The wind was brought about 20° on the starboard bow on a course of about 260° and speed reduced to bare steerageway. The wind continued to blow with unremitting violence throughout the day and night. The vessel laboured and strained as she was tossed from crest to trough in the mountainous seas, and about 0630 on the 27th a mighty crack was heard throughout the ship as the hull fractured just forward of the deck house.

The cracks were observed to extend from the after corners of the number three hatch coamings (a raised steel enclosure around the hatch opening), out to the shell plating and down the side. A quick inspection of the number three upper 'tween deck by the chief officer, 32-year-old Frank L. Bartak, revealed that the damage continued down the sides of the hull for another three to four feet. Daylight was seen through the cracks but as yet the ship did not seem to be making any water. An attempt to reinforce the hull against further cracks was made by stretching wire ropes between bits on both sides and heaving them tight with the cargo winches. Cement boxes were also constructed at the ship's side in the 'tween decks to try to seal them. Carlsen also altered course to a more southerly heading to put the sea abeam and thus reduce the violent pitching that had caused the damage.

The ship at this point was almost due north of Corunna on the northwest tip of Spain and almost due west of Brest. Carlsen must have realized that as soon as the weather improved he would have to put into port for repairs, and just after noon on the 27th he notified his head office in New York of the situation. Up to now the condition of the ship, though critical, was not alarming. The cracks, however, had ominously continued to creep down the ship's sides and the number three hold began to flood giving the ship a slight port list. The vessel continued south on this course during a wretched night with the ship rolling sluggishly through about 20 degrees to either side. Shortly before noon on the 28th *Flying Enterprise* was suddenly flung violently to port by a freak wave, and an ominous dull rumbling was heard on the bridge. Carlsen laconically remarked to second mate Otto Michaels, 'I'm afraid the cargo has shifted', as *Flying Enterprise* assumed a list of about 25 degrees to port. She continued to roll about the same as before, but with the pronounced port list her deck edge on the low side came perilously close to the water.

Even with the list the ship might have been able to limp into port when the weather abated but the sea had done more than shift the cargo; it had carried away the rudder as well. Nothing daunted, Carlsen had the mate attempt to rig a jury (makeshift) rudder, but in that weather and with a 25 degree list the attempt came to naught. The embattled Dane had to face the unwelcome fact that he must ask for help from others if he was to save his ship, passengers and crew.

Until this time the world had no inkling of the drama unfolding aboard the little freighter; a drama that would dominate the front pages for the next fortnight. When the radio operator, David Greene, sent out the distress call it was scarcely noticed by the press. The message was brief and to the point: 'SOS FLYING ENTERPRISE ENCOUNTERING SEVERE HURRICANE AT POSITION 49°20'N, 17°20'W. SITUATION GRAVE. HAVE 30 DEGREE LIST AND JUST DRIFTING.'

Fortunately the ship was in one of the most heavily trafficked areas of the world, and within minutes many ships responded of which five were within less than a day's steaming.

At the time, however, the hours between the sending out of the first message and the arrival of the first ship must have seemed like an eternity. With the vessel listing heavily and almost split in half, lying in the trough of mountainous seas that threatened to engulf her, it was by no means certain that she would stay afloat until help arrived. Abandonment, however, was out of the question until someone reached the scene. A wave had smashed the port lifeboat and the starboard boat could not be lowered because of the increasing list, now almost 45 degrees, following a further shift of cargo.

The nearest ship was the American freighter *Southland*, which was only about 80 miles away. Because of the heavy seas, however, she was unable to reach the scene until after dark. Nothing could be done in the prevailing weather until daylight, so the freighter stood by making preparations to launch a boat at first light. The crew and passengers aboard *Flying Enterprise* spent a miserable night huddling in the passageways of the ship. Carlsen had instructed everyone to wear lifejackets in case the ship started to capsize, and when the main generator had to be shut down during the afternoon because of the increasing list the interior of the vessel became dark, dank and foreboding. Carlsen, however, remained cheerful throughout, confident of rescue.

As soon as dawn broke the *Southland* prepared to launch a boat. The US Army Transport vessel, *General A. W. Greely*, had arrived meanwhile and launched two boats, which helped to support Carlsen's optimistic forecasts. The people aboard the stricken freighter, however, were still faced with the daunting task of reaching the deck of one of the vessels now standing by. Making things even more chancy, the wind had continued to increase in fury, and early on the morning of the 29th it reached a crescendo of 90 knots.[1] From a salvage standpoint *Flying Enterprise* did not appear to offer much promise. It was likely that she would shortly sink, and because of the terrible weather some fifteen ships in the area were in need of assistance, so tugs were in great demand. Of the tugs in the area capable of doing the job, the *Turmoil* was already towing a Shell tanker to Falmouth. The Dutch tug *Zwarte Zee* was towing another British ship, but *Zwarte Zee*'s sister ship, *Oceaan* was still available and was quickly engaged by the owners of *Flying Enterprise*. It was news of that development that had aroused Carlsen's optimism. Unfortunately, as the rescue vessels manoeuvred to take off the passengers and crew, news came that the Dutch tug, now almost in sight, had had to turn around and go the assistance of *Zwarte Zee* herself, which had collided with another vessel and was now in danger.

In the meantime other vessels continued to arrive. The British freighter *Sherbourne*, the American cargo ship *Warhawk*, and the Norwegian tanker *Westfal Larsen* came up as the wind and sea began to abate later that morning. Captain Carlsen asked for volunteers to remain aboard with him as the passengers and remaining crew prepared to leave in the boats from the five rescue vessels now waiting nearby. The first boats came from the two American ships and it soon became clear that the passengers and crew would have to take their chances with the sea as it was impossible for the boats to get safely alongside.

The ten passengers, which included two children, were paired off with the ten best swimmers in the ship's crew, but though they realized that this was their best chance for rescue, it required considerable coaxing to actually get them to leap into the rough sea below. Boats from three of the five vessels participating capsized during launching or were up-ended by seas, though fortunately the crews of all these boats were saved.

The first boat to reach *Flying Enterprise* was one from the *Greely*, which picked up seven survivors on the first attempt. As they headed back to the mother ship, however, the engine failed. Now forced to take to the oars, they pulled for the *Southland* which was closer. The second boat from the transport took off a further seven, but one of the passengers disappeared before the boat could reach him. The first boat now returned to pick up another ten. The boats from the *Southland* meanwhile plucked eleven from the water as the boat from the *Greely*, under the command of her second mate, Robert L. Husband, came back for a third time to pick up the sixteen remaining crew.

Nine volunteers had remained aboard with the beleaguered Danish skipper awaiting the promised tug. The weather, which had abated sufficiently to allow the rescue, now threatened to turn nasty again. Word was meanwhile received of *Oceaan*'s diversion. Carlsen's first responsibility was to the lives of those under him, and much as he wanted to save his ship he could not in good conscience ask those still aboard to take any further risks. He asked the *Greely* to send a boat back again to take off the other nine men. Four, including the chief mate, volunteered again to remain behind with him, but he could not take the chance. Carlsen himself had at first thought his ship was doomed; however, after the rescue of the passengers and the bulk of the crew he took stock of his sitation and felt there was a good chance he might be able to get his ship into port. The list seemed to have stabilized at about 70 degrees, and she seemed tight except for the flooded number three hold. He no doubt would have welcomed the company and assistance of one or more of his shipmates, but he could not ask them to risk their lives any further. He could, however, take that risk himself and he did. The rescue operation over, he thanked the vessels that had assisted and released them to continue their voyages. Meanwhile the USNS *Golden Eagle* arrived and she remained to keep him company on his lonely vigil.

Fortunately for Carlsen he was not completely alone. Ship captains lead a solitary life at the best of times. Neither tradition nor good practice favours them entering into a full social life aboard ship. They tend to remain aloof and, though some no doubt develop a taste for solitude, none would welcome it if it were enforced and as absolute as that which now faced Carlsen. Isolation inclines masters to take up hobbies to alleviate loneliness, and one that has found increasing favour in recent years is amateur radio, with a steady increase in the number of sea-going 'hams', many of them ship's masters. Carlsen was one of that number, and that made his situation just barely tolerable in an otherwise intolerable environment. The phlegmatic but optimistic Dane settled in for a long wait. Tugs of sufficient power were just not available, and *Flying Enterprise* was not a particularly prize salvage prospect under the circumstances. Ocean salvage is no doubt one of the most romantic of businesses, but it is a business and under the standard 'No cure, no pay' terms (if the salvage attempt does not succeed the salvors get nothing) then in effect the slim prospects of *Flying Enterprise* were not such as to unduly excite the salvage world.

For a salvor to realize one penny of reward he must first succeed in getting his prize into port. No matter how superhuman the effort expended or the expense involved nothing is gained if the ship sinks just short of success. *Flying Enterprise* was lying at an angle of about 70 degrees, with a huge crack in her hull all across her main deck and halfway down her sides. Her cargo had shifted and the weather in the dead of winter off the Brittany coast is almost uniformly foul. The lives had been saved. Carlsen was risking his voluntarily, so there was no overriding moral necessity to go to the aid of his vessel. His best bet was the big British salvage tug *Turmoil* at present towing the tanker *Mactra* towards Falmouth. Once that job was finished her owners were prepared to tackle the task of getting the *Flying Enterprise* into a safe haven.

Turmoil was one of eight Bustler class salvage tugs built during the Second World War to save disabled convoy ships. They were at the time the largest tugs of their type in the world. *Turmoil* had a gross tonnage of 1136 tons which was larger than many coastal freighters, and her 4000 shaft horsepower, though small by today's standards, enabled her to tackle any salvage job then on offer. She had a crew of thirty-one, larger than that found on most of the largest tankers today, and she was commanded by a silver-haired salvage master with over thirty years at sea, Captain Dan Parker. Her mate, 28-year-old Kenneth Dancy, had only just joined *Turmoil* as a replacement, but he had gone to sea when young and was an experienced and intrepid seaman as subsequent events would prove.

In the interim all Captain Carlsen could do was wait, though fortunately he did have contact with *Golden Eagle* through his ham radio. By New Year's Day Carlsen's vigil had become front page news, and during the afternoon the American destroyer, USS *John W. Weeks*, arrived to relieve the *Golden Eagle*. One of the first things the commander of the navy ship did was to get some hot food aboard *Flying Enterprise*, as Carlsen had been on very meagre rations. The weather continued foul with strong southwesterlies and heavy rain showers. *Turmoil* experienced unexpected difficulty getting her tow into Falmouth, but finally late on the evening of the 3rd she arrived on the scene.

Captain Parker had a brief consultation with Carlsen and the commander of the destroyer before deciding it was impractical to attempt anything until morning. It was obvious that Carlsen would be unable to do much by himself and Parker reported to the office: 'At daylight, if possible, will put men aboard and connect.' Daylight revealed an unpromising vista. The wind continued strong out of the southwest and it was too hazardous to get anyone aboard *Flying Enterprise* from a boat. During the morning and early afternoon Parker manoeuvred his tug as close as he safely could to *Flying Enterprise*. Seven different times a heaving line was thrown over to which a messenger (a heavier line) was attached. The messenger was connected to the heavy steel towing cable. The plan was to pass the messenger over on the end of the light heaving line. This would then be run round one of the mooring bits and passed back to the tug, which would then heave the heavy towing cable aboard. On several occasions they were near success, but it was too much for a single man no matter how determined.

The wind had meanwhile begun to moderate slightly, and Parker once more carefully backed the stern of the tug close to that of the *Flying Enterprise*. As *Turmoil* stood momentarily poised on the crest of a swell her stern actually touched the rails of *Flying Enterprise*. Dancy saw his opportunity and on impulse leapt aboard. He put out his hand to Carlsen saying, 'Shake.'

Carlsen was by now near exhaustion and they decided to wait until morning, in hope of a further moderation in the weather. During the night another destroyer, the *Williard Keith*, relieved the *Weeks*. At daybreak on the following day, the 5th, Carlsen and Dancy made their way up to the bow of *Flying Enterprise* to resume the attempt to hook up the tow from that point. Again a heaving line was thrown over followed by the messenger, passed round a bit and sent back to the tug. The heavy steel towing hawser was made fast to this and as the tug moved slowly away the hawser was pulled aboard the ship, round the bit and back to the tug where it was made fast.[2] The hawser was a new five-inch steel wire with a breaking strain of 74 tons, and had never been used before. It was not an ideal way to connect up as it resulted in considerable chafing of the hawser where it passed through the chock (an opening in the bulwark on the ship's bow), but it was the best that could be done under the circumstances. After paying out a sufficient scope of towing hawser it was made fast aboard *Turmoil*. According to the log of the tug the long haul to Falmouth began at 0937.

By noon *Turmoil* was towing the heavily listed freighter at a speed of about 3 knots. As they were about 300 miles from Falmouth at that point they expected to reach their destination in about four days' time – about daylight on the 9th – providing the weather did not significantly worsen. In the event *Turmoil* was able to make somewhat better speed than she did at the outset. As the tug and her tow passed the halfway mark it looked like they would reach Falmouth on the afternoon of the 8th. The main concern during this time was the chafing of the hawser. Liberal amounts of butter were applied at first in an attempt to alleviate the problem, and later the destroyer supplied grease for that purpose.

The whole world was now following the progress of *Turmoil* and Carlsen and Dancy aboard *Flying Enterprise*. The city council of Hilleröed in Denmark sent this message to Carlsen: 'Your birthplace Hilleröed in Denmark conveys to you greetings and respects for the sparkling example of heroism and valiant seamanship set by you aboard *Flying Enterprise*.' France awarded him the Officer's Cross of Maritime Merit. A French tug *Abeille* now joined the little convoy and offered to assist. Carlsen, however, was content to place his faith in *Turmoil* and later expressed the view that it was not practical for the two tugs to work together.

Unfortunately the weather started to worsen again early on the 8th. As the wind mounted, heavy rain squalls reduced visibility. *Flying Enterprise* seemed to be lower in the water suggesting that the sea had gained access to other compartments. Captain Parker, concerned about the strain and wear on the towing hawser, reluctantly decided to heave to. Shortly after dusk he turned around and headed into the sea to wait for some improvement. Around midnight the wind began to fall off somewhat and the tow was resumed, though in the last radio contact of the evening Carlsen voiced his concern. They were now about 50 miles from Falmouth, and with any luck they hoped to reach their goal by the following afternoon or evening. There was nothing Carlsen and Dancy could do but hope and pray. Shortly after the tow resumed both turned in. Parker signalled the station at Lizard Head about 0130: 'We are making 3.5 knots. Everything is going well,' but no sooner had that message gone out than the towing hawser parted at the bow chock where it had been chafing.

Parker tried to contact Carlsen on the radio but this blow to their fortunes at first went unnoticed. With the parting of the towing line *Flying Enterprise* fell off broadside to the wind and sea. As she wallowed in the trough Carlsen, sensing that something was wrong, heard *Turmoil* sounding her whistle. The weary Dane climbed up to his cabin where his ham set was and heard the dispiriting news. Parker told Carlsen that the 'Best thing we can do is wait for daylight and come in and try to reconnect. Try and get some rest if you can until then.'[3]

Throughout the next day *Flying Enterprise* drifted east as Carlsen and Dancy struggled on the bow trying to reconnect the tow. At one point Carlsen was almost swept away as the bow of the freighter dug into a sea. The list had increased to almost 80 degrees, and the hazards of keeping a foothold on the dangerously tilted deck that was now beginning to be swept by seas made it increasingly clear that the waterlogged vessel was doomed. Another tug, the *Dexterous* out of Cardiff, was also standing by to assist, but more than dexterity was needed now. By noon it was obvious that the only thing left to be saved were the lives of the two gallant seamen aboard *Flying Enterprise*. Parker asked the coastguard for help and the Lizard lifeboat prepared to put out. Still Carlsen refused to abandon hope and the mayor of Falmouth continued with his preparations for a civic reception of the Danish hero. The Danish naval attaché was also on his way down from London to inform Carlsen that King Frederick IX had made him a Knight of the Most Excellent Order of Danneborg, an honour that dated back to 1219. His parents were also being flown over from Denmark. The governor of New Jersey sent his greetings as did 10,000 French school children, and film and literary agents were in hot pursuit seeking film, book and radio rights. Carlsen, when he became aware of all the fuss being made, was nonplussed and embarrassed. He had suspected what was in store, however, and it was a topic of conversation between him and Dancy during their candlelight dinners aboard *Flying Enterprise*. He later said: 'To be quite frank, we were both scared of it.'[4]

In spite of his lingering hopes and unwillingness to admit defeat Carlsen was too prudent a man not to make provision for the worst. He and Dancy had discussed their predicament in detail and what they should do if *Flying Enterprise* started to sink beneath them. Planes were now circling overhead, and one flier returning to a naval air station in Cornwall recalled, 'As I looked back on my way home a huge rainbow appeared, straddling the whole scene. Let's hope it means good luck.' Luck now was not enough and just after 1500, with the Lizard lifeboat approaching the scene, the destroyer *Williard Keith* sent out a brief message: 'FLYING ENTERPRISE SINKING, ENDEAV-OURING TO RESCUE MEN.'

The ship had assumed a list of 90 degrees and the sea began to pour into the engine room through the funnel. Not long after 1500 Carlsen and Dancy, wearing lifejackets, took up a position near the end of the stack. The *Turmoil*, cautiously moving in towards them, signalled with her blinker light and the two men waved back in acknowledgment. The sudden inflow of water into the engine room down the stack apparently caused a build-up of air pressure in the accommodation spaces above, causing the wheelhouse doors to explode outwards. At that moment Dancy jumped and Carlsen followed. Dancy, who was a strong swimmer, had struck out immediately for *Turmoil* hovering nearby, but looking back he saw Carlsen struggling. He turned around and swam back and the two now made their way slowly towards the approaching tug. They had been in the water less than ten minutes but the brief exertion following prolonged anxiety exhausted them. Dancy pulled himself up the rope ladder hanging over *Turmoil*'s bulwarks, but Carlsen had to be helped aboard. The whole crew of the tug were there to greet them and Carlsen, aware that they had just lost their chance for reward, turned to them saying, 'You've done a good job boys.' To Dancy he said, 'I wish I had ten mates like you.' A strong bond had grown up between the two men during their days of trial aboard *Flying Enterprise*, and Dancy later described Carlsen as 'a truly amazing man'. Both were led below for a chance of clothes, a tot of rum, and a cup of hot tea while Captain Parker turned *Turmoil* towards Falmouth.

Commander Leslie J. O'Brien, the commanding officer of the destroyer *Keith* stayed behind with the other tugs to pay a last tribute to *Flying Enterprise*. As the engine room flooded she began to trim by the stern, her bow rising slowly as the stern sank. Shortly after 1600 with her bow pointing almost straight up, the ship poised momentarily in that position and then slid quickly beneath the waves. The ships standing by sounded a salute on their whistles as *Flying Enterprise* disappeared.

During the days and nights of Carlsen's ordeal endless speculation had appeared in the press, most of it inaccurate and trivial. One story that gained some currency and particularly offended the Danish skipper, was the suggestion that he had stayed aboard the ship because of the financial reward he would receive if the vessel made it back to port. That wounded both his pride and dignity and he vehemently denied it, pointing out that a master can never participate in a salvage award for saving his own ship. He was also a reluctant hero, and he kept insisting that he didn't deserve the ticker tape parade being planned for his return to New York.

It seemed there were a few that agreed with him as the first hints of criticism began to circulate. Most of the crew joined in the praise, but some did not. Carlsen was not the most popular of masters, and that was the way he wanted it. He had grown up in a rough school where the masters were hard and discipline harsh. Times had changed, but Carlsen adapted with difficulty. His aloof attitude and autocratic manner did not endear him to most. He did not look for or expect the sort of widespread devotion given to Captain Smith of the *Titanic*. Some accorded him a grudging respect, but others regarded him with outright dislike.[5] The crew members had gained nothing from the affair, and in fact their jobs had gone down with the ship. One of the messmen asked: 'I want to know why the ship didn't turn around for the nearest port when she had the chance. When the ship's union delegate asked the captain about it, he was told the captain was waiting for orders from New York.' Another crew member, Clark E. Hall, echoed those sentiments: 'It was a question then, and it's a question now, why we stayed there for $28\frac{1}{2}$ hours without sending for help. No one knew about the ship being cracked during that time except the Isbrandtsen office here in New York.' The radio officer, David Greene, testified that only one message was sent out on 27 December when the ship first ran into difficulty. It wasn't until the following day after the cargo shifted that he was given instructions to send out an Urgent signal followed by an SOS.[6]

Whatever the validity of the criticism, Hans Isbrandtsen was known to run 'a tight ship', and Kurt Carlsen had probably felt some concern over his situation in the hours after he first learned of the damage to his vessel. Although the weather was exceptionally bad, it was no worse than he had encountered on other occasions. To finish up on the end of a tow line would not be a feather in his hat, for even though he might escape direct blame he would certainly not be commended. His courageous decision to stay with his vessel changed all that. Once the press made him a hero Hans Isbrandtsen could hardly say otherwise, even if he might have been so inclined.

Whatever his own views, Captain Henrik Kurt Carlsen became a public hero, and he and Kenneth Dancy were treated as such when they arrived at Falmouth. He viewed the welcome planned for him in New York with apprehension. Preparations for the event were thrown into turmoil when the plane carrying him was forced to turn back in mid flight due to faulty de-icing equipment. When Carlsen learned of the delay after sleeping through the landing at Shannon he remarked, 'I guess there is a hoodoo somewhere'. Mayor Impellitteri had declared it 'Henrik Kurt Carlsen Day' in the city. Dressed in a new uniform Carlsen boarded the USCG harbour cutter *Sauk*, flying his personal flag, at pier 69 in Brooklyn. There was bedlam in the upper harbour as *Sauk* made her way through three to four hundred assorted craft assembled to greet the hero. When asked for his reaction he replied: 'I'm overwhelmed. I'm really amazed. I realize now how much trouble I've stirred up. I had no idea. I've seen things like this in the newsreels, but somehow when you're in it yourself, you sort of don't seem to fit.'[7]

When he landed at the Battery the plan for him to walk up Broadway to City Hall was abandoned for fear he would be mobbed by the throng of 300,000 well-wishers lining the street, and he was forced to take a limousine. The motorcade stopped twice along the way, once at 26 Broad Street in front of the offices of Isbrandtsen, and again at Trinity Church, where lay the unnoticed grave of another 'Enterprise' captain, James Lawrence, who had coined the phrase, 'Don't give up the ship' almost a century and a half before.

In a luncheon in his honour given that afternoon at the Advertising Club on Park Avenue, Carlsen refused the present of a gold wrist watch to replace the one ruined when he abandoned his ship. He was adamant in his determination to avoid any hint of commercialization of his exploit, and on the way he told the mayor, 'Frankly, I don't think I am entitled to this. I failed to bring my ship into port.' Impellitterri repeated the remark at a speech he gave at the luncheon saying, 'Doesn't that sum up the type of man he is?'

Hans Isbrandtsen was not one to pass up an opportunity to capitalize on the exploits of his now famous skipper. He quickly put in motion a deal to acquire a replacement for the vessel he had lost, and it was named, not surprisingly, *Flying Enterprise II* and Henrik

Kurt Carlsen was given command. Isbrandtsen also made a generous gesture to those who so valiantly strove to save the original *Flying Enterprise*, and failed on the threshold of success. He gave £750 to Captain Parker of the *Turmoil*, £500 to Dancy and £750 to be shared among the rest of the crew.

Pamir

The age of sail had long been left behind when *Titanic* was launched, yet there were none the less many sailing vessels still trading at that time, and indeed all of *Titanic*'s officers had trained and served in sail. Up until the outbreak of the Second World War sailing vessels were no uncommon sight. Some saw service in that conflict and one of these was the German four-masted barque *Pamir*.

Pamir had been built in the famous Blohm and Voss yard in Hamburg in 1905, along with a sister ship *Passat*, for a shipping line that still specialized in sail, F. Laeisz. She was of 3150 gross tons and carried almost 5000 square yards of canvas. During her early years she was employed in the grain trade to Australia, and after the end of the First World War she, together with her sister ship, were sold to the well-known Finnish shipowner Gustav Erikson who operated a fleet of windjammers trading from northern Europe to Australia via Cape Horn.

Most steam vessels at that time were coal burners and on the long haul out to Australia a number of coaling stops were necessary, which added to the time and expense of the voyage. Such ships were also slow and the windjammers, which required no fuel and could often equal and sometimes exceed the speed of steamers, were able to compete effectively in such a service.

At the outbreak of the Second World War *Pamir* fell into the hands of the British and was placed under New Zealand registry as a training ship. During the course of that conflict she made six voyages to the west coast of South America and back, successfully eluding German raiders and Japanese submarines. When the War finished she was returned to her Finnish owners but they now had no use for her. Almost all vessels were now oil burners and they could carry two to three times the amount of cargo of vessels like *Pamir*. Whereas the vessels *Pamir* had competed against in earlier days rarely had cruising speeds of more than 10 knots many postwar steam and motor ships averaged 15 or more. None the less, a British charterer felt she still had a commercial future but that expectation proved unfounded. When the charter expired after four years it was not renewed and the barque seemed destined for a breaker's yard.

It has long been an article of faith in shipping circles that training in sail produces the finest seamen. Indeed, a number of maritime nations still operate square-rigged sailing ships to train their future merchant officers, and the United States Coast Guard has used the barque *Eagle* for more than three decades as a training vessel. There have probably never been finer seamen than those who took the tea clippers out to China and back. The ability to react appropriately to the unexpected under conditions of great stress, which is the hallmark of the polished seaman, was honed to razor-sharpness on those lovely vessels. Their routes took them through some of the fiercest seas on the globe, and not infrequently these stormy waters were also littered with icebergs such as that which sank *Titanic*. Only the best seamen stood a chance. A young man with any aptitude for a career at sea could hardly help becoming an accomplished seaman in such a school under such men.

While it is all but incontestable that this golden age of sail produced outstanding seamen it does not necessarily follow that fine seamen will automatically be produced through training under sail. The ship itself is simply the vehicle for the training. The key element is the man who sets the example, and particularly the commanding officer or master. If the man who commands a sailing ship and those who assist him are not finished seamen no amount of sail training will produce good seamen.

When it became known that *Pamir* and her sister ship *Passat* were up for sale influential voices in West German shipping circles were raised in support of a plan to acquire them as sail training vessels. A Belgian salvage company had outbid the breakers in the hope that they could find a buyer. The Germans have always been fervent believers in the merits of sail training, and up until 1945 a young man aspiring to an officer's berth in the German merchant service had to have at least fifteen months before the mast before he could qualify to sit for a licence examination. Sailing vessels such as *Pamir* and her sister were becoming rather 'thin on the sea' at this point and it was felt that if the chance to acquire these two fine vessels was missed the future of the German merchant marine would suffer.

A Hamburg shipowner, Heinz Schlieven, decided – against the

advice of friends in the industry – that he would buy the vessels to trade to South America as well as to act as training ships. The blessings of the Archbishop of Cologne, given at the start of the venture, went unheeded by Neptune, and before *Pamir* cleared the English Channel the voyage almost ended in disaster. In heavy weather she lost an anchor and the screw of her auxiliary engine before clearing the Strait of Dover. Fortunately the weather abated, and her other anchor held, keeping her off the shoals. The experience proved an ill omen for the success of the enterprise, and the ships were then impounded in Rotterdam after the second voyage to settle a ship chandler's debt.

There were several unsuccessful attempts to put them back in service but the risks were too great. For the next two years they lay idle in Hamburg. Although there was little advantage in returning them to commercial service there was still widespread interest in using them as training ships. Finally in 1955 forty German shipping companies formed the Pamir-Passat Foundation and aided by subsidies from federal and state governments raised a fund to buy and outfit the ships. In the following years the ships were back in operation under the agency of the Zerssan Shipping Company of Lubeck. As the ships were not required to make a profit in order to stay in service they traded successfully to the Argentine for over a year.

On 1 June 1957, *Pamir* sailed from Hamburg for Buenos Aires where she loaded a cargo of 3103 tons of barley. The regular stevedores in Buenos Aires were on strike and the loading was carried out by young conscript soldiers. A well-known naval architect later testified that he saw evidence of improper loading, and that could explain the shifting of cargo that later caused the ship to capsize.[8] When cargo operations were finally finished late in August the ship was readied for sea and then made her way down the River Platte bound for Hamburg. She was under the command of 61-year-old Captain Johann Diebitsch, who had relieved the regular master on this, the vessel's sixteenth voyage. She carried a crew of eighty-six, fifty-two of whom were cadets between sixteen and eighteen years of age.

The master had considerable experience in sail but he had no previous experience in command of a big square rigger. A number of veteran seamen who had served in sail felt that inexperience in vessels such as *Pamir* by master and crew was instrumental in her loss.

82

Though the novelty of the enterprise initially attracted some seamen, the discomfort and rigours of sailing-ship life soon began to make the berth unattractive. The more experienced seamen tended to seek less rigorous employment, and they were often replaced by less capable men. Even among the experienced sailors few had any substantial sail experience, and none had been trained in square riggers.

Although *Pamir* was over fifty years old she had aged well and was still a very sturdy vessel. She was of steel construction throughout except for her teak decks, and it was never suggested that she was not seaworthy. September is a peak month for hurricanes and there can be little doubt that Captain Diebitsch kept close track of the weather reports as he crossed the Doldrums and moved up into the Horse Latitudes. *Pamir* had understandably found it slow going for the past few months in these belts of calms and light breezes on each side of the equator, and by 20 September she was still some 500 miles southwest of the Azores.

The track taken by the barque would for the most part have kept her well clear of the normal paths of hurricanes in the northern hemisphere. These storms usually form in the Doldrums and drift slowly westward until reaching the vicinity of the Lesser Antilles where they begin to curve to the north and accelerate. Their usual paths ordinarily take them well to the north of *Pamir*'s projected track, at least until near the English Channel. On the 20th a warning was broadcast of a hurricane, code-named CARRIE, in the vicinity of the Cape Verde Islands about 1600 miles to the southeast. Captain Diebitsch probably felt no immediate alarm since the hurricane could be expected to travel at a fairly leisurely pace westward and *Pamir* should have been able to keep well clear. CARRIE, however, was not a conventional hurricane. Instead of moving slowly west the storm curved to the northwest and began to accelerate and intensify.

As subsequent weather reports began to come in Captain Diebitsch must have felt mounting concern. *Pamir* was on an approximately northerly course which normally would have taken her away from the hurricane's path. With a vessel as slow as *Pamir*, however, evasive action in the face of a swiftly moving hurricane is mostly a matter of luck. By the following evening Captain Diebitsch needed no weather report to realize that CARRIE was going to approach dangerously close. The barometer started to fall sharply, and it was clear that the German barque was in for some heavy weather, though the chances of a direct encounter with the centre of the hurricane probably did not seem too great. None the less, extra attention was given to make the ship secure as *Pamir* continued northwards under a full press of canvas.

On 21 September a rapidly falling barometer and mounting winds and waves indicated the rapid approach of the hurricane. As the ship began to roll with increasing violence the cargo began to shift, and it quickly became obvious to Captain Diebitsch that his ship was in grave danger. An SOS was sent out giving *Pamir*'s position as 35°57'N and 40°20'W. A half dozen ships within a radius of 200 miles immediately responded. The American freighter *President Taylor* was nearest and notified Portishead radio that she expected to arrive at the scene at 2300. The *Penn Trader* also arrived at the reported position at almost the same time. There was doubt about the accuracy of the position, and on that dark wild night hope of finding the beleaguered barque seemed slight.

The Blue Star ship *Tacoma Star* joined the search not long after and shortly before midnight lights were seen, but there was no way of knowing if they were near or far. Searchlights revealed only empty, foam-flecked sea. Several hours later the Canadian destroyer *Crusader* arrived. The last message received from *Pamir* was: 'LOST ALL SAILS. BEGINNING TO LIST BADLY. NEED HELP.' After that there was only silence. The powerful searchlights of the destroyer swept the raging sea but no evidence of the ship was found.

As day broke hopes momentarily rose that some trace of the stricken vessel would now be found, but such expectation proved short-lived. Other vessels arrived to join in the search and the US Air Force sent out a reconnaissance plane from their base in the Azores. The plane combined with the US Coast Guard Cutter *Absecon* to conduct a more wide ranging search, but they were forced to abandon it after about four hours because of bad visibility. It seemed the barque had disappeared without a trace. Then, about midday, the British tanker *San Silvester* found a battered lifeboat bearing the name 'Lubeck'. That was *Pamir*'s port of registry, but as the rudder was found lashed in the boat it appeared it had been swept out of its davits and was no certain evidence of *Pamir*'s sinking. That afternoon as visibility improved two more empty boats were observed from planes that had resumed the search. The search vessels headed for the scene of the discovery and recovered the boats, but it was now clear that the ship had gone down and it seemed she had taken all her crew with her. It was recalled that some twenty years earlier another German training square rigger, the *Admiral Karpfanger* had disappeared without a trace in the South Atlantic. Not many years earlier the Danish sail training vessel *Koöbenhavn* had vanished off Tristan da Cunha.

All the rest of the day the search went on without result. Other vessels also continued to arrive to join in what seemed a fruitless task. The world waited as hope waned, and then about dusk on the following day the American Isbrandtsen Line Liberty ship *Saxon* spotted another boat with five frantic exhausted survivors almost twenty miles to the west of the reported position. Cadets Anders, Kraaz and Freidrich along with able seaman Hans Georg Wirth and baker Otto Dummer said there were two boats with survivors aboard. Originally there had been ten men in their boat but five had been washed away or died. The other boat held between twenty and twenty-five men, and not long before their rescue signals from it had been seen so it could not be far away. *Saxon* alerted *Absecon*: 'TEN MEN ON THIS BOAT BUT ONLY FIVE SURVIVED. NOW CIRCLING AREA. CAN YOU TAKE SURVIVORS OFF?'[9]

The search now concentrated on the area where *Saxon* had found the first survivors. Rumour now took over as the press reported any number from forty to seventy rescued, but the search for the second boat turned up nothing. Then, on the following day, the cutter *Absecon* found it with Gunther Hasselbach of Kiel the sole survivor. The others had perished.

One of the six survivors later described the last hours of *Pamir*.

Towards 2000 hours on Sunday evening, 21 December, we received the first warning that a hurricane could be expected two hours later in our area. We were given orders to secure all rigging. All hands were sent aloft but before we could start taking in sail the hurricane was upon us.

Captain Diebitsch immediately gave orders to trim the sails, but his order came too late. A mighty squall tore the foresails away and the mast snapped.

From that moment disaster followed disaster. Things went so quickly that no one could say exactly what happened. The power of the storm forced the ship over on her side. We took on a 30 degree list, which increased to 35 degrees and finally to 40 degrees. The instruments did not record beyond this. The decks were awash.

85

The order 'All hands on deck' was given. The crew put on their lifejackets; the ship heeled over more and more and shivered beneath the weight of the mountainous seas. We could no longer get a foothold on the almost vertical deck.

It was almost impossible to lower a lifeboat with this heavy list. We held on fast to the rail on the starboard side for the port side was already under water.

When our ship suddenly capsized we plunged vertically into the water, one after the other. Many of the boys must have been drowned at this moment. Those who had any strength left tried to swim away, but the suction of the ship drew us after her. Our only thought was to get away from her.

Now it was every man for himself. Small groups reached pieces of wreckage, to which they clung. There were fifteen men in my group. At last we sighted an empty boat drifting ahead of us. It took us an hour to reach it. Only ten of us were left.

We clung fast to the boat while the heavy seas broke over us. After long weary efforts, we managed to climb into the boat, which was full of water. It was only floating on its ballast tanks.[10]

The disaster stunned the shipping world. Sailing ships even in their heyday, when manned by officers and men who were a product of a living tradition of sail, were by their very nature more vulnerable than modern power-driven vessels. What remained of the art of handling large vessels under sail was little more than a fossil. This casualty offers a graphic illustration of how dependent seamanship skills are on a living tradition passed down from master to apprentice for their transmission. It also shows how quickly the essence of the art may be lost if the chain of transmission is interrupted. It should serve as a warning to those who are the custodians of a living maritime tradition how easily this maritime heritage can be dissipated if the national maritime fleets are allowed to dwindle. Once lost this asset is all but impossible to revive or retrieve.

Marine Electric

The United States flag bulk carrier *Marine Electric* was a Second World War-built T-2 tanker converted in 1962 for the carriage of bulk cargoes by the Bethlehem Steel Company. A 327-foot mid-body was constructed by the Bremer Vulkan Schiftbau and Machinen-fabrich of Bremen, Germany, which increased her overall length to

605 feet. The new mid-body contained five cargo holds and five upper and lower wing ballast tanks. The hatches to the cargo holds were equipped with MacGregor single-pull steel hatchcovers. These covers were fitted with steel wheels which, when the covers were in the closed position, slotted into recesses allowing the weight of the hatchcovers to rest on rubber gaskets. Quick-acting dogs (a kind of nut used to tighten a door or port against a gasket to make it watertight) and cross-joint wedges between the steel panels of the cover allowed the hatch to be made watertight. Marine Transport Lines owned and operated the vessel.

In her early years as a bulk carrier *Marine Electric* was employed in a variety of trades carrying various bulk cargoes. Over the years both internal and external members of the hull were subject to considerable wastage. The original bow section, which was over twenty years older than the mid-body, was found to be approaching the maximum allowable wastage limits during an American Bureau of Shipping (ABS) survey in February 1980.[11] The survey was carried out at the Jacksonville shipyard and after completion the vessel was employed in transporting grain between the United States and ports in the eastern Mediterranean. This continued until late December 1980 when the *Marine Electric* again entered the Jacksonville shipyard to undergo replacement of some of the plates and structural members found to be wasted during the previous dry docking in February.

According to later testimony of the chief mate and other crew members as well as one of the company's port captains and a superintendent engineer, the steel hatchcovers had suffered appreciable deterioration, and at an examination of them in March 1981 a manufacturer's representative reported that in spite of some repairs the hatchcovers were, in his opinion, still not watertight.[12] Several days earlier, the Marine Transport Lines port captain had attended the vessel at Brayton Point, Massachusetts and noted many holes in the hatchcovers, although only two weeks earlier an ABS surveyor had conducted an annual hull survey where he found all hatchcovers in a satisfactory condition. On a later visit in May the representative recommended replacing the first panel of the number three hatchcover because it had sagged due to wastage. On 29 May a port engineer found an additional twelve holes in the hatchcovers and three in the main deck. In all it took close to a hundred doubler plates to strengthen the wasted areas. Clearly *Marine Electric* was in a far from satisfactory condition in spite of the fact that she continued to pass both ABS and USCG inspections.

In November 1982 the MacGregor representative wrote a report describing the unsatisfactory condition of the vessel and its hatchcovers. He noted that on his visit in March 1981 the panels on the number three hold 'were in poor condition', and that they 'had deteriorated badly in the interim'. Even allowing for the fact that the representative was interested in selling Marine Transport a new set of hatchcovers for their ageing vessel, his report makes grim reading. He found holes in the wheel tracks of the coamings which were 'so wasted that there is no strength left to support the [weight] of the panels without distortion.'

The report continued, saying:

> The panels themselves are in an even more serious state of decay. The top plates are weak, wasted, and buckled and holed in many places. The cross joint wedges are all [missing], which is a serious omission and although the wedges are on board, the state of the panels is such that extensive welding on them could lead to further rapid deterioration. There are heavy deposits around and on the panels where hatch tape is required. The rubber gaskets are of an incorrect size (required during past repairs) and do not fit correctly to the adjacent panels . . . The judgement as to the seaworthiness and cargo protection capabilities of these panels must be examined in conjunction with the ship's classification society to fully determine their exact state with an eye to the duration of further use, if any.

The report went on to point out that it would be a costly affair to renew all the hatch panels at once, and suggested that alternatively the replacement be carried out one hatch at a time thus 'spreading the cost over several voyages'.[13]

When a port engineer attended *Marine Electric* at Norfolk, Virginia, a few days later he noted in his report that the crew were chipping and scaling the hatchcovers, but that in the process the 'top plating of the covers becomes holed in many cases, especially along the welding of the frame beams, where new beams were welded to existing plating. Such wasted and holed areas are being temporarily repaired with epoxy cement.'[14] He went on to say that MacGregor had suggested to the master that if a substantial number of hatchcover panels were ordered they could be supplied at a 'low price of approximately $12,000 each . . .' which in light of the cost of repairing the panels on a piecemeal basis is 'obviously attractive'.

Although it may have been attractive it was not sufficiently so to warrant taking *Marine Electric* out of service long enough to carry out these repairs. The New England Power Service Company who purchased the coal that *Marine Electric* carried from Norfolk to Brayton Point had asked that Marine Transport Lines keep the vessel in service until 1 April 1983. Marine Transport Lines requested from the USCG that the vessel's scheduled dry docking be deferred until sometime after that date. A USCG inspection was later carried out to determine if that extension could be granted but neither the hull plating or hatchcovers were part of that inspection.[15]

Then, on 2 February 1983, a four-by-one-inch puncture in the ship's shell plating in the number one upper port wing ballast tank was sustained when a bulldozer, being loaded aboard the ship, swung against the ship's side. A cement box was installed over the damage by way of temporary repair, and although the vessel's permanent master requested that the fracture be repaired nothing further was done. Nor was the damage reported to either the ABS or USCG as the law required. Company records also indicate that from the time of the last dry docking in January 1981, until the vessel's loss over two years later, numerous repairs to damage sustained in the holds caused during cargo operations were temporarily repaired without the required report to either the ABS or USCG.

The vessel's permanent master left the vessel three days before her loss to go on leave. He later testified that in spite of a number of defective dogs on the hatchcovers, gaskets in need of repair, and hatchcover panels covered with temporary epoxy patches, he considered the hatchcovers weathertight. He admitted, however, that he had purposely instructed the chief officer to refrain from patching some holes on the after panel of number five hatch so the Marine Transport Lines marine superintendent could see for himself the condition of the hatchcovers when he next attended the vessel. The chief mate testified that although he had never found any evidence of leakage in the hatches he did not consider that they were weathertight, 'because the gaskets were ineffective'.[16]

When *Marine Electric* left her berth at Lambert Point on the night of 11 February she was loaded to within a few inches of her marks with about 24,800 tons of pulverized steam coal bound for Somerset,

Massachusetts. Including the master there were thirty-four people aboard in addition to the Hampton Roads pilot. There is nothing to indicate that *Marine Electric* was improperly loaded, and though the weather outside was nasty it was not unusual for that locale or time of year. It was apparently the practice aboard *Marine Electric* to only put a few dogs on the hatches for the short passage up the coast, relying on the weight of the heavy hatches on the gaskets to give an effective seal. With the weather predicted, however, the mate instructed the boatswain to 'put all the dogs that they could get on around the hatches'.[17]

Three days earlier Captain Phillip Corl had relieved the permanent master in Somerset, Massachusetts. Captain Corl had first gone to sea at the age of nineteen in 1943. He obtained his third mate's licence in 1945, a second mate's ticket two years later, and a chief mate's certificate in 1949. During the following years he sailed in various capacities until he joined Marine Transport Lines in 1976 as third mate. Almost thirty years after obtaining his mate's licence he passed the examination for master, and for the next few years he served aboard various Marine Transport Lines vessels as mate or relief master. In June 1982 he was assigned to *Marine Electric* as relief master.

The pilot disembarked off Cape Henry about 0200 on the 11th. A track was laid down to take the ship out to the Chesapeake light tower. From there a course of about 038° was set. This was direct to the approaches to the ship's destination in Massachusetts. At about 0900 the normal sea speed of about 12 knots was reduced to about half that due to the storm force winds out of the northeast. The seas were estimated to be about 25 to 30 feet in height and green water was breaking over the bow. In light of subsequent events it seems likely that water was finding its way below into the dry cargo hatch and fore peak.

At about 1320 the master of a 65-foot fishing boat, the *Theodora*, contacted the USCG station at Ocean City, New Jersey requesting assistance. She thought she was about 30 miles east of Chincoteague, Virginia, but was unsure of her exact position. She was making water and her pumps were inoperative. The cutter, *Point Highland*, got underway to attempt to find the fishing boat but because of a mechanical fault had to return to port. A helicopter was then launched, but because of poor visibility could not locate the *Theodora*. The coast guard station then broadcast an Urgent message to vessels in the vicinity to look for the beleaguered vessel. The master of *Marine Electric* received the message and took up the search.

An able seaman aboard *Marine Electric* later testified that he sighted the *Theodora* about 1530 while helping the mate secure the mooring lines aft. When the mate returned to the bridge about fifteen minutes later the master informed him that they were going to the assistance of the fishing vessel and had altered course to 270°. Visibility was now about a mile or a little more in thick snow. At 1600 Captain Corl notified the USCG that he had located the fishing boat and had contacted her on VHF and was standing by. The helicopter had meanwhile arrived on the scene and delivered the portable pump the fishing boat had requested. The cutter *Point Highland* had overcome her mechanical problems and was putting out to rendezvous with the two vessels.

At 1738 Captain Corl reported that he was maintaining his westerly heading with difficulty. Some ten minutes later he stated: 'We are in the midst of a very serious rain squall here. A course of 270° from my present position will put me in trouble. I cannot steer 270°.'[18] The USCG requested that *Marine Electric* try to hold her course until the cutter arrived but at 1822 he told the Coast Guard station: 'I don't know if I'm going to be able to keep on this course. I'm taking an awful beating out here. I'm going to be in trouble myself pretty soon.' When the coast guard asked again if he could stand by until the arrival of the cutter he answered: 'I don't know how I can hold – heave to on this course. I'm rolling, taking water, green water – over my starboard side, all the way across my deck.'[19] The master of the *Theodora* now told *Marine Electric* that they no longer needed her assistance and at 1825 she was released by the USCG to proceed on her voyage. The fishing boat later rendezvoused with the cutter about 2000.

When the 8–12 Third Mate, (watches aboard ship are normally divided into three shifts: 12–4, midnight to 4 a.m. and noon to 4 p.m.; 4–8, 4 a.m. to 8 a.m. and 4 p.m. to 8 p.m.; 8–12, 8 a.m. to noon and 8 p.m. to midnight), Eugene Kelly, a 31-year-old graduate of the Massachusetts Maritime Academy, relieved the chief officer about 1945 the ship was on a course of 040° and the weather had moderated a little. He estimated the wind at about 20 knots with head seas about 20 feet in height. Although the speed was increased slightly from 40 to 50 r.p.m. *Marine Electric* was only making about 2 knots through the water. The vessel seemed to be easier and he noticed no change in trim, nor had she developed any noticeable list.

When the watch changed at midnight the A.B. (able seaman) who assumed the lookout watch on the starboard bridge wing thought the ship was down a little by the bow. When he returned to relieve the wheel about 0150 he heard the 12–4 third mate and the master discussing the vessel's trim. About 0230 Captain Corl woke the chief mate saying, 'Come up on the bridge, mate . . . I believe that we are in trouble . . . I think she's going – settling by the head.' When the mate reached the bridge he saw immediately that Marine Electric had indeed settled by the head and he ran down to wake the chief engineer.

At 0251 the master called the USCG station at Ocean City on VHF channel 16 and passed the following message:

> I'm approximately 30 miles from Delaware Bay entrance and I'm going down by the head, I seem to be taking on water forward . . . I am a coal carrier, five-hatch coal carrier, I am loaded with 23,000 tons of coal . . . we are positively in bad shape, we need someone to come out and give us some assistance if possible. Our problem is we don't know exactly what our situation is.[20]

A few minutes later the master reported that he was mustering his crew at the lifeboats and altering course to north to steer for the Delaware Bay entrance. When the coast guard station asked if Marine Electric was in danger of sinking the master replied, 'It's hard to say . . . my bow seems to be going down, we seem to be awash forward, we can't get up there. We don't have any lights to shine up to see what's going on . . . I'm not listing, I seem to be going down by the head fast.'

About 0300 another crew member woke Third Mate Kelly who at once realized that the ship was down by the head. He put on his lifejacket and went immediately to the bridge. He could see seas covering the fore deck back to number three hatch. Attempts were apparently being made to pump out the number one and two starboard wing tanks, though why these tanks had flooded was never determined. The chief engineer was heard to say that the number one hatchcover was 'cracked, or opened, or busted'.[21]

The vessel was becoming very sluggish at this point as it lost stability. About 0355 the master reported to the coast guard that the ship had a 5 degree starboard list and was rolling about 14 degrees.

The list began to increase steadily and attempts were made to correct it by flooding the port tanks and pumping those to starboard. The starboard lifeboat was meanwhile prepared for launching and about 0410 the master passed the word to abandon ship. The abandon ship signal was sounded on the ship's whistle and the chief mate gave the word to launch the starboard boat. At 0414 Captain Corl told the coast guard, 'We are abandoning the ship right now, we are abandoning the ship right now.' The crew were attempting to pull the boat inboard when *Marine Electric* suddenly capsized to starboard throwing crew members attempting to board it into the water.

Third Mate Kelly later testified that at about 0410 the radio operator had reported that two ships were in the area and were proceeding to the scene. It was obvious by then that the ship didn't have much longer and the captain ordered the engine room evacuated. The first assistant engineer called to ask if the fuel oil pumps should be secured. Kelly grabbed the walkie-talkie that was being used for communication and told him, 'Mike, get the hell out of there. We are going down.' By then everyone was making his way down to the boat on the starboard side. The third mate started throwing lifebelts over the side. Kelly expected the ship to go down by the bow and was surprised when it started to roll over. As he watched the water rise he saw the master on the deck above trying to climb over the rail. It was the last time he saw him.

Marine Electric was a little over 30 miles south of Cape May when she sank. The US tanker *Tropic Sun* bound for Delaware Bay was about 24 miles to the north and making for the scene at 17 knots. The Norwegian tanker *Bananger* was slightly closer and somewhat slower. US Navy and USCG helicopters were launched within the hour.

At the time of the capsizing the air temperature was 29° Fahrenheit and the sea temperature was 39°. Of the thirty-four people aboard only three survived. The Chief Mate Robert M. Cusick, the Third Mate Eugene Kelly, and an able seaman. Of the remainder four perished from drowning and the rest from hypothermia. Each of the three survivors weighed over fourteen stone, all wore lifejackets and two were wearing thermal underwear. They were rescued by the USCG helicopter, which arrived on the scene at about the same time as the two ships at 0545.

When the *Marine Electric* capsized she also apparently broke into three pieces. The bow and the stern were located in about 120 feet of water almost in line. The mid-body section was found about 1800 feet away from the rest of the wreck slightly west of south. The starboard anchor had apparently broken loose and inflicted some damage to the hull plating of the bow, which the owners later attempted to claim could have contributed to the vessel's loss. There can be little doubt, however, that the loss of *Marine Electric* was caused by the owner's failure to keep the vessel in a proper state of repair. The wastage of the hatchcovers and deck plating had reached such a point that the crew was patching the numerous holes with epoxy and using waterproof tape for securing the hatches. Unauthorized temporary repairs in breach of ABS and USCG regulations were also carried out, and the cement box used to close a puncture in the ship's side in February 1983 was found to be missing when an underwater survey was carried out.[22]

At the hearing, Chief Mate Robert M. Cusick testified that the patches of duct tape and epoxy used to cover holes wouldn't stay on, and there were many holes with no patches at all. So poor was the condition of the hatchcovers he said: 'I kicked off a piece of paint and another hole showed up.'[23]

When US Coast Guard Captain Dominic Calicchio, himself a former merchant marine officer, questioned the ABS surveyor, who carried out the survey, about the classification society's role it became clear that the inspection of the hatches of *Marine Electric* left something to be desired. The surveyor's memory regarding details of the inspection of the vessel's hatchcovers seemed to be as leaky as the hatchcovers themselves. He claimed that he did 'not test the hatchcovers for watertightness or for thickness,' but insisted he 'examined them for strength'. When a member of the Board of Investigation asked, 'How can you judge the strength without knowing the thickness?' The surveyor replied, 'I visually checked this thing out.'

It was pointed out at the investigation that the vessel might have survived had the master reversed his heading and run before the sea when he first had reason to suspect that he was making water in the forward compartments. That may well be, but it was not the poor judgement of the master that was ultimately responsible for this casualty but the willingness of his superiors to avoid the hard and unpopular decisions required to maintain the vessel in a satisfactory state of repair, and how far up in the corporate hierarchy the responsibility for these decisions extended is a matter for further speculation.

4

Fire

In a hierarchy of marine disasters fire is the ultimate hazard. Complete fire prevention aboard ship is an unrealistic goal if for no other reason than if someone wants to start a fire aboard a vessel it is next to impossible to prevent it. Fortunately most fires are not due to such causes, but it is unrealistic to believe that arson can be eliminated aboard ship. Hence the only practical approach to the problem of shipboard fire is to construct vessels in such a manner that fire cannot readily spread once it breaks out, and to establish effective routines for coping with such emergencies.

Although the most feared of all shipboard hazards fire is one the average mariner hardly ever experiences in any serious manifestation. Occasional waste basket or 'mattress' fires occur, but they are almost always quickly extinguished. The weekly fire drills do tend to remind everyone of the danger, but the memory is fleeting. There are just too many other immediate and pressing duties and details demanding attention to dwell much on the remote possibility of fire. None the less, it is a matter to which any master worth his salt must give long and serious thought. If he does not make some attempt to consider the manifold manifestations this hazard might take, and how he should react in each case, he will be singularly ill-prepared to take decisive action should fire break out on his ship. Having said that, the reality is that the possibility of fire aboard is not a matter often considered outside of safety meetings.

The planned fire is probably the most hazardous of all shipboard fires since the arsonist, or terrorist, will usually go to great pains to see that the outbreak occurs in places and under conditions most conducive to its rapid spread. The fire aboard *Morro Castle* appears to have been such an example. The only effective defence against such attacks is an equally well planned and executed response.

Unlike regulations in respect to safety in the more advanced maritime nations, which can realistically be designed to address the hazards and strictly enforce them, the international world of shipping must reach compromises that usually fall far short of what is required. Vessels which, from the standpoint of safety, should by any reasonable standard be scrapped are instead sold to ship operators who register them under flags of convenience where minimal standards are the norm. The international regulations governing such things usually provide for exceptions for vessels built before a certain date, since the cost of compliance with the regulations for new construction would relegate them to the scrap heap where they rightly belong.

The *Morro Castle*

When Captain Robert R. Wilmott died suddenly on the night before *Morro Castle*'s scheduled arrival at New York it was assumed that he was the victim of a heart attack. It was only later that suspicions were raised that he might have been poisoned. That would in itself have been no more than a minor sensation had not the ship he commanded caught fire and burned to the waterline early the next morning, causing the deaths of 124 passengers and crew in what became one of the most celebrated marine disasters since the *Titanic*.

When *Morro Castle* sailed from Havana on Wednesday, 5 September 1934, she had 318 passengers and a crew of 231. One of the crew was a 33-year-old Californian, George W. Rogers, the chief radio officer, who was to become the unlikely hero of the disaster. As the flames invaded the radio shack he coolly remained at his post sending out distress messages and guiding rescue ships to the scene. When the heat and fire finally drove him out he continued to show great courage and resourcefulness by improvising auxiliary transmitters with which to carry out his duties. The press not unnaturally made him a hero, which he certainly appeared to be, and he gained great publicity for his exploits and appearances at hearings into the causes of the disaster. With all this exposure it is remarkable that it was only after he was jailed for murder years later that it was discovered he had had a long previous criminal record. If Captain Wilmott was indeed poisoned, Rogers was also a prime suspect, and he made admissions in prison that strongly suggested it was he who started the fire which made him a hero.[1]

*

Morro Castle was built in Newport News in 1930 for the Cuban Mail Line which operated a small fleet of coastal passenger ships under the Ward Line house flag in the New York to Havana tourist trade. The Cuban Mail Line was itself a subsidiary of Agwi (Atlantic, Gulf and West Indies) Lines. *Morro Castle* (along with her sister ship *Oriente*) was the largest ship in the fleet, being 528 feet long with a gross tonnage of 11,520, and was the flagship. Her turbo-electric engines drove twin screws giving her a speed of over 18 knots. She had berths for more than 400 passengers, but the bite of the Great Depression made it difficult to fill her to capacity.

Her master, Captain Robert Wilmott, a big-boned, heavy-set, and florid-faced man of fifty-six, was the senior master of the company. He had been born in London and first went to sea as a deck boy on a freighter. His great ambition was to command a passenger liner and prospects for advancement appeared greater in the American merchant marine. In 1902 he obtained a berth on a Ward Line vessel and ten years later he had risen to third mate on one of their cargo ships. One of his most vivid memories was viewing the Cunard liner *Carpathia* from the bridge of his ship as she entered New York harbour with the survivors from *Titanic*. He, and the chief engineer, Eban S. Abbott, were assigned to *Morro Castle* while that vessel was under construction, and they had been with her ever since. Only the year before Wilmott had surprised everyone by marrying a recently widowed first-class passenger, Mrs Mathilda Reed. They spent their honeymoon on a two-week cruise to Mexico and Havana, but since that time they saw one another only for a few hours each Saturday as *Morro Castle* changed passengers and took on stores for another run to Havana.

The chief officer, William F. Warms, was a tall, wiry, no-nonsense seaman with a receding hair line and a dour, rough and ready manner. Warms's life was the sea. He had come up the hard way and was passionately proud of the promotion he had earned. He had first shipped out as a cabin boy while a youth, and later joined the navy, making bosun's mate second class before leaving to resume his career in the merchant service.

He obtained a third mate's ticket in 1909 and was soon given a job as third officer on one of the Ward Line freighters. Through hard work he gained steady promotion, and by the end of the First World War his dedication to his job and loyalty to the company earned him command of a fruit boat. His devotion was noted with approval and

97

other commands followed. In 1926 he was made master of a small passenger vessel, the *Yumari*. He expected others to work as hard as himself and hence was not a popular commander. Unfortunately his zeal led him to view fire and lifeboat drills as a waste of time, and disgruntled engine staff reported this dereliction to the authorities. Warms had his licence suspended for ten days and lost his command, forcing him to cool his heels ashore for a year. His dedicated professionalism, however, was appreciated by his employers and they gave him command of the *Agwistar*, another cruise liner. However, several mysterious fires on board resulted in criticism of safety procedures on the ship and Warms found himself again without a job. He felt he had been made a fall guy, and was determined he would never be victimized again. In spite of these setbacks he still regarded himself as a 'company man', and as jobs were becoming scarce he was forced to accept employment as chief officer of a Ward Line freighter. Warms's devotion to the Ward Line paid off, however, when he was appointed to *Morro Castle* as chief officer. Experience had soured him though, and he had little respect for or faith in anyone who was not a 'seaman'.

The chief engineer was one of those who fell outside the pale. In his formative years Warms had served with a number of 'down easter' masters of a puritanical cast, and the impressionable young seaman had grown up as a God-fearing man with little appreciation for frivolity, fancy living and their trappings. Eban Abbott was 'no seaman' in Warms's estimation. He appeared to the chief officer as a man 'who liked the uniform and not the job',[2] and affected airs giving the impression that he was ashamed of his less cultivated colleagues. Warms had no time for such as Abbott, and showed it. He referred to him as that 'stuffed tailor's dummy in the engine room', while the chief engineer called Warms that 'worm on the bridge'. At best it made for an awkward working arrangement, and it placed Captain Wilmott, who had to depend on both men, in a most uncomfortable position.

Wilmott had achieved his ambition and wished only to be allowed to enjoy it. He had acquired a taste for classical music and literature, and also enjoyed good food and the company of women. Yet he could also project the image of an old sea dog when that seemed appropriate: he was a bit of a romantic and liked to regale his passengers with tales of his adventures. The friction between his chief officer and chief engineer threatened to disturb the pleasant pace of life aboard his ship. While he felt more affinity for Eban Abbott, who was something of a dandy and also enjoyed a good time, he depended more on his chief officer. He promised Warms he would have Abbott transferred to *Morro Castle*'s sister ship *Oriente* as soon as he could arrange it. Although Warms was a bit too rough for Wilmott's taste he had no compunction about weeding out troublemakers, and *Morro Castle* had her fair share of those.

Communists had gained a firm toehold in the seamen's union and the Cuban authorities strongly suspected there was more than a casual connection between the troublemakers on the ship and those on the island. *Morro Castle* regularly carried munitions in her cargo. Only a few months before Captain Wilmott had been served a meal that made him violently ill causing him to suspect poison.[3] Less than a month later a fire was discovered in a hold carrying explosives, and there was evidence it was deliberately set. Since that time he had become increasingly agitated and began to shun the social obligations he had before relished.

It was later alleged that Captain Wilmott had a history of heart disease. His widow testified that she had overheard him on two occasions tell the operations vice-president, Henry E. Cabaud, that he suffered from heart trouble. This was denied, and there is no evidence that Wilmott had ever consulted a doctor either aboard ship or ashore about any heart complaint. Whether or not he had a weak heart Captain Wilmott was, according to Chief Officer Warms, a highly nervous individual. He had, moreover, more than enough to worry about on that voyage. In the depths of the Great Depression life aboard ships everywhere was no bed of roses, and American ships were no exception. Maritime unions were either nonexistent or so feeble that employers could ignore them with impunity. Wages were paltry, the food was meagre as well as poor, and job security was a concept not yet born. There weren't many happy ships in those days, and *Morro Castle* was certainly not one of them. She docked in New York in the morning and sailed the same day. Since vacations were as common as job security a berth aboard *Morro Castle* had a certain similarity to a prison sentence, except it could be terminated by quitting and joining the dole queue.

Masters enjoyed better wages and conditions, and Captain Wilmott was even granted a brief vacation each year, however, their continued employment was at the pleasure of the employer, which encouraged a hardhearted ruthlessness in keeping with those grim times. On ships engaged on long voyages some relaxation of the tension might result, but in a ship like *Morro Castle* whose round voyage was a mere week the pressure was constant and was reflected in the relationships aboard ship. Radio operators had only appeared on ship's rosters in the first decade of the century, and though the *Titanic* saga had highlighted their value in emergencies they were not usually accorded the esteem to which they commonly thought they were entitled. There was a history of friction between the radio shack and the bridge on *Morro Castle*, and a sinister element had lately been added with the recent promotion of George Rogers to chief operator.

Rogers had joined *Morro Castle* as second operator several months before, and though he soon succeeded in ingratiating himself with most of those aboard he thought worthy of his attention, he had incurred the wrath of George Alagna whose place he took, but who remained as a junior operator. Alagna had only recently graduated from the Indiana School of Technology at Fort Wayne, but he was naive and Rogers quickly won him over with a tale that he had been put aboard by their employers (the Radio Corporation of America) to investigate recent happenings. Alagna was a hothead and an idealist with leftish tendencies. Shocked by the conditions he found aboard *Morro Castle* he wanted to do something about them. A year before militant seamen had staged a successful sit-down strike on a ship named *Diamond Cement*, and Rogers suggested to Alagna that he undertake the organization of a similar event, though Rogers, because of his position, would be unable to participate. Although Alagna succeeded in delaying the departure of the ship for several hours the strike was a failure: company officials agreed to some of the demands but promptly forgot their promises once the ship had sailed. Alagna succeeded only in establishing himself as a troublemaker, and only escaped being fired on the spot because the Radio Marine Corporation said they could find no replacement at such short notice.

Rogers was a large, blubbery, pear-shaped man with a sluggish demeanour that hid a sharp intelligence and dangerous cunning. Unknown to anyone else on the ship his attentions could be deadly though they might appear amicable and even pleasing. Rogers was a psychopath with a criminal record going back twenty years. According to a subsequent psychiatric report he was a 'sociopathic personality; a shrewd individual who attempts to manipulate his environment.'[4]

The first person to suffer directly from Rogers' attentions was his immediate superior, Stanley Ferson, the chief radio operator, whose job Rogers wanted. Ferson had unwisely become involved in some of Alagna's activities, thereby compromising his position, and Rogers chose to exploit that. With the aid of a friend he convinced Ferson through the use of several clever anonymous letters that unless he resigned he was possibly in danger of losing his wireless operator's certificate. As Rogers had already ingratiated himself with J. B. Duffy, the Radio Corporation of America official responsible for appointments and promotions, he was confident of succeeding Ferson. Ferson fell for the ruse, and so successful was Rogers in covering his tracks that Ferson shook his hand on departing.

Wilmott was well aware of the dissatisfaction aboard his ship, and particularly the friction between the bridge and the radio shack. While in Havana a drunken seaman from another American passenger vessel had been aboard and boasted about ways of 'getting even with the company', through the use of stink bombs in the passenger spaces. News of the incident reached the master's ears, and perhaps caused him to speculate on the possibility of sabotage on his vessel. On the day *Morro Castle* sailed from Havana the second mate, Ivan Freeman, had had a run in with Alagna over the use of the RDF, and Wilmott sent for Rogers to sort out the dispute. Just what transpired during that interview cannot be known, but Rogers later said that Wilmott told him that he was getting rid of Alagna in New York because he was a troublemaker.

However, according to a passenger with whom Captain Wilmott was friendly, Rogers himself was the original object of Captain Wilmott's suspicions. He had told him: 'his first act on reaching New York would be to fire Chief Radio Operator Rogers, that Rogers was capable of acts which might endanger both the passengers and the ship.'[5]

The fabrication and dissemination of rumour is rife aboard most ships, and there is no reason to believe that *Morro Castle* was immune to this malady. Information had reached the captain that a bottle of sulphuric acid and another containing material from which a 'stink bomb' could be fashioned had come aboard in Havana. Whether Rogers was initially suspected of involvement in a plot is not known, but the next morning, the 7th, Captain Wilmott called Rogers to his office for another interview, and Rogers must have used his considerable powers of persuasion and deception to shift the suspicion to Alagna. Immediately afterwards the master sent for the chief officer, who later said, 'Wilmott called me into his quarters on Friday morning. He told me that he was very worried that something would happen. He said he could feel it; that he had definite information that Alagna had two bottles and that Rogers had taken them away from him. The captain said he was afraid Alagna would harm him and he kept his door locked.'[6]

Warms later repeated this conversation to Fourth Officer Howard Hansen, who stood watch with him, saying that he had suggested to the captain that Alagna be put in irons, but Wilmott had rejected that proposal. Wilmott reacted to the situation by keeping to his quarters and even having his meals there. That was noticed and added to the rumours, but on the afternoon before *Morro Castle* was due to arrive in New York, Wilmott had relaxed sufficiently to invite a few guests to his cabin for drinks. September is one of the worst months for hurricanes, and a vessel running between New York and Havana is particularly vulnerable to this hazard. This gave him a focus for his worries, and he regaled his guests with an account of his experience the year before when *Morro Castle* was hit by a hurricane off Hatteras. The radio apparatus was damaged and they were out of touch with the outside world for two days.

The last night at sea is traditionally the time for the 'captain's dinner', and Captain Wilmott had promised he would attend. When the time came, however, he sent word that 'due to unforeseen circumstances' he would be unable to put in an appearance. The master had ordered some food sent up to his quarters and while eating a piece of melon he suddenly clutched his stomach and keeled over. The waiter who had brought the food summoned the ship's surgeon, Dr de Witt van Zile. The captain suffered from chronic indigestion, and van Zile was not unduly alarmed but he mentioned the master's indisposition to Warms whom he met in the passageway as he left the captain's quarters. The chief officer looked in on Captain Wilmott before he returned to the bridge, but Wilmott assured him all was all right saying it was only something he had eaten. The time was half-past seven. About a quarter of an hour later Warms looked in to see how Wilmott was. There was no answer to his knock and he stepped inside. Looking into the night cabin he saw the captain in the bathroom sprawled over the bath with his trousers down. His eyes were open but he was dead, or at least he appeared to be. Warms's first reaction was to pull up the master's trousers, for appearance sake. Memories of Wilmott's apprehensions and all the peculiar developments of the past twenty-four hours gave Warms momentary pause, but then realizing the gravity and strangeness of the situation he called his junior officer on the bridge and told him to locate the ship's surgeon, Dr van Zile, and Chief Purser Robert Tolman. They both appeared within moments along with the chief steward. The chief engineer, who had just come up from the engine room where he had been summoned because of problems with a boiler, appeared shortly. The master, according to the purser, 'was quite blue', and van Zile, finding no trace of a heartbeat with his stethoscope, pronounced him dead.

Tolman was now told by Warms to alert everyone concerned and have wireless messages sent to the chief company officials ashore. Tolman would have sent the first message to Henry E. Cabaud, the operations vice-president, but he could not remember his address which was locked in the captain's safe. Instead he sent a radiogram to Victor M. Seckendorf, the passenger traffic manager and the marine superintendent, Thomas S. Torresson. The message sent to Seckondorf simply read: 'WILMOTT DECEASED 7.45 P.M. ACKNOWLEDGE' and was signed 'WARMS'. The death of a ship's master is no everyday occurrence, and this cryptic announcement of so rare a happening elicited an unusual response. It was later alleged that Warms did not inspire much confidence in those who served under him, and that Wilmott himself shared these views. If that was indeed the case it is likely that Wilmott's reservations concerning his chief officer had been communicated to his superiors ashore. That then might explain why Warms's message was answered not by a request for further details from Warms himself but by a radiogram addressed to Purser Tolman to: 'PLEASE CONFIRM QUICKLY MESSAGE SENT BY WARMS TO SECKENDORF REGARDING WILMOTT GIVING DETAILS.'[7]

The weather had meanwhile turned foul with heavy rain squalls and the vessel began to ship water over the bow. *Morro Castle* was approaching New York from the south and Warms was on the bridge with the now acting First Officer, Ivan Freeman. At about 0210 a passenger discovered a fire in a locker in a writing room on the port side forward on B deck. He alerted some stewards in the vicinity and they attempted to put it out with hand extinguishers without reporting it to the bridge. Regulations pertaining to fireproof construction were rudimentary at that time, and wood was widely used as panelling and trim, particularly in passenger vessels. The wood was often varnished, so a fire once started would spread rapidly if not checked almost immediately, as happened here. Warms remained ignorant of the developing disaster until shortly before three o'clock when two night watchmen belatedly reported the outbreak to the bridge. Warms went outside and saw smoke issuing from a ventilator behind the bridge, whereupon he had the fire alarm rung and sent the lookout below to call out the bosun and crew. The junior officer of the watch was sent to warn the passengers and acting Second Officer Clarence Hackney was detailed to take charge of fighting the fire. By now it had gained such headway that it is doubtful it could have been brought under control even if the crew and the ship's equipment were equal to the occasion. Unfortunately that was not the case, and within minutes of the moment Warms learned of the fire raging inside his ship it must have been clear that only a miracle could save her. When the acting chief officer reported that the fire was out of control Warms ordered the first distress message sent at 0318.[8]

Acting promptly Warms summoned the crew, and the passengers were alerted to the danger. By now the fire had spead to both the deck above, A Deck, and the deck below. Six of the ship's twelve boats were launched but only ten of the three hundred passengers aboard escaped in that manner, though eighty-seven crew members did so. The flames now barred access to the remaining boats and the passengers were ordered to go to the decks below and make their way aft. The spread of the fire was accelerated by the effect caused by the vessel steaming at full speed and creating wind currents that fed the fire.

Unfortunately for Warms the ship's bosun had been celebrating *Morro Castle*'s impending arrival in New York with a jug of Cuban rum and was in no state to respond to his summons. Had Warms himself been acting in his usual role of chief officer his more familiar relationship with the deck crew might have enabled him to mitigate some of the confusion arising from the bosun's absence. Warms, however, was now acting master and his proper place was on the bridge. On first learning of the fire Warms had himself roused acting Chief Officer Freeman (whose quarters were just abaft of the bridge) and told him to 'Get up. There's a fire on board. Get down and take charge.' Freeman dressed quickly and when he reached the scene he found the fire in the writing room blazing furiously and no water in the fire mains.

Ship's officers rarely have much experience in fighting fires, and their reactions when faced with such an emergency can be tainted by the confusion inherent in such a situation. Confronted with a raging fire and no pressure on the fire mains Freeman ran to the engine room himself to see why the pumps weren't delivering pressure.

Even after the seamen were turned out, attempts to fight the blaze were severely hampered because a number of the fire stations, including the one nearest to the writing room, had no fire hoses, the hydrants were capped and the spanners (a sort of special wrench needed to remove the caps and hook up the hoses) had been taken away. It was claimed that the hoses had been removed a month previously on the orders of Captain Wilmott after a lady passenger had filed a claim for an injury sustained when she had fallen on a slippery deck caused by leakage from a hydrant. The master was well aware that the expedient he adopted was an illegal one. None the less, he made it the practice to have the hoses removed and the hydrants capped after the vessel left New York and the fire stations restored to their proper condition before the ship's return.[9]

The practice was not only illegal, it was also highly dangerous as subsequent events proved. Captain Wilmott's disdain for safety practices, however, did not stop there. The law required that fire and boat drills be held once a week. Drills are sometimes logged that are never held, and on vessels flying flags of nations inclined to turn a blind eye to such seemingly inconsequential infractions of their regulations, the weekly drill may become a fortnightly or even a monthly affair. On *Morro Castle* it would have been injudicious of Captain Wilmott to have ignored or sidestepped the regulations pertaining to drills as with the many disgruntled crew members aboard such an infringement would probably have been reported. As previously noted, Chief Officer Warms, when master of the Ward Line ship *Yumari*, had in fact been given a ten day suspension for just such an infraction,[10] and would have been an unwilling partner in any attempt to twist the regulations. Wilmott's view of drills, however, was that they were an unwelcome interruption of the ship's routine, and should be accorded no more time and effort than that required to comply with the law. The fire drills were so organized as to cause the least inconvenience to passengers, and were indeed held at locations on the ship where passengers were unlikely to even see them carried out let alone participate.

Warms found himself in a most unenviable position. Although a very experienced officer, he was no doubt a somewhat harrassed and even confused man in the few hours after he assumed command. He had unexpectedly been thrust into a strange situation, and he undoubtedly was subject to considerable stress having the master's duties suddenly added to those of chief officer. A nor'easter was brewing just as he was nearing the pilot station at Sandy Hook in the approaches to New York. Custom and prudence both required his presence on the bridge. It was then, just as the navigation of the vessel was demanding his undivided attention, that he was informed that *Morro Castle* was on fire. His proper and natural response was to call out the crew under the bosun who, unknown to him, was stupefied by drink. He also notified the acting chief officer who was as bemused by his new responsibilities as was Warms. To add to this recipe for disaster the chief engineer, who alone of all the principal officers involved was acting in a familiar role, failed to respond to his duties in a manner appropriate to his station and therefore compounded the confusion.

Chief Engineer Eban Abbott was asleep when the general alarm went off shortly before three. Ordinarily he would have donned a boiler suit and gone directly to the engine room, but for a reason never satisfactorily explained he put on dress whites and then called the engine room. The first engineer, Antonio Bujia, who had also been roused by the alarm answered the phone, and in response to Abbott's query as to conditions there told him that some smoke was coming in through the air vents but no flame. Abbott, finding the elevator that he would normally take to the engine room filled with smoke, then descended to A deck where he found seamen leading out hoses. When the hydrants were opened, however, there was no pressure. Abbott continued down to D deck where he was surprised to meet Bujia.

Abbott asked him where he was going and Bujia replied: 'To the bridge. I called you through the telephone and speaking tube and got no answer.' When Abbott enquired how everything was below Bujia told him that though the plant and machinery were functioning perfectly, the smoke coming in through the ventilators made it questionable how long the men could remain at their posts. Although the chief engineer had apparently intended to proceed to the engine room he had no great enthusiasm for descending into the bowels of the ship with a fire raging above. As his conduct later proved, he was no leader of men and his chance meeting with his first assistant gave him an excuse to avoid the confines of the engine room. 'You go back and stand by,' he instructed Bujia, 'I'll go to the bridge myself. Keep the men below by all means. Don't let them leave until they have to. If and when you do have to leave, shut the turbines off, shut off the fuel system to the boilers and leave the steam fire pump running.' By now, as Abbott suspected and intended to find out, the fire was out of control. It was only a question of trying to stem its advance until the passengers and crew could be safely evacuated in the ship's boats.

The smoke generated by the fire made it difficult to see what was going on though Warms at first took this as a sign for optimism, believing that the application of water to the fire was responsible. His confidence quickly turned to dismay when tongues of flame began to break through the cloud of smoke. The alarms in the fire-detecting cabinet in the wheelhouse then began to show red. Warms had just entered the wheelhouse when the red light corresponding to a cabin on A deck lit up. At first he stared at it in disbelief, then suddenly the whole board was alight. 'My God!' he shouted, 'They're all going.' He rang the general alarm and lunged for the engine room telegraph ringing 'Stand by' as he yelled to the helmsman for left wheel to head the doomed liner towards the Jersey coast. This brought the wind abaft the beam on the starboard quarter on the side away from the seat of the fire. It was now just after 0300.

Meanwhile in the radio room Third Operator Charles Maki was on watch, and shortly before 0300 he noticed some smoke coming from a wastebasket in the corner of the radio shack. What caused this was never determined, but Maki rushed to the radio operators' sleeping quarters nearby to wake his mates. He burst into the room just as the general alarm went off. Alagna jumped from his berth immediately but Rogers seemed to be sleeping soundly and had to be shaken. Alagna was first to reach the radio shack where he found that the emergency power supply to the main transmitter was dead, but as the main supply from the engine room was still on line this created no immediate problem. Rogers arrived with Maki a few minutes later and assumed charge. He sent Alagna to the bridge for orders and tuned the transmitter to the distress frequency.

Some 10 miles to seaward the freighter *Andrea S. Luckenback* was also heading for the Ambrose light ship that marked the entrance to the port of New York. As the master was plotting a radio bearing given to him by the radio operator, the second officer on the port wing of the bridge noticed a glow on the horizon. As he trained his binoculars on the spot the captain stepped out on the wing with the radio operator. It looked like a ship was on fire, and he thought it might be the passenger ship that had overtaken them some time earlier. It was about 0310 and the master turned to the radio operator saying, 'Call the coast station at Tuckerton. Ask them if they know anything about a ship burning off Sea Girt.'

On the bridge of *Morro Castle* Acting Captain Warms was rapidly trying to sort out the disastrous situation now facing him. Only a few short hours before he had been contemplating the implications of his unexpected promotion and its effect on his career. He was, of course, concerned about the fire aboard his ship, but he hadn't foreseen that within minutes he would be faced with catastrophe. The appearance of Alagna on the bridge asking for instructions was not particularly welcome, and in light of his suspicious status Warms was inclined to postpone the decision that Alagna was demanding.

On the dark rain-swept wing of the bridge, with confusion mounting with every passing moment, Alagna wasn't even sure Warms knew who he was. He had made several futile trips back and forth between the shack and the bridge and when he returned to the radio shack at 0313 he was choking from exertion and inhalation of the smoke sweeping over the bridge. 'The whole place is afire,' he gasped. 'What about the distress signal?' Rogers asked. 'They're madmen on the bridge and I can't get any co-operation,' was Alagna's bitter response.

But Rogers' attention was now focused on his receiver. The *Luckenback* ship was asking Tuckerton radio about the liner burning off the Jersey coast. The shore station could shed no light on the mystery, and Rogers who could have solved it remained silent. Alagna was almost beside himself with frenzy by now and pleaded with Rogers to send out a CQ even though they had no authorization as yet from the bridge. Rogers was still strangely reluctant and delayed a few minutes more until the 'silent period' began at 0315. (There are two 'silent periods' each hour, of three minutes duration, at 15 and 45 minutes past the hour. During this time radio operators are required to refrain from transmitting so that the distress frequency, 500KC, which is also the calling frequency, is clear for the transmission of distress and urgent messages.) As he began to transmit Tuckerton broke in and told him to wait until the silent period was over. They obviously thought that *Morro Castle* had also seen the burning ship and was reporting it, but Rogers answered saying that it was his ship that was on fire.

He repeated his call again when the silent period ended, and as he finished the main transmitter went dead as the main generator in the engine room failed. The whole ship was now blacked out, though the flames from the fire supplied ample illumination. The three men quickly set up the emergency transmitter. Then Rogers ordered Alagna to go back to the bridge for orders. The insulated deck beneath his feet was now so hot he had to put them on the rung of his chair. The flames from the fire began to encircle the shack.

Chief Engineer Abbott had meanwhile made his way up to the bridge where he cowered in a corner on the weather side of the bridge wing. The unco-ordinated efforts to fight the fire had resulted in fire hydrants being opened indiscriminately, with an attendant drop in the water pressure. Full pressure could only be maintained on a maximum of six hydrants. If as many as twelve were open the pressure at each hydrant would drop to no more than a third of normal capacity. On the upper decks it had diminished to a trickle and this development must have convinced Warms that fate had turned on him. He became aware of this while issuing orders to lower the boats to the embarkation deck, and he rushed to the other wing of the bridge in search of the chief engineer shouting, 'Chief – God damn it, where are you?'

When he found Abbott whimpering, 'What are we going to do? What are we going to do?' Warms shouted, 'What's happened to the water pressure?' To which the chief replied, 'It's too late – a hundred hoses couldn't hold this fire now.' 'Answer me!' Warms bellowed. 'What's happened to it?' Abbott was well aware of the capacity of his pumps. If he had been equal to the occasion he wouldn't have allowed mismanagement to disable the fire system.

A shout from the quartermaster that the ship was not answering her helm reminded Warms there were better things to do than rage helplessly at a man who could no longer respond to anything beyond a blind urge to save his own skin. The fire had apparently disabled the steering system and Warms tried to turn the ship away from the wind by backing and filling with the engines. It was simply too much for any one man and Warms was trying to fill the shoes of two, master and mate. While attempting to conn his disabled ship he was also issuing orders to those engaged in fighting the fire, while at the same time giving directions for the abandonment of *Morro Castle*. Acting Chief Officer Freeman now reappeared on the bridge. On seeing him Warms cried out, 'For God's sake, get forward and prepare to let go the anchor. We have a powerless ship!'

As Freeman ran forward a hysterical passenger grabbed the master screaming, 'You've got to save my girlfriend! She's trapped in one of those cabins.' Two seamen pulled the man off as they explained that the captain was trying to save everyone. Warms told them to take him down and put him in a boat. Abbott was mumbling that it was hopeless to try to do any more. As Warms ran into the wheelhouse to ring 'Stop' on the engines before dropping the anchor Abbott called after him, 'I'm going to leave now.'

He turned and bolted down the ladder from the bridge wing to the number three boat just below. Although it had a capacity for seventy persons, there were only eight in the boat, but Abbott was determined to leave the burning ship and, once seated, shouted 'Lower away.' Warms, looking down from above, countermanded the order and told them to 'Keep it at the rail for passengers.' One of the falls had jammed anyway and Abbott, seeing that his chances for a quick escape looked slim if he stayed put, climbed out and made his way to the number one boat just ahead, which was also a motor lifeboat. He climbed in and sat down in the bow of the boat, wringing his hands, oblivious to what was going on round him.

Under the circumstances it was remarkable that panic amongst the passengers was not more widespread. By the time acting Captain Warms learned of the fire it was so far advanced that it would have been difficult to contain let alone extinguish even if everyone had done their duty. During the half hour or so between the first detection of the fire and the report of it to Warms, the rest of the ship's passengers and crew remained blissfully unaware of the impending disaster. By the time Warms learned of the fire it was a full blown emergency, though the acting master did not at first recognize the seriousness of the situation. When the fire was first reported to the bridge Warms was approaching the pilot station in deteriorating visibility with all his attention directed towards the navigation of his vessel. The fire at first seemed no more than an irritating distraction, though in retrospect it is clear that it should have claimed the major portion of Warms's attention from the time he learned of it.

The chief engineer, who alone of those able to play a critical role in the developing emergency was not also faced with unfamiliar duties and responsibilities – and could have been a tower of strength and support to Warms – cracked up and fueled the sense of uncertainty and confusion prevailing from the beginning. He now was nothing more than a frightened witness to the unfolding disaster. At the least he could have assisted in helping passengers to escape. The decks were now becoming so hot that it burnt one's feet to walk on them. One passenger had cut his chest stumbling through a window he had broken with his cane. Dressed in pyjamas which had caught fire he hopped about barefoot on the hot deck as his pyjamas flaked off his back like burning newspaper. While other passengers stared at him in horrified amazement, he fluttered about screaming as he ran his hand through the charred remnants of his hair burnt off by the fire. In his pain and fright he ran wildly aft until he came to the stern where he vaulted over the rail into the sea below.

The fear that had momentarily reduced Abbott to a cowering wretch now wrenched him out of his apathy. He assumed that escape was the first consideration of all aboard and he shouted to Warms on the bridge to join him. When that was ignored he ordered the seamen assigned to the boat to 'Lower away! For God's sake, lower away.' Fortunately they had more regard for their duty than respect for his authority and they waited for an order from the bridge. At this moment a can of black powder used to charge the line-throwing (Lyle) gun, and stowed in the mate's cabin abaft the bridge, fell into the heart of the fire as the deck collapsed. The explosion killed four crewmen outright.

Until now it did not seem to have occurred to Warms to ask for assistance. Perhaps the idea of abandonment of his 'new command' was so abhorrent that he had pushed it from his mind, but Radio Officer Alagna had returned to the bridge once the CQ had been sent and was shouting in his ear. 'Captain, listen to me. What about a distress signal?' Warms at first looked at him with incomprehension. 'Rogers is dying in there,' Alagna shouted over the roar of the wind and flames. 'He can't hold out much longer. What do you want us to do?' He then told the master that another ship had sighted them, and with that news Warms seemed to snap out of his shock and despair. 'Is there still time to send an SOS?' he asked. 'Yes,' the radio officer shouted. 'Send it,' yelled Warms and gave *Morro Castle*'s position as '20 miles south of Scotland light. About 8 miles off the coast.' Alagna first tried to call the radio room from the bridge but the circuits were dead, and he stumbled out of the wheelhouse to attempt to make his way aft through the smoke and flames.

Warms now told the quartermaster Charles Hoffman to leave the bridge and take charge of the number one boat. At first the sailor declined to leave but Warms insisted. The woodwork on the bridge was afire and Hoffman jumped from the bridge wing to A deck below. He landed by the number three boat and was helped in by another seaman. There was no time to wait and though the boat paused at B deck it was an inferno there so it continued down amid howls and shrieks from those trapped by the fire.

The number one boat was next to follow under the direction of acting Second Officer Hackney. The hull of the boat was too hot to touch and several of its occupants burnt their hands when they grabbed the gunwale when the rear davit jammed almost upending the boat. A young seaman jumped out to clear the fall and after the boat was waterborne he scrambled down the Jacob's ladder, but before he reached it the falls unhooked when a wave lifted the boat. There was nothing to do but jump and swim for the boat now dancing on the waves. Fully-loaded the boat might have handled better, but light as it was it moved in a most lively and unpredictable fashion. Try as he might he couldn't gain the boat and he finally slipped beneath the waves. All the while Abbott sat motionless in the bow on a coil of rope that if used could have saved the gallant young sailor's life.

Alagna had meanwhile made his way back to the radio room through smoke and fire. Rogers sent an SOS. Halfway through a battery explosion interrupted the transmission. The explosion wrecked the receiver but the transmitter was still operating. What they didn't realize was that, though the message went out, static generated by the heat of the fire had interfered with the part of the message that gave the ship's position. Had Rogers given up then many more would have died than actually did, as it would probably have taken much longer for assistance to arrive.

The auxiliary generator had stopped and there were no lights. Hot sulphuric acid from the ruptured batteries was bubbling over the steel deck, but Rogers found the generator and, working by touch in the dark, repaired the loose connection that rendered it inoperative. The acid had soaked through his shoes and burned the soles of his feet but he stumbled back to the table where the transmitter lay. As he reached it he lost consciousness, falling across the table. The pain of the radio keys digging into his forehead revived him and he began sending out the SOS received by the *Monarch of Bermuda*: 'CQ – SOS – TWENTY MILES SOUTH OF SCOTLAND LIGHT. CANNOT WORK MUCH

LONGER. FIRE DIRECTLY UNDER RADIO. NEED ASSISTANCE IMMEDIATELY.'
No sooner had this gone out than the generator exploded ending all
possibility of further transmissions. Rogers was slipping off into
unconsciousness again when Alagna grabbed him by the shoulders
and shook him awake. 'The whole place is afire. Come on.' But
Rogers was still reluctant to give up. 'Go back to the bridge,' he told
Alagna, 'and see if there is anything else.'

With both transmitters and receivers dead this was a futile gesture
and one that would mean both their lives if indulged. Alagna shook
Rogers again saying, 'Warms says we are to abandon ship. Let's go!'
He pushed Rogers towards the door and out on to the fiery deck.
They managed to make their way to the burning bridge only to find
it deserted. From there they descended to A deck where they climbed
down a ladder to the deck beneath the bridge. They then joined
Captain Warms and about a dozen others on the bow.

After acting Chief Officer Freeman dropped the anchor *Morro Castle*
came to rest with the wind ahead. As the fire had not yet reached
forward of the bridge the bow was clearly the safest place on the ship,
and Warms and a few members of the crew including those deck
officers left aboard found refuge there. The ship was now effectively
divided in two with the Captain and his few remaining men isolated
on the bow, while those passengers and crew who had been unable to
get away in one of the ship's boats had sought safety on the stern.

Many of the surviving passengers later alleged that the crew had
offered them no assistance at all and that it was every man for
himself. Of the first ninety-eight people to escape in the ship's boats,
ninety-two were crew members.[11] The fact is, however, that the
emergency developed so rapidly there was simply not enough time to
organize an orderly evacuation of the passengers. By the time word
was passed to abandon ship the fire had gained such headway that
the 'safest' avenue of escape seemed to be away from the smoke and
flames and towards the stern of the vessel. Perhaps the best explanation was offered by one of the seamen: 'When the crew was called,
the situation had already become critical. The call came too late.
Then there was no direction as to "what to do". So everyone did
what he thought should be done.'

Once the ship was anchored Warms and his men could do no more
for those driven aft by the fire. One of the real heroes of the disaster
was Third Engineer Arthur Stamper who had the watch when the
alarm was raised. The forced draught system which serviced the

main engines also provided ventilation for the engine room, which had the unfortunate result of sucking in smoke from the fire, and the only way to turn it off was to stop the main engines. By the time the order was given to stop the engines the machinery spaces were almost uninhabitable. First Engineer Bujia called down to Stamper from the grating on E deck to secure the boilers but leave the fire pump running and then get out. He then made his own escape. Stamper knew that unless the fuel was shut off to the boilers there was the risk of an explosion and preventing that became his first objective.

He first stopped the main propulsion engine and then descended to the lower engine room. Crawling on his hands and knees to try to escape the smoke he made his way towards the boilers. Just as he began to make out their shape he bumped into his junior engineer, Lewis Wright, whose station was in the fire room. Thrusting his flashlight into his hand he told him to cut off the oil to the boilers. Saying he would be right back, he returned to the operating platform to secure the turbines to save the remaining steam in the boilers to drive the fire pumps. Once that was done the silence was almost as deafening as the roar of the machinery it had replaced.

Stamper then went below again to make sure that all the valves supplying oil to the boiler fires were shut. He and Wright then adjusted the steam valves which were driving the fire pumps before they abandoned the engine room. Stamper knew there was no escape upward as fire blocked that route. The only way out was through the propeller shaft tunnel, leading aft to an escape hatch at the end. The tunnel was itself filled with smoke, but as they moved further aft it began to thin and breathing became easier. As they climbed the escape ladder up to the open deck on the stern they could hear passengers singing hysterically, 'Hail, Hail, the Gang's All Here'. As Stamper and Wright emerged covered in grime the passengers stopped their singing and surged towards them seeking advice and reassurance. 'Will the ship blow up?' 'Should we jump now?' 'Where are the lifeboats?' 'Is help coming?' He tried to calm them and assured them the ship would not blow up. 'Now be calm, and don't jump unless you have to. Maybe you won't have to.' He then got some of the male passengers to help him take a nearby hose out of its rack. Leading it forward towards the flames he called out to have the valve opened. Because they were low down on D deck the pressure was still fairly good and Stamper was able to slow the advance of the fire towards the stern.

Rescue vessels were now beginning to converge on the stricken liner. First to arrive was the 30 gross ton fishing boat *Paramount* from Manasquan Inlet who, hearing radio reports of a large ship burning off the coast, called the USCG and volunteered her assistance. On arrival the *Paramount* found many passengers in the water clinging to debris or simply supported by their lifejackets. Thirty-five were rescued. The *Andrea S. Luckenback* arrived not long after and picked up twenty-six. The tanker *City of Savannah* was next on the scene and saved sixty-five. Last to arrive was the British passenger ship *Monarch of Bermuda*. She had been 30 miles away when the first message was received, but though she was last to arrive she plucked seventy-one persons from the storm-tossed sea. She herself was to fall victim to fire in dry dock thirteen years later.

Warms persistently refused offers to take him and his fellows off, instead directing rescuers to the threatened passengers on the stern of the burning liner. This was in accordance with his responsibility for their safety but he also still had a faint hope of salvaging something from this horrendous affair. Although a glance aft might have told him that *Morro Castle* had little future other than as scrap, custom and tradition informed another view. As long as he remained aboard his ship, his owner's rights of salvage were secure. That he was protecting a claim of dubious value was a matter he chose not to consider. The New York pilot boat first raised his hopes by an unrealistic offer to tow the ship to Gravesend Bay off the Brooklyn shore. While Warms considered this unlikely prospect the 1800 ton USCG cutter *Tampa* appeared on the scene. The coast guard vessel was almost half as long as the *Morro Castle* herself and easily capable of taking the ship in tow. It was the intention of the commanding officer of *Tampa*, Lt Commander Earl G. Rose, to put a 12-inch hawser aboard and tow *Morro Castle* to Gravesend Bay where New York City fireboats could extinguish the blaze.

On the other end of the vessel pandemonium reigned. Many of the elderly were simply too frightened to jump from the blazing liner. Others were persuaded to climb down ropes hanging over the stern, but when they reached the end there were no boats to take them aboard. Some clung to the bodies of others who had already perished and others found bits of wreckage to support them. Thankfully the first rescue boats then reached the scene. The few ship's boats successfully launched had long since departed.

The first boat to reach the shore was the number one boat carrying

Chief Engineer Abbott. The boat had twenty-nine crewmen and only three passengers, and as it approached the shore Abbott began to take stock of his situation. In his white uniform and insignia he stood out like a sore thumb, and he realized that people would find it very strange that the chief engineer was one of the first to reach safety. One of the passengers saw Abbott remove his shoulder boards with the four stripes of his rank, mumbling, 'I will be jailed for this'. At the first opportunity he changed his clothes completely.

By now the media was fully alert to the drama and its potential for exploitation. Already there were rumours of sabotage and some said that on her way south the ship had carried ammunition in her holds destined for one of the political factions in Cuba. The mysterious death of the master fuelled the speculation. They were looking for heroes and scapegoats and the representatives of the press were careless of reputations in their search.

George Rogers was a willing accomplice and succeeded in bamboozling everyone. He became the star witness in the investigations and court trials that followed. He followed up those performances with a vaudeville booking in which, dressed in a dazzling white uniform, he recounted his version of events from the stages of RKO theatres. His home town of Bayonne, New Jersey, gave him a hero's welcome and he ended up by going to work for the local police force repairing radio equipment. Several years later he was convicted of the attempted murder of one of the detectives on the force by means of a bomb he had fabricated. He emerged from prison in 1942 on a conditional parole arranged through influential acquaintances, whom Rogers had convinced he was framed. The condition was that he enter military service, but none would have him. In 1953 he murdered an elderly couple who had befriended him and was sentenced to life imprisonment where he died in 1958.

The first of the scapegoats was George Alagna, whom Rogers helped frame to deflect suspicion from himself. Alagna was indicted on suspicion of sabotage but the charge was later dismissed for lack of evidence. None the less, the experience was so traumatic that Alagna later attempted suicide.

The attention of the court was next directed not surprisingly in the direction of Warms and Abbott. Warms as commanding officer of the ship was a natural candidate for the role of fall guy. In the situation into which he was thrust he could only emerge as a hero or a villain, and as almost a quarter of the passengers and crew perished in the disaster he was destined for the latter role. Abbott was in a less vulnerable position but his conduct during the fire and abandonment was so craven it was inevitable that he be charged. It required little ingenuity to assemble a catalogue of failures and oversights with which to burden Warms. Mistakes were made and Warms was in command.

In the case of the chief engineer there was little doubt that he had abdicated his duties and responsibilities almost at the outset of the affair. Warms's failure was not through lack of trying, but Abbott had quit at the outset and was clearly culpable. A jury heard the case, but even with the best will in the world they were incapable of judging the guilt of Warms in the difficult and foreign (to the jury) circumstances in which his conduct was framed. Abbott's conduct required no special knowledge or experience to evaluate. Both men were found guilty and the judge sentenced Warms to two and Abbott to five years in prison.

Somewhat surprisingly the grand jury also indicted Henry E. Cabaud, the tall, white-haired executive vice-president of the Ward Line. They found him guilty of misconduct and negligence. He was given a suspended sentence of one year in prison and fined $5000. The Ward Line was also fined $10,000 and the judge regretted that the law did not provide for a greater penalty.

Warms and Abbott both appealed and in 1937 the US Circuit Court of Appeals unanimously set aside the verdicts noting: 'Warms had maintained the best traditions of the sea by staying on the vessel until the bridge had burned under him.' The court could find nothing in Abbott's behaviour worthy of commendation, but they did not feel he was guilty of criminal conduct requiring a prison sentence. Cabaud and the Ward Line did not appeal.

Dara

Although there were no doubt any number of vessels as vulnerable to fire as was the British India Steam Navigation Company's passenger vessel *Dara* when she sailed from Bombay on 23 March 1961 on a voyage to Karachi and Basra with a number of other stops along the way, she was nevertheless an extremely attractive target for a planned disaster. Classed as a passenger ship, *Dara* in fact more nearly resembled a ferry in her pattern of trade, though not in design. Her ports of call were for the most part less than twenty-four hours apart and though she had berths for seventy-eight first and second class passengers, the bulk were unberthed and 'camped out' either on the open deck or in the specially constructed 'tween decks provided for them. When the unberthed passengers come aboard they stake out a territory where they 'make camp' so to speak, and for as long as they remain on board they regard this territory as their own and guard it jealously; any intrusion is most objectionable and may be greeted with outright hostility. *Dara*'s certificate allowed her to carry up to 948 passengers of this class though only 537 were aboard when she caught fire on her fateful last voyage. The cabins were as usual all taken, and there were in addition seventy-four persons of various description temporarily aboard in addition to her crew of 132.

Dara was built in 1948 for the British India Steam Navigation Company by Barclay Currie and Company Ltd. of Glasgow. She was a single screw motor vessel of 5029 gross tons with a length of 382 feet and was constructed especially for the trade in which she was employed at the time of her loss. She was one of four similar vessels, *Daressa, Dumrah* and *Dwarka*, in service between Bombay and Basra with a number of way ports in between. She was named after a great Persian prince, and commanded by Captain Charles Elson, a stocky, square-faced man of medium height, with a receding hair line. He had been at sea for thirty-two years, all of it with the British India line. He had served eleven years as chief officer before being appointed to his first command two and a half years before, and had been in *Dara* for almost exactly a year.

All of the deck officers and most of the engineers were British. They tended to be career officers, who joined the company at the beginning of their working life and worked their way up. The company was the successor to the John Company, the name by which the seafaring branch of the British East India Company was known. It had been in existence for over a hundred years and occupied an honoured place in the estimation of the seafaring fraternity. The chief officer, Peter Eugene Jordan, had been with British India since 1947 and had served as chief officer in *Dara* for the past eight years. He was a tall, dark-haired man of thirty-five and a thorough professional. The balance of the crew were almost all Indian nationals, many of whom had served on *Dara* or her sister vessels for many years.

The weather in the Persian Gulf during most of April was, according to one of the passengers who later wrote an account of the disaster, Mr P. J. Abraham,[15] altogether exceptional with heavy rain storms and high winds that were almost unheard of at that time of year. *Dara* and her sisters were built primarily for the pilgrim trade carrying thousands of devout Muslims from the subcontinent to Saudi Arabian ports in the Gulf from whence they made their way overland to Mecca. April, however, was not the season for pilgrimages, so the ship was nowhere near full. Of the 600 or so passengers aboard there were numerous nationalities speaking many languages and dialects, though most were Gulf Arabs, Indians and Pakistanis.

When the inquiry into the disaster was held in London almost a year later the leading attorney for the Ministry of Transport, Mr Waldo Porges, QC, questioned Captain Elson at some length about the conduct of drills aboard *Dara*. When earlier questioned about this the master had advanced the view that having a proper fire and boat drill was just not practical. Waldo Porges now asked him to elaborate. Captain Elson said that on first joining the vessel he had given some thought to the problem and considered trying to have a proper drill while at sea but had given it up as impractical. When he discussed with the chief officer the possibility of having a fire drill muster the mate, who had been on the ship a long time, said 'that it just couldn't be done, there would have been trouble among the passengers if you tried drawing a hose across their personal effects – there would have been – well – relations were not always happy between the Indian crew and the Arabs anyway, and that sort of thing made it quite impossible – well, impracticable.'[16]

He went on to recount how some years before a friend of his had been stabbed, and was now partially paralysed, during a riot that broke out when an attempt was made to have a drill aboard one of the ferries. Three of the Indian crew were also killed. Since that incident the company had issued the ships with bullet-proof, or 'stab-proof' vests. With such volatile passengers any real emergency aboard *Dara* was a most unwelcome prospect.

Dara had had a regular fire and boat drill in Bombay before leaving on the voyage and before embarking passengers. The crew were mustered at fire and boat stations, fire hoses led out and charged and the offshore boats launched. Captain Elson admitted that this was far from ideal since in any real emergency the ship would be filled with passengers who must be cared and provided for, and there was no way of simulating such conditions at the drills. He admitted there was room for improvement but he offered no specific recommendations, nor did the court come up with any.

Even aboard well-found conventional passenger ships the most that can be expected in an emergency is that the passengers will be instructed in how to don their lifejackets and know their boat station. The law requires that drills be held to accomplish those aims, but aboard ferries that is not ordinarily practical. The passage is too short so reliance on printed notices in cabins and around the ship is the norm, and the fact that they infrequently attract the attention of the passengers is no matter for remark. Aboard a ferry such as *Dara* the problem is even more complex and intractable.

Another problem was that *Dara*, though a small vessel could carry a relatively large number of passengers because most were not berthed, and that required equipping her with enough lifeboats to handle her maximum capacity. There was simply not enough deck space to accommodate so many boats (sixteen) easily, so twelve of the boats were nested, or superimposed, one above the other, with only a single set of davits and falls for each such pair. Launching those boats under the best of circumstances was awkward, and under conditions of actual emergency could be very difficult if not impossible. In retrospect it can readily be seen that the deck was stacked against Captain Elson and his crew, and in the actual circumstances it is somewhat remarkable that the loss of life was not substantially greater.

On 23 March 1961 *Dara* sailed from Bombay, calling at Karachi, Pasni, Muscat, Dubai, Umm Said, Bahrain, Kuwait, Mina Al Ahmadi, Korramshahr, and Basra. The vessel then began the return leg with stops at Korramshahr, Kuwait and Bahrain before returning to Dubai about noon on 7 April. Cargo was discharged and loaded and passengers embarked and disembarked, but before all the passengers could be taken aboard the weather suddenly began to deteriorate and everything was brought to a halt. The rain came down in sheets and then turned to hail. Almost within moments it was blowing a gale. The holding ground at Dubai is very poor and the storm had caught the vessels anchored there unawares. A Panamanian freighter named *Zeus* loaded with cement and anchored close ahead, began to drag anchor, and before anything could be done, she struck *Dara* twice as she drifted past. The damage was slight but Captain Elson felt his vessel would be safer at sea and he decided to get underway. There were still some seventy visitors, port officials, tradesmen and longshoremen aboard and the sea was now too rough to disembark them. They became unwilling and unfortunate temporary passengers, but that could not be helped. After getting underway *Dara* proceeded slowly to the north. The wind was blowing in gusts of up to force 9 by this time attended by rain in sheets and lightning of such intensity that it was almost like daylight. The ship was rolling and pitching most uncomfortably in the short, steep seas and dinner was rather sparsely attended as a result. After clearing the anchorage Captain Elson reduced speed to bare steerageway so as to get no further from Dubai than necessary. The weather slowly began to improve and not long after the second officer took over the watch at 0400, the master decided to put about and return to Dubai. The second mate fixed the ship's position at 0425 by a visual bearing of the light on Jazirat Tunb (a small island to the north of Dubai and just off the Iranian coast) and a radar distance off. From the position thus obtained the master laid off a course of 190°, and after Dara had steadied on that heading he turned the conn over to the watch officer and went below.

Second Officer Charles Alexander had checked the course with the secunny, as the Indian quartermasters were known, and noted that one of the vessels that had followed *Dara* to sea from Dubai had also turned around and was heading back. She was about 5 miles off just abaft the starboard beam. The vessel was a converted tank-landing craft, or LST, the *Empire Guillemot*.

About a quarter to five a severe explosion shook the ship, knocking the quartermaster down and setting off the alarm bells in the fire detection cabinet in the wheelhouse. Alexander thought that the explosion had come from the engine room as did everyone else at the time. That impression was strengthened by the fact that the power had also failed. Captain Elson reappeared on the bridge almost immediately and found the second officer trying to pinpoint the source of the fire that the explosion had almost certainly triggered through the Kidde fire detection cabinet.

The secunny reported that the light in the compass binnacle was out, but that really made little difference since the engines had stopped and the telemotor steering had been put out of action by the explosion. The secunny was told to light and hoist the oil 'not under command' lights and Captain Elson sent the second mate to call the chief officer.[17]

Mr Alexander met the mate at the foot of the ladder leading to the bridge. He had needed no call as he, as well as almost everyone else, had been awakened by the blast. The second mate said, 'The captain wants you to find out what's wrong,' so the mate returned to his cabin, hurriedly dressed, and was informed by an American lady passenger on the deck below that there was a fire in the bar. He went aft to the first class smoking room where the bar was located and, peering through the glass door, saw what looked like a chair on fire. He grabbed a fire extinguisher off the bulkhead and extinguished the blaze only to see it break out again a few seconds later. The extinguisher was by now exhausted but he was joined by the extra third officer who was unrolling a fire hose. The flames had now enveloped the chair and Jordan kicked it to one side to see a hole about a foot in diameter through which the flames were funnelled from the deck below. The explosion had in fact blown a hole right through the bridge and promenade decks creating a funnel effect through which the flames were sucked by the natural draught.

Unfortunately the fire main was not charged because of the failure to activate the fire pumps in the engine room. Only a trickle of water came out of the hose. At first the mate could not believe it, but after he had tried another nearby hydrant he realized he was faced with a raging conflagration without any means to check it. He then reported to the captain on the bridge that the first class smoking room was in flames and that there was a hole in the deck from which the flames were coming that he thought extended to the engine room. The explosion had also apparently knocked out the telephone to the engine room as there was no response to calls there. The emergency lights came on about this time but the system did not extend to the bridge or chart room forcing them to rely on electric torches for illumination.

At this point it never occurred to anyone that the source of the explosion was anywhere else other than the engine room. After reporting to the bridge the mate returned to the scene of the fire to see what could be done. The captain told him to 'Get the CO_2 operational and make sure everything is battened down'; a logical step to be taken with a fire in the engine room, which was a natural assumption. The master had meanwhile rang the general alarm bell and ordered the radio operator, to send out a request for assistance.

On reaching the boat deck just below the bridge Jordan met several engineers with the two deck cadets, Ian Tew and John Grimwood. One of the engineers said the engine room was filled with smoke and they needed a breathing apparatus. Grimwood was sent to fetch one while the chief officer continued below to the First Class Smoking Room. He found it engulfed in flames and continued down to the Upper Deck just above the engine room where the CO_2 room was located. On reaching it he found the port side alleyway alight with flame and filled with smoke. Realizing he could do nothing there he hurried back to the bridge.

The fire had spread with alarming rapidity and, with no effective means of fighting it, the chief officer informed Captain Elson that the situation was hopeless. The captain replied without hesitation, 'Make it boat stations and abandon ship as soon as you can.' It was now 0451, less than ten minutes since the explosion had rocked *Dara*. As no more than a few moments had passed since 'Sparks' was instructed to send out the first alarm, he was now told to 'make it an SOS.' The radio shack was now filled with smoke and he was driven out before he could get a message out. Next he attempted to send out the distress call over the portable emergency radio but the rapid spread of the blaze made it impossible to rig an effective antenna.

Jordan had meanwhile rung the abandon ship signal on the general alarm, but when he tried to repeat it on the ship's whistle he found there was no steam. The master had the second officer try to contact the ship abaft the port beam on the Aldis lamp. Either the battery was dead or the explosion had damaged it so Captain Elson then tried to use his electric torch to attract the vessel's attention.[18]

It was now shortly before five and the watch officer aboard the other vessel, the *Empire Guillemot*, spotted the outbreak of the fire on the ship on his starboard bow almost immediately. The master, Captain Francis E. Godley, later recalled, 'Immediately we came to the conclusion the ship was on fire I told the chief officer to call all hands. I called the radio officer and questioned him as to whether there were any distress signals going out. He reported back that there was nothing on the air, and I said, "The best thing you can do is to send out a distress signal because apparently the ship cannot do it."' *Dara* was about 5 miles off and Captain Godley hauled to port and steamed up to within about half a mile, by which time *Dara* was ablaze from the bridge to the poop deck.

The confusion above decks was reflected below. Like those on the bridge the watch engineers assumed the explosion had occurred in the engine room. The second engineer, Ramsay Birrell, was standing on the manoeuvring platform with uncertified Fifth Engineer Durham at the time. The explosion kicked out the circuit breaker on the generator distribution board causing a blackout. The second engineer thought the explosion had come from the crankcase. He stopped the engines and together with his junior engineer he went up to the next level to see if he could find out what had happened. At this point there was no evidence of fire, and it did not occur to him to start the fire pumps. As they worked their way up they encountered smoke, which got thicker by the minute. It soon became so dense as to drive them out of the engine room, and he decided to report to the chief engineer. He found him outside the engineers' accommodation on the boat deck.

Chief Engineer Cruikshank ordered the skylights and funnel flaps closed and sent the fifth engineer aft to try to start the emergency fire pump. He was unable to find the starting handle in the darkness though it was found close by later that day. The fire frustrated an attempt to start the forward emergency pump. The chief instructed the second engineer to flood the engine room with CO_2 but he was unable to get to the controls because of the smoke. Cadet Grimwood then appeared wearing a breathing apparatus, but he was unable to reach the control cabinet either. The situation by now was obviously desperate and Grimwood, who displayed remarkable coolness and courage throughout, said to Durham whom he met on coming out, 'You better get to your boat station.'

Within less than half an hour flames enveloped the whole starboard side of *Dara*, making the use of the boats on that side impossible. The chief officer had descended to the boat deck after ringing the abandon ship signal on the general alarm. He found several people including the chief engineer standing by the number four boat, and he shouted 'Get the boats away. Clear the boats away.' He then went to the railing on the after end of the boat deck and shouted down the same instructions to Cadet Grimwood standing in a group of people by the number eight boat.

From that vantage point Jordan could see that the number ten boat on the poop deck was also being cranked out so he then busied himself with getting the number four and six boats on the boat deck away. Unfortunately, panic had now become widespread. The determined efforts of the ship's officers to instil some kind of order into the chaos was ineffectual because in their haste to respond to the emergency they had not donned their uniforms. They were thus unrecognizable by most of the frenzied passengers as figures of authority.

The possibility of coping successfully with a serious emergency aboard *Dara* and her sister vessels was intrinsically difficult at best, since the nature of her service prevented any drills or effective measures of instruction of the passengers in what to do in case of an emergency. With a rapidly spreading fire at night and with no readily identifiable figures of authority – indeed rumours quickly spread that the officers had abandoned them – it is small wonder that panic took hold of the passengers, and that the ship's officers and crew did as well as they did.

Most of the passengers had fled either to the bow or the poop deck as the fire spread. Very few remained amidships and when the number four and six boats were swung out, the fire, which had by now spread to both sides of the promenade deck, which was also the embarkation deck, prevented anyone from boarding.[19] It was obvious that any attempt to try to put passengers in the boats before launching would be extremely hazardous, so word was passed to get the boats in the water as quickly as possible from where they could be boarded from the ladders provided for that purpose.

All but four of the sixteen boats were nested, and the power failure made recovery of the falls very difficult, especially since during the drills the falls were always overhauled by mechanical means. In the event only the top boats were used, and only those on the port side. The number two and eight boats, which were not nested, were located on the bridge or main deck, which at least at the outset was relatively free from fire. These boats were launched with passengers in them; the number two boat under the supervision of Mr Alexander, the second officer. This boat got clear without too much difficulty, though the drain plug in the bottom could not be found, which allowed the boat to fill and it was only kept from sinking by its flotation tanks.

The number eight boat was the motor boat, and it was launched under the supervision of Patrick Jackson, the third officer. There was a great scramble for places in this boat, and when it was lowered it was jammed to overflowing. After it became waterborne the number six boat came alongside. As this boat was practically empty there was a great rush by those in the crowded number eight boat to climb into the number six boat. Unsurprisingly, that caused the number eight boat to capsize, throwing its occupants into the water: some were pulled aboard the number six boat but some were drowned.

The number ten boat from the poop deck was also overcrowded

and very unevenly loaded. That, and the jostling of those in the boat, made it unstable, and when it floated free it overturned. The number nine boat, the only boat on the starboard side, was launched with less difficulty than the others because most of those aft had crowded into the number eight and ten boats. When the number nine boat was lowered there was less competition for places and hence less panic.

After seeing the number four and six boats away Chief Officer Jordan, together with the chief engineer, attempted to recover the falls of the number four boat so as to launch the lower one of the pair. He soon realized more men were needed if that effort was to succeed and he went up to the bridge and told the captain who told him to 'at least clear the gripes away and prepare the boat for launching.' Jordan did so and then came back to the bridge, now burning fiercely. He and Captain Elson spent some time throwing chairs and other wooden objects over the side that might help support a person, but when the heat from the fire began to melt the glass windows in the wheelhouse they descended to the boat deck where there was still a small area free of flame. From there Jordan saw a lifebuoy and several pieces of wood caught in the ship's accommodation ladder two decks below. He decided to go down and free these and scrambled down the side. He found the heat there quite intense and shouted up to Captain Elson, 'It is very hot here,' to which the master replied, 'Well get off the ship,' so Jordan jumped. Day broke not long after, and the *Empire Guillemot* came quite close, but several lines thrown to Jordan fell short. He was later rescued by the Norwegian tanker *Thorsholm*.

Had *Empire Guillemot* not been so nearby and acted with such commendable alacrity and initiative the toll of those lost would have been much higher. In addition to *Thorsholm* a Japanese tanker *Yuyo Maru No. 5*, the *British Energy*, and another British India ship *Barpeta* had picked up *Empire Guillemot*'s call and hastened to the scene.

The master, together with Sinclair, the chief radio operator, were now alone on the boat deck and it was clear that they couldn't stay there much longer. They both climbed over the rail and Elson said, 'Come on, we'll have to go,' and let go. Sinclair hung on for a few minutes longer before following. Elson drifted aft where he had a narrow escape when hit on the head by the lower block of one of the falls of the number eight boat. He was dazed but when his head cleared he found himself floating free. He saw Grimwood and also the chief engineer together with a young lady clinging to a grating from the bridge. He was eventually pulled aboard the Norwegian ship that rescued Jordan.

There was considerable apprehension on the part of some of danger from sharks and the deadly sea snakes that infest the Persian Gulf. Fortunately no sharks appeared, but Jordan claimed he later saw a large sea snake attempting to get in his boat when he was on his way back to reboard *Dara*.

The entire midships house was now ablaze but the poop deck was still untouched by the fire. Third Officer Jackson together with the second engineer and Grimwood the cadet had seen the number eight, nine and ten lifeboats away. Jackson now turned to the number seven boat but the heat drove him off. Attempts to recover the falls of the number ten boat in order to launch its twin, number eleven, were abandoned because of the difficulty, and they turned their attention now to throwing the rafts and wooden hatch boards and benches over the stern. The rafts were made fast to the railings on the stern, and Third Officer Jackson tried to induce the remaining passengers to slide down the lines to the rafts below. Perhaps they thought the ropes too slender and would not go. So Jackson sent Grimwood down hoping they would follow his example. Still they held back, but after one of the native seamen slid down an elderly lady followed. There were now only two women left and the third mate and second engineer took one each in their arms and jumped. As the raft was on a short tether the sea, which was still quite rough, imparted a violent motion to it throwing its occupants off. The line was therefore cast off. As they drifted away they spotted Chief Radio Operator Sinclair, who seemed to be in some difficulty. Grimwood swam over to him with a lifebelt and a boat from *Empire Guillemot* rescued them soon after. A boat from *British Energy* later picked up those on the raft.

There were more than ample boats on *Dara* for everyone aboard, and there were in addition twenty-eight liferafts or buoyant apparatus. Twenty-three of these, however, were stowed on the bridge deck above the engineers' quarters and the rapid spread of the fire soon made them inaccessible. The other five on the poop deck were lauched without difficulty. The fire also prevented access to the boats on the starboard side except for the two nested boats on the poop. The rapid spread of the flames also made it very difficult to move easily about the vessel. Moreover, there were not enough experienced crew members available to assist with the difficult task of launching the lowermost of the nested boats. None of these were used. Though there were also more than enough lifejackets many people had none because they were either unaware of where they were kept or were prevented from getting to them by the fire. Many of those lost died simply because they could not gain access to the safety equipment provided.

Grimwood found the second mate aboard *Empire Guillemot*, and he suggested they go back to *Dara*. They made several trips back and forth taking passengers off before climbing back aboard using one of the ladders hanging over the stern. They found several badly injured women together with some children whom they lowered into a boat from one of the rescue vessels. The master, chief engineer and chief officer, who came aboard as they had done, joined them not long after. Because of the brisk wind on the port beam the fire had still not progressed aft of the mainmast, which was abreast the number seven and eight boats, but forward of that was a raging wall of fire. The chief engineer managed to start up the after emergency fire pump but it couldn't deliver much pressure and was used to cool down the davits of the number seven boat so the falls could be recovered. The falls from the number ten boat were also overhauled and both boats were then swung out so that there was a boat on each side.[20]

A little while after they had cleared the boats a loud 'whoosh' was heard on the port side forward, and as they looked over the rail they saw fuel oil pouring out of the ship's side (it was suggested afterwards that the deep tank in the engine room had exploded though this was later disputed). It quickly took fire and in a matter of moments the whole port side was ablaze. The number seven boat was hastily lowered and the master and mate jumped over the stern as the others scrambled down the ladders into the boat from where they made their way over to the *Barpeta*. In all 584 persons were rescued, though three of these later died as a result of injuries or shock. The total number of those who died either as a direct result of the explosion or fire, or were drowned in the attempt to escape, was 238.

That evening three Royal Navy frigates arrived, *Loch Alvie*, *Loch Ruthven*, and *Loch Fynne*, and Captain Elson, together with his chief engineer and chief officer, went aboard *Loch Alvie* where the master had the ship's doctor attend to his broken toe. A fire fighting party was put aboard but later withdrew for the night. The frigates confined the fire fighting activities that evening to playing their hoses on *Dara*'s hull and superstructure. The following morning Captain Elson transferred to *Loch Ruthven* where he had breakfast with the commander of the frigate and the senior officer present, Captain Desmond Law, before going back aboard *Dara*. The midships house was now gutted and the fire was confined to the engine room and holds.

At dawn fire-fighting parties from the frigates, as well as one from the USS *Laffey*, which had meanwhile arrived, went back aboard. They had cooled the superstructure sufficiently so that the men could make their way around the vessel without difficulty, but the ship had begun to list to starboard about 4 degrees. Pumps were put aboard to pump out the water that had been put into number three hold the previous evening, but, by the time the salvage tug *Ocean Salvor* arrived at about 18.00, the list had increased to over 6 degrees. Later that evening a salvage expert, Mr Cowasjee, arrived and went aboard *Dara* to assess the situation. After the inspection he recommended beaching the ship and then flooding her to extinguish the fire below, but they decided to wait until daylight before beginning the tow. A site about 3 miles north of Dubai was selected and at daybreak the tug got a line aboard what remained of *Dara* and prepared to tow her towards the selected site. The list by now had increased to about 10 degrees. Captain Elson and the commander of *Loch Ruthven* decided to transfer to the tug and on the way over saw heavy smoke beginning to pour out of the gutted ship. As he boarded the tug Captain Elson noticed that the starboard gangway door had swung open. As the tug began to tow the list seemed to increase, and the bottom of the open gangway port which had originally been well clear of the water drew closer and closer to the sea level. About nine that morning the sill of the port became submerged and water started to pour into the ship.

During the evening following the frigates' arrival the stability of *Dara* was probably reduced to almost zero as a result of the water poured into her by the naval ships. The loss of weight from her ruptured deep tank on the port side probably accounted for the initial list to starboard. Loose water in the public spaces and alley ways then probably began to find its way to starboard thereby increasing the list until the gangway port came under water. The pull of the tow may also have imparted a heeling moment to the listing vessel as the ship sheered considerably when the tow got underway, and at 0920 *Dara* rolled over and sank in about sixty feet of water.

*

It was not until the wreck had been examined by a diver some six months later that the cause and nature of the explosion were finally revealed. The place of the explosion was in the port alleyway of the upper deck just above the engine room and outside of cabin number twenty-eight. It blew large holes in the engine room casing, which formed the inboard bulkhead of the passageway and in the outboard bulkhead separating the alleyway from the cabin. A somewhat smaller hole about four feet in diameter was blown in the deck above, and a hole of about a foot in diameter in the deck above that, into the First Class Smoking Room. The explosive charge was estimated to be about twenty pounds in weight and it was calculated that the explosion generated a fireball eight to twelve feet in diameter with a temperature of 2000 to 3000°C, which explains the extreme rapidity with which the fire took hold and spread. It was thought to be the work of Omani rebels but that was never firmly established.

Charges and accusations were originally levelled against the master, chief officer, chief engineer and second and fifth engineers, but the final verdict was that given the extraordinary nature of the emergency there was no substance to the charges except some minor criticism of judgement on the part of the two watch engineers. It was accepted, however, that the organizational procedures for coping with such an emergency were not effective. It was not suggested, however, that either the master or the owners were at fault in any way. Aside from the extraordinary circumstances attending the case, alluded to above, the procedures and practices aboard *Dara* differed in no significant respect from those on similar vessels in the trade.

Frequent references were made during the hearing to the lack of realism in the drills carried out aboard ship. As this is a very difficult and complex problem it is largely ignored. Undoubtedly much more could be done than is usually done, but that would require an expenditure of time and resources devoted to the drills that owners would not ordinarily encourage. Although an individual master might occasionally attempt some innovation in this area, it is the present writer's experience that it is very difficult to generate much enthusiasm among officers and crew in such a seemingly pointless exercise.

Lakonia

The Dutch built Greek owned liner *Lakonia* had undergone a number of transformations during her lengthy career. Built in Amsterdam in

1930 as the Dutch Nederland Line *Johan van Oldenbarneveldt*, she was designed to carry 770 passengers in four classes between the mother country and the flourishing Dutch East Indies. When the war broke out in 1939 the Dutch Line underwent her first conversion from which she emerged as a troop ship, and she spent the war years carrying troops across the Atlantic and around the Mediterranean. A year after the end of hostilities she was returned to the Dutch who used her during the next few years in a service to Indonesia. She continued in that employment until the early 1950s when she was returned to her former owners and reconverted back to a passenger ship to transport immigrants to Australia.

As the postwar surge of immigration to Australia declined her Dutch owners looked for a more profitable use for the ageing liner. The burgeoning cruise trade seemed to offer what they were seeking and in 1959 *Johan van Oldenbarneveldt* went into the shipyard for a major refit. Her accommodation was altered to turn her into a one-class luxury cruise vessel for round-the-world voyages with berths for 1210 first class passengers. Competition from newer and more comfortable ships, however, frustrated the expectations of profits and in September 1962 she was withdrawn from service and entered lay-up. Britain was beginning to emerge from her postwar austerity and Greek interests were looking for a vessel to cater to the booming winter cruise trade out of Southampton to the Canary Islands. The Greek Line acquired the Dutch ship for little more than scrap value and renamed her *Lakonia*.

Her new owners spent £500,000 on a face-lift at Marriotti's in Genoa, the bulk of which was spent on redecoration of her public rooms and giving her a glossy exterior. Most of the rest of her equipment was neglected, but her engines in particular had seen hard service and were badly in need of repair. An extensive retrofit programme was decided on, and over the next twelve months much work was done. The finishing touches were applied during the ship's annual overhaul before her 1963 Christmas cruise.

As *Lakonia*'s 650-odd passengers began to board her on 19 December the 20,238 ton liner gave an initial impression of glamour and luxury, but experienced travellers soon found that her beauty was only skin-deep. She was thirty-three years old and only two other ships of her class still in service were older. She was like an old beauty queen covering the ravages of age with make-up. The glossy brochures that had attracted many of the elderly Britons who were looking for a warm Christmas reminded one of publicity photographs of ageing film stars. More than one of the passengers were tempted to cancel their holiday before it began, and the purser's office was deluged with complaints before the vessel sailed. As it was, the fitters in the engine room were still hard at work at 1700 on sailing day, and it was two hours later that the last of the repair force trudged down the gangway as the crew went to undocking stations.

One of those who considered cancellation was Joseph Samuel Wright, a retired engineer and company director who, together with his wife, was a veteran cruise ship traveller.[21] When they boarded after lunch they found their cabin cold, and without hot water. After settling in he decided to have a good look around the ship, and what he saw appalled him. Except for two nested lifeboats marked 'Not for Passenger's Use', the remainder were clinker-built boats from an earlier age. 'The diagonal planking was dry and sprung,' he noticed, and 'You could have pushed a penny between them.' Rust and corrosion was as much in evidence as lubrication of moving parts was not. He found the other boats 'in very much the same condition . . . My impression was that it had been a very long time since these boats had been off the davits.' He remarked to his wife: 'God help us if we have to go down in these.'[22]

Not all of the passengers were as critical – or as perceptive – as Mr Wright. The owners seemed to view their venture as a floating hotel business, and the food was first class. A 73-year-old housewife from Richmond, in Surrey, Mrs Ada Lassally, said: 'Prior to the fire I had been having a wonderful holiday and everything had been perfect. . . .'[23] However, no one who survived remembers being impressed with the ship's safety procedures or boat drills. The one conducted at 1015 on the day after sailing was perfunctory in the extreme. No boats were swung out. No instructions were given to passengers in the wearing of lifejackets, and there were few of the crew in evidence. It was a formality to be got out of the way and forgotten, and it allowed a truthful entry in the vessel's log book that a drill had been held, which was what the regulations required.

Another who came to have reservations about *Lakonia*'s lifeboats was Mr Harry Craige of Putney. On the day of the boat drill he and his wife Margery were standing on the boat deck, and as he glanced up at the boats a disturbing thought crossed his mind. 'I wonder,' he said to his wife, 'if these boats have ever been lowered?' When she looked at him questioningly he continued his ruminations, 'I don't believe they would lower even in an emergency.' Although he said no more at the time he continued to brood over the matter, and later he told his wife: 'I don't think we'll come back on this ship. I don't like it at all. I'm going to the wireless office to send a cable to Cook's. We'll cancel our return trip and come home by plane from Las Palmas.'[24]

A drill was held the day before sailing from Southampton. All the boats on the offshore side were swung out and four had been lowered into the water. It must be remembered that this was done alongside the dock with nothing to distract or excite the seamen involved. Nor should it be forgotten that many of the crew were new to the ship, and that it was a crew composed of a number of nationalities of different temperaments speaking different tongues. The master and officers, as well as the seamen and engineers, were Greek, but the rest were Germans, Italians, Dutch, French, Belgians, and Chinese with a sprinkling of English thrown in for seasoning. Although almost two thirds of the crew had sailed in the ship before most of these were German stewards. Over 20 per cent of the crew had very little or no previous sea time.[25]

Captain Mathios Zarbis was a small, stocky, jovial man in his middle fifties with thinning hair and an expanding waistline. He thoroughly enjoyed the social side of his position as master of a cruise ship, and no doubt he was picked for the job as much for his convivial nature as for his professional qualifications. He enjoyed joking and dancing with the lady passengers. He was also fond of talking about his home in Greece and how he looked forward to retiring to it in another six or seven years. He had been apprised of the complaints pouring in to the purser since the ship had sailed on the evening of the 19th, and he had taken steps to placate and mollify those passengers he thought might carry their grievances further than the ship. The distinguished-looking English cruise director George Herbert planned a tramp's ball and other entertainments for the night before *Lakonia*'s arrival at Madeira. The weather had been cold and wet for the first few days out of Southampton. It would have been remarkable if it hadn't, but as dawn broke on the 22nd more moderate temperatures hinted at the pleasant weather expected in the Canaries.

At the ball that evening in the Lakonia room on the promenade deck Captain Zarbis had invited both the Wrights and the Craiges to sit at his table. The captain was determined to erase or at least ameliorate the impression these guests had formed of his vessel and he laid on the charm. He danced with Mrs Craige and told her about his home and family in Greece. She found the situation somewhat embarrassing since she and her husband had been complaining bitterly ever since they arrived aboard *Lakonia* and here Captain Zarbis was treating them as if nothing had happened. They had no sooner finished dancing and sat down at the table than they noticed thick black smoke rolling in through the door. An instant later a crew member dashed in to inform Captain Zarbis there was a fire in the hairdresser's salon on the deck below.

Shortly before 2300 the fire watch patrolman making his hourly rounds about the vessel noticed smoke seeping through the sides of the door to the hairdresser's salon on the port side of the upper deck. As he ran to the bridge to report his discovery, Assistant Chief Steward Konstantine Papadimitriou, smelling smoke, traced it to the source and dashed down the corridor to the chief purser's office. Purser Antonio Bogetti was sitting in his office with the staff captain and several others when Papadimitriou rushed in and he immediately called the bridge. The others, led by Staff Captain Dimitri Valmas, hurried to the hairdresser's salon.

Staff Captain Valmas, mindful of the panic that might ensue if an alarm was raised, and apparently confident at this stage that the fire could be extinguished, attempted to play down the incident. He gave orders for fire hoses to be laid out and extinguishers fetched, and Papadimitriou was sent to get the keys to the salon.

Although the staff captain tried to keep everyone calm and avoid confusion the lack of organization among the crew quickly made itself felt. Second Mate John Hallas had meanwhile been sent from the bridge to investigate (there were three chief officers, a provisional master, and two second mates in addition to the master and staff captain). When he arrived at the scene he found the door to the hairdresser's salon broken down. The fire had by now spread to the barber's shop, just adjacent.

Captain Zarbis had gone directly to the bridge on leaving the Lakonia room. Once there he ordered the general alarm bell sounded and the engine room was instructed to start the fire pumps. The chief enginer, John Serafirmides, had been alerted to the danger when the fire was first discovered, and he had already given orders for additional fire pumps to be put on the line. He also had speed reduced, and Captain Zarbis now ordered the engines stopped. The master then went to the chart room and marked the position of the ship on the chart. He then instructed the radio officer, Dimitris Zegenis, to send out an SOS, 'On the principle,' as he later said, 'that it was better to be safe than sorry, although at that time I had every hope that we would put out the fire ourselves.'[26] He then attempted to make an announcement over the public address system but found that it wouldn't work. He again 'sounded the alarm a second and third time to make sure that even sleeping passengers would hear it.'

Unknown to the master the fire had even now reached a stage where the ship was in jeopardy. Accounts are confused as to just what happened but it is clear that the breaking of the door to the hairdresser's salon was the first in a chain of mistakes and oversights that allowed the fire to spread and get out of control. When the door was broken down thick, acrid, black smoke poured out into the corridor. There were a large number of bottles of hair-care preparations in both the barber's shop and the hairdresser's salon which were not only highly inflammable but gave off toxic fumes and smoke when ignited. As the heat intensified the bottles began to explode and thereby feed the fire.

Lakonia was built in an era when safety regulations concerning methods of construction and the materials used were in the nature of an afterthought. Wood was widely used in both the construction and decoration of the cabins and public rooms, and over the years it had become liberally coated with layers of paint and varnish. Moreover, a fresh coat had just been applied in the refit *Lakonia* had undergone, so the ship was literally a tinderbox.

To compound the difficulty the crew were ill-trained and many were inexperienced. Moreover they were of mixed nationalities, which added a communications dimension to the problem. The turnover rate amongst the crew was also high, so unfamiliarity with the vessel and its organization, such as it was, created confusion and uncertainty.

Vessels such as *Lakonia*, purchased for a price little more than would be fetched at a wrecker's yard are also often crewed on the cheap, and when that happens the vessel becomes a prime candidate for disaster. Seamen that come cheap are as often as not changed almost as often as the linen so standards of organization, which are probably low already, are even further degraded. Thus ships that present the highest risks are often those least capable to cope with emergencies.

Lakonia, unfortunately, though able to meet the ridiculous standards that allowed her to satisfy the requirements of the underwriters and the flag under which she sailed, was by any reasonable assessment both unfit to carry passengers due to her physical condition and also to her standards of manning. It would perhaps be invidious to level charges of incompetence in specific cases, however, the crew of *Lakonia* as a whole were clearly incompetent to cope with the emergency that resulted in her loss.

The perfunctory nature of the fire and boat drill the previous day is clear evidence that neither the master nor those who served under him regarded the possibility of being faced with a serious emergency as high on the list of priorities. It was, moreover, a Christmas voyage, and Captain Zarbis was no doubt very aware that *Lakonia* had a reputation to maintain if she was to survive in the highly competitive cruise trade. This consideration would explain in some part the reluctance, later severely criticized, to subject his 'customers' to more than a bare minimum of disturbance in drills. Given the age and condition of the ship, and the unfamiliarity of many of the crew with her, a great deal of effort should have gone into organization and training to bring standards up to a level where there would have been a reasonable hope of coping effectively with the emergency that arose.

After Captain Zarbis had taken what measures were required on the bridge he went to the scene of the fire to assess the situation. What he found cannot have been reassuring. Not surprisingly there were no co-ordinated efforts to fight the blaze because there had been almost no realistic preparation for such an emergency. Chief Mate Spyridon Angelopoulos, who was the safety officer and, in theory directly responsible for the organization of fire-fighting procedures, had been awakened by a seaman sent by the officer of the watch after the discovery of the fire. He had gone first to fire station number two located about amidships on the promenade deck where the locker containing safety equipment was situated. The asbestos fire suit and air pumps for the fresh-air breathing apparatus had already been taken so, with the four seamen assigned to him, he proceeded to take the balance of the safety equipment to the scene of the fire. Dense smoke was already beginning to make it very difficult to approach the blaze and on reaching the purser's office he had hoses from the two hydrants in the vicinity laid out.

Second Mate Hallas, who was one of the first to arrive on the scene, had taken charge of the men assembled at fire station number one in the vicinity of the hairdresser's salon. One of the men donned a fire suit while others put on smoke masks, and together they advanced on the fire, down the port passageway, using hoses fitted with conventional fire nozzles.

Angelopoulos also donned a mask and attempted to approach the fire from the starboard side. From there he was able to direct a stream of water through the open door of the barber's shop. The smoke had by now become so intense that in spite of his smoke mask he was able to man the hose for no more than five minutes at a time before a seaman relieved him.

The staff captain had meanwhile undertaken to try to close off the area by having seamen dog down open ports and close fire screen doors in the area. Unfortunately this also hampered those who were trying to fight the fire, so some of the doors were kept partially open to allow hoses to be led through them. At the beginning the hose pressure was quite adequate, but as more hoses were brought indiscriminately into play the pressure began to drop. The fire which had been growing in ferocity in spite of the efforts to contain it now spilled out into the passageways, and the smoke thus generated billowed in great clouds down the corridors.

The passengers attending the tramp's ball in the Lakonia room were among the first to know of the fire because of the smoke creeping in from the deck below, however, those in other parts of the ship were unaware for some time that anything was amiss. A Bob Hope film, *Call Me Bwana*, was playing in the ship's cinema, and even when one of the passengers attempted to raise the alarm there, no one would at first take him seriously. The failure of the public address system added much to the confusion since that was the only effective means of communication throughout the ship. Someone issued instructions for the passengers to assemble in the restaurant which was three decks below the promenade deck and on the same level as the upper part of the engine room on the waterline – an insane order, as it was the worst possible place from which to effect an orderly evacuation of the vessel. Many recognized it as such and ignored it. One of the passengers, a Mr Taylor, took his wife and two sons down, but as he said later: 'There must have been about three hundred people there, and more and more people were coming into the restaurant. We realized that if anything was seriously wrong we were going to be trapped down there.'[27] They made their way back topside, and others soon followed their example.

It could easily have led to panic and it did add to the confusion. Mr William Scott, who had been feeling ill, had retired to his cabin just down the corridor from the hairdresser's salon. His wife, who was asleep, woke up saying, 'I can smell smoke.' When he ignored her she persisted: 'I can smell smoke. Why can't you smell it? You've been smelling paint all week.' She then jumped out of bed, put on her dressing gown, and opened the door. Thick black smoke poured into the cabin, and they ran choking down the corridor. Scott turned back to collect some clothes but was met by a steward shouting: 'Go down to the dining room. Go down to the dining room.' No sooner had they reached the restaurant than another steward told them, 'Go to your cabins. It's all right now, it's all right,' but as soon as they reached the promenade deck another steward met them shouting: 'Go back. Go back.'

Scott described the scene as 'Absolute chaos. We didn't know where to go.' People were running in all directions in obedience to conflicting orders and the questionable advice of other passengers. Others were trying to find children or friends, or attempting to retrieve valuables from their rooms. Some later accused the crew of giving way to panic, but the vast bulk of the passengers were British, and what to them might seem to resemble panic was no more than excited behaviour by others of a less phlegmatic background. George Herbert, the cruise director, struck a realistic note: 'This is rather typical of the Greeks. They tend to shout at each other even in the ordinary way, and while they shout nothing is being done.' A building contractor from Sheffield, Mr Eric Field, commented: 'Perhaps a normal Latin temperament has been mistaken for panic. There was a lot of shouting, arm-waving and running about. I would hesitate to say there was panic.'

In spite of the confusion there were also acts of self-sacrifice and even heroism by stewards and seamen. One young Greek Cypriot steward, André Vasilades, particularly distinguished himself. Small, and slight, Vasilades seemed to be everywhere, fighting the fire, carrying messages, and helping passengers to safety. When Reg Fishenden frantically sought help from George Herbert to rescue his ten-year-old son Nicolas, trapped in a cabin on a deck below, the young Greek immediately volunteered to go over the side on a thin line to pull the child through the port hole. When he reached Nicolas the boy whimpered, 'I don't know what to do.' 'You don't have to do anything,' Vasilades told him, 'Just give me your right hand.'

Gripping the rope with his left hand he pulled Nicolas out the port hole with his right. For a moment he thought the slender line might break under their combined weight. It held, however, as they dangled precariously high above the water, and he shouted for the men tending the line above to haul away. In a moment that must have seemed an eternity they reached the safety of the deck above where the boy's anxious father waited to haul him over the rail to temporary safety. However, by a cruel twist of fate, both Nicolas and his mother were killed only minutes later when the forward davit of the lifeboat they were in collapsed, spilling them into the sea and allowing the boat to fall on top of them.

About half an hour after the discovery of the outbreak of the fire the staff captain reported to Captain Zarbis on the bridge that the fire was out of control. The master told him to go back to the Promenade Deck and see to the preparation of the boats for launching. The same order was also given to First Mate Andreas Paterakis. The cruise director, George Herbert, next appeared on the bridge to ask if he might use the public address system to inform the passengers of the situation. Captain Zarbis told him it was not working and gave him instructions to pass the order verbally to prepare to abandon ship. Herbert went down both sides of the promenade deck, which also served as the boat embarkation deck, shouting: 'On captain's order, as the loudspeakers do not function, you are requested to go to your positions near your boats.'[28]

The chief steward sent his men around to those cabins that had not yet been made uninhabitable by smoke or fire to see that no one was overlooked. Hope had been all but abandoned of being able to contain the fire yet efforts to fight it continued. This had the unfortunate result of keeping the officers and the seamen under them, who were those most qualified to prepare the boats and launch them, from participating in what was now the prime objective of a successful abandonment of the ship. Again the lack of organization was critical and the only one who might have been able to stem the chaos, the master, was denied the means through the failure and breakdown of the communications system.

Once the decision to abandon ship was taken there was no reason for delay. Unfortunately, Captain Zarbis apparently did not realize the extent of confusion prevailing, and the necessity of issuing specific instruction to his officers to take charge of the abandonment. He perhaps thought his staff captain had assumed direction of that operation, but when George Herbert returned to the bridge shortly after midnight the master told him to 'tell the passengers to enter the boats, first on the starboard side.'[29]

Captain Zarbis then gave the order for left wheel and slow ahead on the starboard engine to create a lee on the starboard side. The wind was out of the northeast at about force 4 with a moderate sea and swell. The wireless operators had meanwhile continued to send out distress messages and five ships within a radius of less than 50 miles had already responded and were heading for the scene. Another three would join them in the rescue operation.

The order to lower the boats to the embarkation deck was given originally as a precaution, and as those who ordinarily would have carried this out were engaged in fighting the fire, it is not surprising that when the order came to abandon ship many of these men were absent from the boat stations. The drill for abandon ship is quite distinct from that for fire, and when the drills are supplanted by reality, confusion is inevitable if the fighting of the fire is not suspended before ordering abandonment. While Captain Zarbis had given specific orders to several of his officers to lower boats no general order was passed by anyone with clear authority. The cruise director had, it is true, been given specific instructions by the master to pass the word to abandon ship. But his job was entertainment and while no one could deny that this was high drama he was hardly the person to direct it, willing as he might be.

The situation would have been less desperate had the boats been well maintained and of recent design, but both boats and their davits and associated gear had been badly neglected. Some of the boats, moreover, lacked synchronized winches for lowering, a process which required some skill and careful supervision to accomplish safely. When the task was entrusted to those with neither skill nor experience, the difficulties became daunting, and when there was no one to supervise the enterprise it became dangerous as well as difficult. The motion of the ship had furthermore been aggravated by putting the wind and sea abeam. The ship's embarkation ladders had also not been stowed and they interfered with the lowering of those boats above them. The removal of the gates in the ship's railings, which would have allowed easy access to the boats, and should have been done as a matter of course, was overlooked in the confusion and added to the difficulties. Finally, the drains in the bottom of the boats, that allow rain water to drain out when the boats are in their stowed position, also will allow the sea to run in when the boats are launched if the plugs are not put in place. Seamen know this as a matter of course. Stewards may or may not. Many of *Lakonia*'s did not.

Staff Captain Valmas, who had been sent to see that the boats were prepared for launching, had given orders to that effect and then returned to the fire. He unwisely decided to enter spaces fouled with smoke and was overcome. He was taken to the stern to recover and by the time he had done so the boats were being lowered. The flames were now spreading with great rapidity and threatened to engulf the promenade deck from where the passengers and crew were attempting to embark.

The first boats were lowered within less than half an hour after the original order to abandon ship. Chief Mate Angelopoulos gave the orders for the launching of most of the boats on the starboard side, but few of those assigned to the critical tasks involved with launching the boats were available to assist. Overboard discharges from the engine room partially flooded several of the boats during launching. Some passengers were inebriated as were a few of the crew. Others became seasick, and in most of the boats there was no officer to take command so confusion took charge. Most of the boats left the vessel only partially full, and one of the few that was – boat number twenty-three – spilled most of its occupants into the sea when the forward davit broke. Some were crushed when the boat fell on top of them. Mrs Fishenden and her son were among them.[30]

The last of the boats were lowered about 0130 by which time tongues of flame were dangerously close. The eight boats nearest the bridge were nested, four on each side, and because of the difficulties associated with launching them they had been ignored. The spread of the fire, which had driven the master from the bridge, now prevented access to these remaining boats, and about 150 passengers and eighty crew, including Captain Zarbis and the chief engineer, were left to their own devices.

A number of the boats left the vessel less than three quarters full, so even without the eight boats that were not launched there had been sufficient room to take everyone off. The haphazard and even reckless manner in which the boats were handled caused many of the passengers to wait for rescue from another source. It was known that other vessels were nearby and would reach the scene shortly. Captain Zarbis, who had more optimism than the rest, still felt there was a chance that the fire could be brought under control. The engine room was still manned and the fire pumps were still working. The bridge was now a blazing inferno and shortly collapsed in a mass of flames, but the stern of the vessel was still free of fire.

Many of those remaining aboard had gathered in the Mocambo lounge where crew and passengers mingled in a ludicrous holiday atmosphere. A steward appeared out of nowhere still clad in his black silk quilted jacket with his arms full of fruit, which he proceeded to distribute. Other stewards, less helpful, were enjoying the hospitality of the bar and chatting amongst themselves. George Herbert felt a sense of impropriety and indignation: 'there were far too many of them there. They could have been organized into fire-fighting parties to help the few men who were working jolly hard and had been working all night.'[31]

The scene could have served as a setting for the film *Ship of Fools*. Most of the passengers remaining aboard were the elderly and infirm, who were either unable or too frightened to forsake the comparative security of the ship for the uncertainty of an open boat. Many were clad only in nightdresses though there was also the occasional mink. To take their minds off the ordeal drinks were passed round and someone started to play 'Silent Night', followed by 'Good King Wenceslas' on the piano and some began to sing. Others played cards, and some fell asleep in their arm chairs. About ten minutes later part of the superstructure collapsed with a tremendous crash. The sleepers woke with a start, the singing stopped and fear flitted across the faces of the women. Then someone cracked a joke, the ladies tittered, and the singers resumed their chorus. It was a typically British, but increasingly unreal situation.

George Herbert, who was afraid that panic might set in when the shock wore off, went to find out how things were going elsewhere. He found the staff captain and chief purser who told him that a Norwegian ship was expected on the scene at about 0300. Herbert went back to the lounge to spread the word and just about that time lights were seen to starboard.

The cruise director later said: 'Everyone thought that these ships would come in fairly close, certainly to within a few hundred yards

FIRE

and somehow get boats across to us and take everyone off.'[32] What those aboard *Lakonia* did not realize was that the rescue ships were unaware of the extent of the confusion aboard the vessel. They assumed that the evacuation of the ship had been complete and did not realize then that some were still aboard the blazing liner.[33]

A retired company director from Bognor Regis, Mr Ernest Neary, who had been one of those most active in organizing activities to keep people's spirits up, had gone to the starboard side of the promenade deck to get a better view of the ships approaching, when he spied some of the food laid out for the festivities interrupted in the Lakonia room. Together with a companion he picked up some silver salvers laden with roast duck, and some with bread and butter and took it into the lounge where everyone tucked in with delighted surprise.

The distraction was only momentary, however, and it was soon apparent that the ships had stopped much further off than anticipated. They appeared to be about four to five miles off. The fire was much closer now and obviously out of control. As if to emphasize the gravity of their situation some of the stewards who had been drinking with the passengers at the bar appeared wearing top coats over their best suits and carrying cases. They were all dressed up with no place to go, and this incongruous sight brought home to at least some of the passengers the need to prepare for departure from their temporary and now endangered haven.

The captain appeared just then, his dress uniform torn and blackened with smoke, his face drawn and drained of hope. Before he could say anything the ship was shaken by an explosion in the cinema just forward of the lounge, and in the twinkling of an eye it was engulfed in flame. That brought an end to any vestige of the pseudo-festive atmosphere still lingering. The chief purser now herded the passengers into the shopping parade aft of the lounge and just forward of the stern.

The first vessel to arrive on the scene was the 12,053 gross ton Argentinian liner *Salta*. She was about 30 miles slightly north of east of *Lakonia* when her wireless operator picked up the first SOS and, as soon as they knew the position of the stricken ship, course was immediately altered to go her assistance. The burning liner was sighted about the same time as the last of *Lakonia's* boats was launched, and shortly after 0200 *Salta* started to reduce speed as she approached the first boats. It was 0430, however, before the Argentinian vessel took the first survivors aboard and they fished the last one from the water almost eleven hours later.

143

The next ship to arrive was the British freighter *Montcalm*, a smallish vessel of about 5000 gross tons on a voyage from the Great Lakes in America to Casablanca. When the auto-alarm woke her radio operator shortly after 2300 she was several miles north of *Salta* but being somewhat slower she arrived about half an hour later. Her master, Captain E. J. Kempton, played a considerable part in the rescue. In the three to four hours it took him to reach the scene he had taken steps to provide for the rescue, care and comfort of the survivors.

Although *Montcalm* picked up only 236 passengers and crew to *Salta*'s 490, the British ship was later on the scene and lacked the capacity and facilities to care for large numbers in addition to her own complement. By 0630 the American freighter *Rio Grande*, the Belgian *Charlesville*, the Pakistani ship *Mehdi*, and the American Export Line's *Export Aid* were also on the scene. The P&O liner *Stratheden* and several other vessels followed later.

Captain Kempton, who had only assumed command of *Montcalm* the year before at the age of twenty-eight, had the memory of the *Empire Windrush* (a classic example of how a vessel should be abandoned) fresh in mind, and had assumed that the evacuation of *Lakonia* under somewhat similar conditions should pose no great problems. The handling of the boats suggested a less than orderly evacuation, however, and the testimony of some of the survivors reinforced his suspicions that his initial assessment was incorrect. The people in the boats were in no immediate danger and as dawn broke he decided to examine the smouldering hulk more closely. He soon found that his fears were justified, and as he closed on *Lakonia* he found scores of people in the water. He spent the next seven hours fishing passengers and crew from the sea. By about 1500 he felt fairly sure there were no further survivors in the water but went in for a final closer look.

The *Montcalm*'s master later described the operation: 'I went in very close to the *Lakonia*, within a hundred yards, and we went all around it very slowly and had a good look with binoculars, and tried to see if there was anybody left alive on board. It didn't seem possible at the time that there could be, because the ship was completely gutted. She was on fire fore and aft and the flames were raging inside as well. We could see the glow of fire through the portholes so we left that particular area, went back upwind, where all the people had

Titanic: the last photograph, taken as the ship left Queenstown (now Cork) harbour. (Popperfoto)

An artist's impression of the sinking of the White Star liner on 15 April 1912. (Popperfoto)

Townsend Thoresen cargo ferry *European Gateway* lies half submerged on a sandbank off Harwich after collision with Sealink's Speedlink Vanguard at the entrance to the harbour on 19 December 1982.

Salvage of the Townsend Thoresen passenger ferry *Herald of Free Enterprise*.

A mourner pays homage to a relative lost in the Zeebrugge disaster during a memorial service held on 11 March 1987 in front of the ferry. (Popperfoto)

Salvage workers stand on the side of *Herald of Free Enterprise* as the vessel slowly makes its way upright four weeks after the disaster. (Popperfoto)

The badly-listing *Flying Enterprise* on 8 January 1952, only a day away from Falmouth, and almost a week since the list to port first developed. (Popperfoto)

The *Andrea Doria*.

The ill-fated sailing vessel *Pamir*. (Popperfoto)

The still-burning *Morro Castle* beached at Asbury Park, New Jersey in September 1934. (Popperfoto)

The Swedish passenger liner *Stockholm* after the collision with the Italian passenger ship *Andrea Doria* in the summer of 1956 off Nantucket Shoals.

he Greek VLCC *Atlantic Empress* ablaze after colliding with the Liberian *Aegean Captain* in the aribbean in the summer of 1979, causing the largest oil spill in history.

he wreck of the *Amoco Cadiz* seen from the air after stranding on the northern shores of Brittany in arch 1977 where she spilled a quarter of a million tons of crude oil, occasioning widespread arine pollution.

(*Above*) *Exxon Valdez* surrounded by fishing boats working to keep oil containment booms around the tanker and its spill and beside a sister Exxon tanker engaged in pumping off the remainder of the oil. 27 March 1989. (Popperfoto)

(*Left*) Sea lions rest on a rock in the oily waters of Prince William Sound after the stranding of *Exxon Valdez*; by 2 April the oil spill covered over 1000 square miles. (Popperfoto)

been swimming, and continued to search that area until the *Stratheden* arrived.'[34]

Aboard *Lakonia* the remaining passengers and crew clustered on the stern around George Herbert and the chief purser, Mr Rodenberg. It was still about an hour and a half before dawn at 0730 but the time for decision was now. The Promenade Deck was almost entirely engulfed in flame, and when two more explosions shook the ship Herbert cried out, 'Where is the captain?' That beleaguered gentleman was elsewhere, however, and between them the cruise director and the purser began the task of persuading their fellow unfortunates to take the dreaded step of plunging into the sea some thirty feet below. Herbert, recalling the grim scene later said: 'I found it a most harrowing affair. They were old people, obviously in many cases incapable of fending for themselves in the water. I felt I was pushing some of them to their deaths. I am sure I did.'[35]

Several crew members had appeared with rope ladders which they made fast on the rails. Slowly the desperate people clambered over the rails and down the ladders. At first the going was awkward but not too difficult. As they made their way further down the ladders began to swing. Some dropped off and others slid down the ropes landing on those already in the water below. Screams and cries for help rent the night air, and wives became frantic when separated from their husbands. Pandemonium raged below yet those still on deck queued in contrasting orderly British fashion above.

Reg Fishenden, who had seen his wife and young son crushed under a falling lifeboat only an hour or so before, later described the scene: 'They were coming down in their dozens and I saw them passing me. Some of the old ones were falling off, screaming, into the water. There was no scrambling and they were quite orderly until they fell. The cries were terrifying and I thought the best thing I could do was to stay where I was. I didn't see myself having any chance in the water at all.'[36]

Fishenden and about thirty others stuck with the ship until the choice became one of certain roasting or possible drowning. George Herbert, Rodenberg the purser, and the intrepid young Cypriot Vasilades still stayed behind to give whatever help and encouragement they could. The passengers peeled off in pairs and singly until less than a dozen were left. Captain Zarbis and his second in command, Dimitri Valmas, were now among them. The captain was urging those left to take to the water. Waving his arms and shouting,

'Jump! Jump! No deaths here!' Fishenden was one of the last to go, and when he finally fell into the sea he passed out but was somehow saved.

George Herbert, who had put on the performance of his life, saw the last of the passengers off and felt he could now ring down the final curtain. Turning calmly to the master he said: 'Well, captain, there's nothing much more I can do. I think I'll go now.' Captain Zarbis replied almost as casually, 'I'll have to stay to the end,' adding almost as an afterthought, 'Besides I have no lifejacket.'[37]

Although panic had been largely avoided by the passengers as long as they felt a solid deck under their feet, it began to take hold once they were in the water. Vasilades continued his valiant effort to keep their spirits up and succeeded in retrieving one of the rubber dinghies dropped by American Air Force planes circling overhead. He collected sixteen people dangling from rope ladders before he pushed his overloaded craft free of the ship's side.

Captain Zarbis was now alone on his blazing vessel where he stayed until ten o'clock in the morning. Satisfied that everyone else was gone he climbed into one of the rubber dinghies that was alongside and drifted off.

Of the 1027 souls aboard *Lakonia* when she sailed from Southampton 128 – thirty-three crew and ninety-five passengers – perished in the fire and subsequent abandonment. The Greek court of inquiry that was eventually convened to look into the disaster, while taking note of the fault and responsibility of the owners of the vessel for what happened, found the master, staff captain and safety officer guilty of gross negligence, while the other deck officers were held guilty to a lesser degree. The master was, in what seems a monumental miscarriage of justice, also convicted in a criminal court of manslaughter and sentenced to fourteen months in prison. First Mate Andreas Paterakis was sentenced to nine months for abandoning ship in a motor boat capable of holding over fifty with only eight people aboard.[38]

Captain Zarbis's greatest mistake and fault was in accepting employment from the owners of *Lakonia*, who are the true culprits in this affair.[39] They, of course, were indulging in practices accepted as customary by many who had gone before them, so they alone should not be singled out for blame. This is not a political book and the author has little sympathy for systems that evade or ignore the responsibilities of ownership. But there seems little doubt that a system which allows individuals either singly, or in groups, to escape responsibility for sending a ship and crew to sea under the questionable cover of a dubious seaworthy certificate is seriously flawed.

5

Explosion

The closing of the Suez Canal during the Arab-Israeli war in 1967 caused ship designers to turn to their drawing boards to seek an economical way of transporting oil cargoes via the Cape of Good Hope. The obvious solution was to increase the size of the ships and it was not long before vessels of 100,000 tons and more appeared. The commercial success of these ships led to the design and construction of even larger vessels. The first VLCC entered service in 1968 and the ULCCs began to appear several years later.

Ships that carry petroleum cargoes have always been highly vulnerable to fire and explosion, but the huge new ships that came into service in the late 1960s and early 1970s were to prove exceptionally susceptible to these hazards. Within the space of a few weeks at the end of 1969 the *Kong Haakon, Marpessa*, and *Matra*, all in excess of 200,000 dwt, were victims of explosion and fire. This caused some momentary concern but during the decade that followed tanker casualties seemed to resume a normal pattern. Then, on the last day of 1978 the 218,000 dwt Greek tanker *Andros Patria* exploded killing thirty crew members. In March 1979 the 300,000 dwt Portuguese owned tanker *Neiva* caught fire while discharging a cargo of crude. Luckily there were no fatalities but the ship was later declared a constructive total loss. A couple of months later the 213,000 dwt Liberian registered *Atlas Titan* suffered an explosion in which five crewmen died while cleaning tanks off Lisbon. In addition to the casualties presently to be described (the first three being explosions at sea, the last two in port), the 235,000 dwt Spanish *Maria Alejandra* exploded and sank within a minute off the coast of Mauritania in March 1980. Among the thirty people who perished were the owner and his wife and daughter. In the previous fifteen months no less than thirty-five tankers or combination oil/bulk carriers of over

100,000 dwt were the victims of fire or explosion. Clearly there was something gravely wrong.

Berge Istra

Berge Istra was one of four sister ships laid down in 1972 for the General Ore Navigation Corporation in the Uljanik shipyard and diesel engine factory of Pula, Yugoslavia. The vessels were designed as combination oil/ore bulk carriers, or OBOs, with a displacement of about 260,000 tons, a deep draught of just under 67 feet and an overall length of 1030 feet. *Berge Istra* had a crew of thirty-two including her master and was registered in Liberia. The deck officers, engineers and the majority of the key ratings were Norwegian while most of the rest of the crew were Spanish.

The vessel and her sister ships were operated by Messrs. Sig Bergesen D. Y. & Co. of Oslo and were employed in a regular trade carrying oil and ore in turn. The voyages normally began in the Persian Gulf where crude oil was loaded for northern Europe. From there the vessel proceeded in ballast to Brazil where a cargo of ore was loaded for Japan, from where the vessel returned in ballast to the Persian Gulf to repeat the cycle.

Captain Kristoffer Hemmnes, a 45-year-old Norwegian citizen, commanded *Berge Istra* on the voyage in question. *Berge Istra* had arrived at Europoort, Rotterdam, on 13 November 1975, carrying a full cargo of crude loaded at Kharg Island in Iran. After discharging she had sailed the following day for Tubarao, Brazil, where she would load a cargo of iron ore for Kimitsu, Japan.

Exactly what happened aboard *Berge Istra* after departure from Rotterdam can only be inferred since the vessel and all her documents and records were lost and we only have the sketchy testimony of the two seamen who survived. Normally the tank cleaning began after the vessel had cleared Ushant. The second and third officers would then begin the questionable practice of standing watch on watch of six hours each, in order to free the chief officer from his watch standing duties so he could supervise the tank cleaning. The tank cleaning would normally proceed uninterrupted for about a week during which the chief officer was on 24-hour call.

The ships had engines and accommodation aft with five large holds or tanks forward of the machinery spaces. On each side were ten wing tanks capable of carrying either oil or ballast. The aftermost wing tank (number ten) on the starboard side was used as a slop tank in which oily residues were collected during tank cleaning. Forward of number one hold were two fuel oil deep tanks between which was located the forward pump room. There were also two fuel oil tanks in the engine room just abaft the number ten wing tanks. Just forward of the engine room in number five hold was situated the main pump room. When the vessel was originally constructed only the slop tank (number ten starboard) was connected with the inert gas plant, but later the coverage was extended to all of the vessel's tanks and holds.

Inert gas systems (IGS) were developed in the 1970s to meet the threat of explosion in the large tanks of vessels designed to carry liquid cargoes which gave off explosive fumes. Flue gases, such as carbon dioxide generated during the combustion process in the ship's boilers, are used to creat inert gas which is piped into the ship's cargo compartments to displace the air in the void spaces. The double bottoms of the tanks were not used for the carriage of either oil or ballast, and served primarily as a space through which the piping ran. The normal procedure in cleaning the tanks was to start with the wing tanks, washing them with portable Butterworth-type machines, with the oily residues being discharged into the slop tank. The centre holds, or tanks, would then be cleaned in the same manner. During the washing all tanks would be inerted, but after washing all tanks, holds, cofferdams, double bottoms, etc. would be gas-freed by means of mechanical ventilating units rather than by re-inerting them. The reason for this was that the 'Riken' explosimeter would 'not record an accurate hydrocarbon content in the presence of inert gas.'[1] This had the disadvantage of possibly allowing the tanks to gas up again from either undetected residues or a leak from the slop tank. It would appear that the tank cleaning was accomplished without difficulty since the cargo spaces were accepted as free for loading on arrival at Tubarao.

Berge Istra arrived there at 1030 on 28 November and loading of iron ore began shortly afterwards. 185,244 long tons were loaded in her centre tanks or holds during that day and the next and the morning of the 29th. She departed shortly before three o'clock in the afternoon heading across the South Atlantic to the Cape of Good Hope and across the Indian Ocean for the Sunda Strait.

Little of any significance is known of what took place during the intervening weeks. *Berge Istra*, though capable of 15 knots, was steaming at a regulated speed of 13.75 knots for reasons of economy.

The owner's instructions allowed the master to use his own discretion whether to inert the cargo spaces and tanks after loading. Although we have no evidence as to his decision in this respect it was the normal procedure not to inert them after they had been gas-freed.[2] It was furthermore usual, after the tanks were cleaned and gas-freed, for these vessels to be regarded as dry cargo carriers, 'with freedom to carry out any work which would be appropriate for such a vessel.'[3]

According to testimony of others who had sailed recently in the vessel, as well as written evidence supplied by the owners, we know that a number of the steel pipes passing through the double bottoms were leaking and in need of replacement. Indeed on 19 December a radio message, later confirmed by a telephone call, asked that arrangements be made to supply lengths of pipe at Kimitsu so this condition could be corrected. Under the circumstances some 'hot work' was probably in progress on the afternoon of 29 December. According to the ship's normal routine it is also likely that fuel was being transferred from the fuel tanks forward to those in the engine room, and that pumping of oil and water leakages into the double bottoms was also being carried out.

We know that during the late afternoon just before supper, while south of the Philippine island of Mindanao (though even this can not be certain as all navigational information disappeared with the ship), a series of violent explosions occurred in the after part of the vessel, followed by fire. The ship took an immediate heavy list to port and started to settle rapidly by the stern. Within a matter of a few minutes she sank in one of the deepest parts of the Pacific Ocean.

At the time four of the crew were working in the fore part of the vessel, and two of these four were the only ones to survive. One of them, 40-year-old Able Seaman Imeldo Barreto Leon, said that he was clearing debris from the deck on the port side when the first explosion shook the vessel. He felt a heavy tremor but it didn't knock him off his feet.[4] He looked aft and saw smoke and flames in front of the forward part of the after deck house. His immediate reaction and that of his three fellow crew members working in the vicinity was to run forward away from the source of the fire and explosions. As they were climbing the ladder from the main deck to the raised fo'c'sle head a second explosion occurred, again causing a heavy tremor throughout the ship.

Berge Istra had begun to list to port after the first explosion and this increased rapidly following the second. The other three men had by then reached the fo'c'sle head and ran across the deck to the other side, scrambled down the ladder to the main deck on the opposite side and set about releasing a six-man liferaft situated there. Before they succeeded in this effort, a third and even stronger explosion, which Mr Leon thought to be on the starboard side, racked the vessel. As he looked aft he could see the whole of the deck house enveloped in smoke and flame. The ship was by now listing heavily and settling quickly by the stern. The other seamen had meanwhile succeeded in releasing the liferaft but were unable to launch it because of the heavy list to port. By now Leon could no longer see the after part of the vessel. The ship was sinking rapidly by the stern and the sea had advanced as far forward as the number eight hatch (number four hold).

His fellow crewmen had since abandoned their efforts to launch the raft and were trying to make their way back up to the fo'c'sle head, but the going was difficult because of the heavy list. He had himself just reached the after part of the fo'c'sle head when the ship sank underneath him and he found himself in the water.

As the vessel sank Leon was pulled down with it, but he fought his way back to the surface to find the liferaft floating about thirty feet off. It had evidently floated clear when the ship sank but it had sustained considerable damage in the process. Leon, however, had fortunately escaped without injury, and he swam to the raft and pulled himself aboard. As he looked around he saw Ordinary Seaman Epifanio Lopez in the water not far off and managed to pull him aboard. He looked around for the other two but they were nowhere to be seen, nor was there any sign of other survivors. There was a fair amount of wreckage and debris but nothing else.

Lopez was unconscious, having apparently suffered a knock on the head as well as injury to one of his legs. Leon at first thought he was dead, but after giving him the 'kiss of life' Lopez revived. However, his injuries were so serious he was unable to fend for himself, and for the whole of the time aboard the raft until the rescue Leon had to tend his injured shipmate.

Leon showed remarkable tenacity and determination in the days that followed. It was almost certain that there had been no time to get off a distress signal before the ship went down. The foundering of *Berge Istra* had therefore most probably gone unnoticed, and though her disappearance would become apparent when she did not arrive on schedule there would be no way of knowing when and where she had gone down. The prospect of a successful rescue effort, once it was mounted, did not look promising, but the plucky Spanish seaman did not become disheartened. The food and water stowed in the raft lasted for about eleven or twelve days, after which Leon was able to catch fish with the gear he found aboard the raft. Fortunately there was frequent rain which he collected with the canopy of the raft.

To add to his difficulties the pyrotechnic signals with which the raft was equipped had instructions only in English and Norwegian. As he could read neither of these languages the instructions were useless. At first he did not worry about this as he thought he knew how to ignite the flares, but in the event he was proved wrong. During the next few days he twice sighted ships but was unable to fire off the flares. He now had only one left as the remainder had been damaged by water.

Because all records were lost and no one involved in the navigation of the vessel survived virtually nothing is known about the voyage from the time *Berge Istra* left Tubarao until the explosion almost a month later. Even the route taken can only be surmised since, contrary to the accepted practice aboard *Berge Istra*, which Captain Hemmnes had before always faithfully followed, the vessel didn't participate in the AMVER reporting system provided by the US Coast Guard (see appendix 6).

In the event *Berge Istra* did not participate on this voyage, and neither her owners nor anyone else had any accurate knowledge of her position during the voyage. Although this would in no way have effected the outcome of events up to the time *Berge Istra* disappeared, it might have helped to establish her probable position once the search operation was mounted. On Monday 29 December the owners received a message giving her ETA (estimated time of arrival) at Kimitsu as 0800 hours on 5 January. As she was known to be steaming at a regulated speed of 13.75 knots the owners were hence able to calculate a rough positon when her loss became known.

It was customary for *Berge Istra* to transmit a routine message each Wednesday to the owner's office in Oslo. On Wednesday the 31st no message was received but this was not noticed by those who normally would have handled such traffic. As this was the day before the New Year's holiday the oversight is not remarkable, but the investigating board expressed some concern that in the main office of such an

experienced and responsible owner this was allowed to go unnoticed.
Not until 5 January when the vessel's agents in Japan notified the
Oslo office of *Berge Istra's* failure to arrive as expected, and she failed
to answer a message enquiring as to her whereabouts, was any
concern felt.

Captain Stangeland, the operating manager of Sig. Bergesen
immediately got in touch with several other of the company's vessels
in the area and instructed them to begin a search. This they
proceeded to do until it was called off on 22 January. On the 6th
Captain Stangeland contacted the AMVER office in New York only
to be told that *Berge Istra* had not logged in. On the 7th he reported
the disappearance to the Bureau of Maritime Affairs in New York,
and the US Air Force, as well as the Japanese Maritime Safety
Agency. When none of these organizations was able to come up with
any clue about the fate of the missing vessel through enquiries of
ports and vessels along the supposed route an intensive air search
was initiated, which lasted until the 17th but produced no result.

On the 18th Able Seaman Leon, using his last flare, was able to
ignite it when he sighted the Japanese fishing vessel *Hachimo Maru*.
After nineteen days he and Ordinary Seaman Lopez were finally
picked up. They were taken to the island of Palau from where a US
Coast Guard plane flew them to Okinawa for much needed medical
attention. It was later calculated that the raft had drifted in an
easterly direction at a rate of about 25 miles per day, so when they
were rescued they had reached a position north of Halmahera Island
and south of Mindanao Island in the Philippines.

On the basis of the testimony of witnesses and the available
evidence the Board concluded that the initial explosion most likely
took place either in the double bottom space where inflammable
mixtures had gathered due to the leakages already mentioned, or in
the after pump room. In either case they felt that in order to account
for the magnitude of the explosion the port fuel tank in the engine
room must have been involved in a chain reaction. The ignition of
the inflammable vapour was considered to have originated most
probably from the inert gas plant.[5]

The Board made a number of recommendations inviting IMCO
(now IMO) to consider a variety of measures mainly concerned with
inert gas systems, and the desirability of carrying out hot work at sea
on such vessels was questioned. Almost four years later, however, one

of the sister ships of *Berge Istra* exploded and disappeared with all hands in the eastern South Atlantic, suggesting that the lessons that might have been learned from this earlier tragedy had been ignored or incompletely understood.

Berge Vanga

There can be little doubt that the explosion and loss of *Berge Istra* caused considerable concern and soul searching among those directly responsible for her ashore and those who manned her sister ships. It should have been apparent – and almost certainly was – to those who sailed the vessels (and particularly the masters) that practices normally regarded as routine did in fact represent a grave threat to the ships they commanded and the lives of those aboard them. They were duly provided with copies of the *Berge Istra* report and it is unthinkable that they did not give it the closest study and consideration. None the less, the major recommendations made by the Board concerning the use of inert gas and the carrying out of hot work while underway seem to have been ignored. Adoption of the recommendations would have required basic changes in both the way the vessels were operated, and repaired and maintained, which would have been both costly and inconvenient. There can be little doubt, however, that for a time much greater attention was paid to safety procedures and practices, but as the impact of the incident was eroded by the passage of time the awareness of the necessity for constant vigilance diminished.

On the voyage on which *Berge Vanga* was lost a representative of her charterers, Shell International Marine Ltd. of London, Mr Nigel Page, travelled on the vessel from Rotterdam to Brazil to observe the tank cleaning procedures used on board. He later criticized the effectiveness of the cleaning methods in respect to the wing tanks, which presented a much more difficult problem than the more easily accessible and structurally simple centre tanks. Although Mr Page established a good working relationship with the ship's personnel he gained the impression 'that the officers of the *Berge Vanga* were more easily satisfied than he was accustomed to in the case of the officers of Shell ships, and that they generally showed some laxity in their procedure for testing and entering tanks.'[6] He experienced running eyes and slight dizziness on entering one tank after cleaning and found a 'substantial quantity of residue in the form of a sticky deposit' in several of the wing tanks. In spite of this the vessel had no difficulty in obtaining a gas-free certificate from the ore terminal surveyor in Sepetiba Bay, Brazil, on arrival there on 22 October.

After docking at the ore terminal loading began without delay and was completed on the 24th at 14.20. 208,396 long tons had been distributed throughout the ship's five holds and *Berge Vanga* proceeded directly to sea. Except for the AMVER reports and those to the owners in Oslo nothing further was heard from the ship until her meeting with the m/v *La Ensenada* later on in the voyage.

The Board of Investigation that was convened in London in the following year came to the conclusion that *Berge Vanga* probably suffered a similar fate to that of her sister ship *Berge Istra*. It felt that an explosive atmosphere had probably been created in the pipe lines passing through the pump room or double bottom space, or in pockets within some of the cells of the double bottom itself. Although it was claimed that the whole of the double bottom spaces were cleaned on the voyage to Sepetiba Bay, the Board discounted that evidence; believing that with the time and manpower available that job could not have been effectively carried out.[7]

A decision had been taken by the owners to install a crude oil washing system (COW) to replace the water washing machines in anticipation of a compulsory requirement. Three experienced welders were engaged to join the vessel at Sepetiba Bay to carry out the necessary work. Some preliminary work had already been done while the ship was in dry dock at Sasebo, and other work of a preparatory nature was to be done by the crew on the voyage from Rotterdam to Sepetiba Bay under the direction of a young and relatively inexperienced engineer employed by Messrs. Tofte & Jorgensen Ltd., of Copenhagen, who were given the contract for the job.

This task almost certainly continued after the ship sailed from Sepetiba Bay, and while some work remained to be done on deck, the weather conditions at the time that *Berge Vanga* encountered *La Ensenada* were such that it would be unlikely they were so employed. They would thus be going ahead with the work below. It is therefore probable that they were carrying out 'hot work' in either the after pump room or the double bottom, and that this provided the source of ignition for the explosion that destroyed *Berge Vanga*.

In July 1979 *Berge Vanga* had been surveyed when she had dry-docked in Sasebo, Japan, by a representative of the Bureau of Maritime

Affairs and no substantial defects were noted. She had also had her certificates renewed by Det Norske Veritas. Although the ship disappeared without trace, except for several pieces of wreckage later identified as belonging to her, she had had a VHF contact with the m/v *La Ensenada* during the day on 29 October, whose watch officer had obtained a satellite position from the bulk carrier. Visual contact was lost about 1345 but as *Berge Vanga* was due to make a routine report to her head office and AMVER at 1600 of the same day, and no report was ever transmitted, it can be inferred that she disappeared sometime during the above interval. This inference is to some degree confirmed by the discovery of wreckage, referred to above, in that area and the further discovery of a large oil slick some 45 miles to the eastward of her assumed position.

Once again there was an appreciable delay between the first evidence that there was something amiss aboard the vessel and the raising of an alarm. On the afternoon of the 29th, when no report was received by the owners in Oslo, there would probably have been no immediate concern since the report was of a routine nature. When no message was received the following day doubts that everything might not be as they should be aboard *Berge Vanga* should have given rise to an attempt to contact her. But that was not done until the next day, and it was not until the early morning of 1 November that confirmation was received from AMVER headquarters in New York that they had also received no message. Not until late that evening was the ship officially reported missing, and the first steps to mount a search were not taken until the following day. Once the search was undertaken, however, it was pursued with the utmost vigour by both aircraft and surface vessels until 12 November, five days after the discovery of her wreckage.

At the time of her loss *Berge Vanga* was commanded by Hakon Johansen. The ship had a crew of thirty-six in addition to the three Norwegian welders and the Danish engineer. Her chief officer, Alf Lauritzen, and the chief engineer and his assistants were Norwegian, but the rest of the crew including the second and third mates were Filipinos. The Board felt that *Berge Vanga* had been adequately and competently manned but they were severely critical about the manner and method of tank cleaning and the way the supervision of repairs was carried out.

They commented that the desirability of indisputably empty tanks while 'cargo oil residues remain on board was not fully appreciated.'

They went on to say: 'The use of "check lists" prior to tank cleaning and tank entry to ensure compliance with safety precautions, and the use of "permits to work" before hot work or potentially hazardous operations were undertaken, as recommended in the 'International Safety Guide for Oil Tankers and Terminals', do not appear to have been practiced on this ship.'[8]

Although these defects in the ship's organization can be laid at the door of the vessel's master, the owner and his representative cannot escape some responsibility for the way one of their vessels was run, and the Board was highly critical of their performance.

The Board concluded that the evidence showed:

'considerable confusion exists regarding regulations and instructions to ship operating personnel in connection with procedures on board combination carriers for tank cleaning, inerting, carrying of slops, etc., and for changing over from oil to dry cargo and vice versa. For example, a number of directives had been issued to the *Berge Vanga* from the owners and from various authorities, during the period following the loss of the *Berge Istra*, dealing with the desirability or otherwise of inerting empty tanks during voyages with dry cargo. Unhappily these various directives contained mutually inconsistent instructions, and the officers on board could well be forgiven if they were left in a state of bewilderment as to what they were supposed to do. . . .'[9]

The Board also made note of some of the design shortcomings and defects in the *Berge Vanga*, which can perhaps be explained though not justified by the fact that OBOs were, like container ships, ro-ros and VLCCs, blazing new trails in ship design and construction. The naval architects were learning by the old trial and error method, and several significant errors were made in the design of these ships. At the time the contracts for these ships were signed, 'no explicit requirements for the arrangement of double bottom spaces or slop tanks in combination carriers were included in the rules of the ship's classification society, Det Norske Veritas, or in the regulations for such ships promulgated by IMCO, Liberia or Norway. Such requirements came into existence at a later date.'[10] By the time these requirements were announced *Berge Vanga* was in operation.

The Board also noted that while the Norwegian Maritime Director-ate had issued regulations pertaining to these defects, it pointed out that *Berge Vanga*, 'being under Liberian registry, did not have to meet these requirements which apply to vessels under Norwegian registry.'[11]

Mycene

Less than six months after *Berge Vanga* disappeared off Tristan da Cunha, the Spanish built, Italian manned, Liberian registered VLCC *Mycene* was broken in two by explosion and sank off the west coast of Africa while cleaning tanks during a ballast voyage from Genoa to the Persian Gulf. Like many Liberian registered vessels the 238,889 dwt ton *Mycene* was owned by a single-ship company, the Mycene Shipping Company, itself part of a larger group, d'Amico Società di Navigazione of Rome. The management was largely vested in a company located in Monte Carlo, known as Compagnie de Gestion Maritime, Societie Anonime Monegasque, which usually obtained officers for its ships from the Genoa agency Hugo Trumpy Società per Azione.

Mycene had loaded a full cargo of crude at Kohr al Amaya in the Persian Gulf in early February 1980, and after sailing for the Mediterranean made a number of crew changes on 15 February off Dubai. The positions changed included those of master and chief engineer. The new master, Emilio Sormirio, held both Italian and Liberian master's licences. Captain Sormirio, though new to *Mycene*, had served in another VLCC, the *Oceania*, as both mate and master over a period of some three years, but his last command had been a dry cargo vessel. In spite of his unfamiliarity with the vessel he was destined to command he spent only a mere twenty minutes in relieving the master he replaced. He was told that the acting chief officer, Mr di Cecca, the regular second officer temporarily promoted to mate, was thoroughly familiar with the ship. The vessel then continued up through the Strait of Hormuz, down the east coast of Africa, round the Cape of Good Hope and up the west coast of Africa to the Strait of Gibraltar.

Captain Sormirio used the month it took for this passage to familiarize himself with his new ship and its equipment. The VLCC he had previously served in had been fitted with an inert gas system and he had also been given instructions concerning such installations while standing by another vessel which was being retrofitted with an inert gas system. He later claimed that he had looked for instructions for *Mycene*'s gas inerting plant but could not find them though they were in fact on board along with the ICS (International Chamber of Shipping) and OCIMF (Oil Companies International Marine Forum) 'International Safety Guide for Oil Tankers and Terminals', both in English, with which Captain Sormirio had some difficulty. The master also personally tested the portable oxygen analyzer and combustible gas detector and found them in good operating order.

Before reaching Gibraltar instructions were received instructing him to proceed first to Melilli in Sicily to discharge 136,000 tons of *Mycene*'s cargo before continuing on to Genoa. Shortly before arrival at Melilli Mr di Cecca, who was due to be relieved by the regular chief officer in Genoa, informed Captain Sormirio that the regular practice aboard *Mycene* was to log crude oil washing (COW) during discharge at Melilli as required by the charter party, but not actually to do so as it would prolong the discharge time. In case a surveyor for the charterer (AGIP) should come aboard during discharge cargo was discharged from all the tanks in order not to empty any and reveal that COW was not used during the discharge. On the passage to Genoa cargo could be transferred to empty some of the tanks so they could then be crude oil washed en route.

After arrival at Melilli the master telephoned the managing agents at Monte Carlo and learned that certain repairs to the inert gas system, viz., the replacement of the oxygen analyzer unit which had been left behind on the previous voyage for repair, and the installation of a new gas pressure and oxygen level recording unit would be done at Genoa. Captain Sormirio also learned that the regular chief officer would not be rejoining as planned. A new first assistant engineer and a new pumpman also joined at Melilli.

Captain Sormirio then came across a telex from a previous voyage where instructions had been given to arrive with the tanks 'de-inerted'. Since he did not intend to use the inert gas plant during discharge because crude oil washing would not be done he chose to take that previous directive as authorization to dispense with the use of inert gas during discharge. His previous experience, however, should have warned him of the hazard of that action. Hence the discharge at Melilli was carried out with the tanks open to the atmosphere and without the use of inert gas.

Mycene fortunately completed partial discharge at Melilli without incident and sailed about 1230 on 22 March for Genoa via the Strait of Messina. After clearing the strait the master instructed the mate on the morning of the 23rd to inert the tanks and begin emptying some of the tanks in preparation for crude oil washing. The time available was very limited and after about six to seven hours of operation of the inert gas system (IGS) – the time required to effect a one-volume change in the tanks – the level of oxygen in the tanks was still above 14 per cent. This is the lowest level deemed safe to carry out crude oil washing. Had the chief officer persevered he could have obtained a lower value, but he either did not understand that or decided it was not worthwhile to continue, so *Mycene* arrived in Genoa without any crude oil washing having been done. It would have been desirable, however, to have continued use of the IGS, but this was not done because the master understood it could not be used while the repairs and alterations to the system scheduled for Genoa were being done. That was later disputed, but when Mr Caforio, the technical manager for the parent company and senior owner's representative in attendance, came aboard in Genoa he was extremely upset to find that the IGS was not in use nor had it been used at Melilli. He initially considered having the tanks purged before allowing discharge but decided against it because the harbour regulations prohibited purging within the port and it might have delayed the installation of the recorder unit of the system. It would also have delayed the dispatch of the vessel, though that was not mentioned, and since no crude oil washing was being carried out discharging on atmosphere was considered safe.[12] Mr Caforio hence contented himself with instructing the master to have the tanks inerted as soon as possible after leaving Genoa. The next day, however, before departure Captain Sormirio said to the marine superintendent, Mr Luciano Merani, that he thought Mr Caforio had 'something against the use of inert gas.' This at least suggests there was some degree of confusion in the mind of the master about the use of inert gas when *Mycene* began her fateful voyage on 25 March.

To add to the confusion at Genoa a new chief officer, Mr Cosimo Spadavecchia, who was not only new to his employers and the ship but had no experience or knowledge of IGS, replaced Mr di Cecca.[13] A new bosun also reported aboard, and as the mate must rely heavily on the bosun in normal operation of the vessel, not to speak of an operation such as tank cleaning, the disabilities this officer faced in taking over his new post were daunting. The second officer was also leaving and his replacement, for some unexplained reason, decided he did not care to sail on *Mycene* (a decision he must later have viewed with some satisfaction). As he never signed articles, which would have legally bound him to make the voyage, he felt free to leave the vessel before she sailed.

Liberian regulations prohibited the vessel sailing with less than three deck officers besides the master. One of the advantages of Liberian registry, however, (and the same is even more true of other flag of convenience registries) is that their regulations can so easily be ignored when it is convenient. The master was promised that a new second officer would join the vessel by helicopter off Las Palmas in about five days' time, so he consented to sail without a second mate, which entailed his standing a watch until one was obtained. On departure from Genoa Captain Sormirio not only had no second mate, but his chief mate was a total stranger and his third officer had only just completed his cadetship and this was his first appointment.

To understand the master's handicaps at this point let us review the personnel changes that had taken place since he assumed command of this strange vessel about a month before. The chief engineer had joined the vessel at the same time he had, though he had been aboard the ship previously. A new first assistant engineer had come aboard at Melilli along with a new pumpman. A new chief officer and bosun (though the bosun had been on the ship before) had joined in Genoa and he had lost a second mate. The owners and the agency that was responsible for supplying officers and crew to *Mycene* should have been well aware of the personnel handicaps under which Captain Sormirio was operating, but the men were all properly certificated, and as far as those ashore were concerned (at least after the second mate joined), the vessel met the legal manning requirements and what happened aboard was a matter for the captain and the insurers.

Before sailing from Genoa the repairs to the IGS had been completed except a 'small job' of installing a thermocouple for the reading of temperatures which could be done by the ship's engineers. The master was informed of this but he misunderstood its implications. The IGS was in fact tested briefly before departure and found to be operating satisfactorily, but Captain Sormirio understood that until the thermocouple was installed the system was inoperable.[14]

On the day after departure the master had a discussion with the chief engineer and first assistant about the manner of accounting for the diesel oil consumed in tank cleaning. To obtain a clarification on this point the master telephoned Mr Merani, and during the conversation Mr Merani enquired if the minor repair to the IGS had been accomplished. The captain did not know. Mr Merani said it did not matter as the system could be used without it. Captain Sormirio took this to mean that tank cleaning could be carried out without the IGS if necessary, though his experience should have told him this interpretation was nonsense.

Following this conversation the master consulted with the chief engineer again and asked him about the status of the IGS, whereupon the chief engineer told him that it was in the same conditon departing Genoa as on arrival there. That led to another misunderstanding, for though there were some alterations scheduled to be made to the system at Genoa it was none the less operational on arrival there. The master, however, believed that they could not use the system until the repairs were made. So he assumed that the IGS did not work and claimed that when this matter was discussed he said that if inert gas was unobtainable it was 'too bad' and they would just have to do without it. What is suggested is that both the master and the chief engineer totally failed to appreciate the implications of the matter they were discussing. Both of them should have known that cleaning the tanks without inerting them was a highly dangerous task, yet here the master was suggesting that if it wasn't available they would get on without it. The chief engineer, who knew it was available for the asking, none the less never seemed to realize what the master was suggesting.

After departure from Genoa the new chief officer quite understandably suggested to Captain Sormirio that because of his unfamiliarity with the ship and the task facing him that the tank cleaning be delayed for some fifteen days or so until he had time to study the manuals and familiarize himself with the operation of the equipment. The request was eminently reasonable given the circumstances, but the mate might have had more success if he had not suggested such an extensive delay. This would have meant that no cleaning would begin until the passage was half over leaving little time for unanticipated delay. The idea of arriving at Ras Tanura without being able to go on to the loading berth at once was one the master did not care to entertain, as he was sure his employers would view such an eventuality unsympathetically. He therefore told the chief officer to get on with the tank cleaning. Preparations were apparently begun on the morning after departure and actual cleaning commenced after lunch on the same day.

The use of high velocity jets, such as were installed on *Mycene*, in cleaning cargo tanks in which crude oil has been carried tends to generate enough hydrocarbon gas to create an explosive mixture. The tank washing process using high capacity tank washing machines is also capable of producing isolated cylindrical lengths of water known as 'water slugs' that can accumulate a sufficient electrostatic charge to ignite hydrocarbon gas in a compartment when they come into close enough proximity to an earthed probe to cause a discharge of the electrostatic energy. The huge tanks found in VLCCs are particularly prone to such phenomena, and within a few years of their appearance on the scene a number of explosions such as that which wrecked *Mycene* resulted in the development and introduction of the IGS as a means of neutralizing this hazard. Inert gas systems either utilize the low oxygen content gas produced in the combustion process in steam turbine plants, or in inert gas generating plants designed specifically to produce such gas, to create a non-explosive mixture in the cargo tanks. It creates a non-explosive blanket or cloud either on top of oil cargoes or in tanks where they have been carried. Such a system is so efficacious, when used properly, in the prevention of conditions whereby explosions are possible, that to fail to use it where available cannot be justified under any circumstances.

The system, particularly on a vessel with diesel propulsion where the gas must be generated independently (as was the case on *Mycene*), does cost money to run and involves some additional expenditure of time and effort in the tank cleaning process. However, that additional expense is more than justified in the degree of protection it affords from the danger of explosion. The adoption of so cavalier an attitude by Captain Sormirio towards the use of inert gas can only be explained by the assumption that he lacked a proper appreciation and understanding of its use. That is perhaps excusable in the case of the chief officer who had no prior experience with the equipment, but not, surely, in a master with such experience. The owners, and those employed by them to advise and instruct the seafaring staff, were clearly delinquent and culpable in failing to ensure that the master, chief officer, and chief engineer were all trained in the use and understanding of the IGS and provided with clear and unambiguous instructions for its use. It is true that manuals were aboard that if understood and followed would have prevented this tragedy. But so important was this matter to the safe operation of the ship that the mere provision of these instructions cannot be said to absolve the owners of any further responsibility in this matter.

Under the circumstances one would think that the master would have taken an active and even dominant role in the planning and implementation of the tank cleaning operation, but the reverse appears to have been the case. Captain Sormirio apparently did suggest to Mr Spadavecchia that he should ask the chief engineer to provide inert gas, but he qualified those instructions by saying, 'there is no point in waiting and you can start washing.'[15] The chief officer apparently interpreted those vague instructions to mean that the use of inert gas was not essential, and so he proceeded to get on with the washing. The master, perhaps because he was standing a watch, took little further direct interest in how the tank cleaning was being carried out. What little discussion he had with the chief officer about it was more in the nature of a progress report. The master's reluctance to become involved in the tank cleaning was perhaps due to his own lack of knowledge. But whatever the reason he left it to the mate, and he in turn tended to rely on the bosun, Onofrio Patruno, and the pumpman, Giacomo Zaccaria, since they were experienced in the matter. Unfortunately, the bosun did not survive the explosion so we are denied his testimony which might have shed considerable light on a rather confused situation.

To make matters worse the closed circuit system of tank washing was adopted since this had been the procedure employed on previous voyages *when the IGS was used*. This method consisted essentially of filling the port and starboard slop tanks, which were cross-connected by an equalizing line, about three quarters full and recirculating the oil from one tank through the COW system and back into the other slop tank. The water thus removed from the tanks in this process was hence a mixture of water and oil. By drawing the water from the bottom of the slop tank a degree of separation was achieved so the recycled water was relatively clean, but this method was not considered safe by experts unless it was used in conjunction with inert gas.

Even so the tank cleaning was almost completed without incident, and by the morning of 3 April only the number one centre tank remained to be cleaned. These centre tanks were huge compartments, almost 200 feet long by 86 feet deep and 65 feet wide, giving them an internal capacity of over one million cubic feet. So large were they that small clouds would actually form in them during the washing process, giving rise sometimes to miniature thunderstorms, though these discharges in themselves were not of sufficient intensity to ignite the vapor.

The cleaning of the number one tank began early in the morning under the direct supervision of the bosun. Four high velocity Gunclean machines with a capacity of 165 tons per hour were used and possibly some portable machines as well, though that was disputed by the first assistant engineer. About mid morning the bosun reported to the chief officer that he had temporarily shut down the machines, whose capacity for delivering water outstripped the capacity of the eductor to remove it, to allow the eductor to catch up. After the stripping operation had been completed the bosun restarted the Gunclean machines and walked forward towards the number one tank, passing a young ordinary seaman named De Palma who was working on the starboard side of the after deck. About two to three minutes later the ship was shaken by a severe explosion, and De Palma looked up to see flames shooting up out of the number one tank. This was followed almost immediately by several other explosions of such severity that they lifted the fore part of the vessel, bodily causing *Mycene* to trim heavily by the stern. The frightened ordinary seaman ran aft and actually stepped into the water from the stern of the ship.

The force of the explosions and the stress set up by the lifting action caused *Mycene* to break in half about 30 feet forward of the main deck house aft. Almost immediately the forward section sank. The after section, which had been severely shaken by the explosions, was badly damaged but remained afloat. There was nothing left but to abandon the shattered hulk remaining, though no orders were actually ever issued to that effect. The radio room had been demolished so no distress message could be sent. Oil from the starboard slop tank, however, had spilled into the water and been ignited, prohibiting the use of the starboard lifeboat and the port one could not be moved because the explosion had apparently distorted the forward davit. Several of the crew had succeeded meanwhile, on their own initiative, in launching a liferaft on the port side, and the master together with several crew members launched the raft on the starboard side. Unfortunately they were not made fast and no one had thought to rig painters so the rafts drifted away. It was now everyone for himself, though the master was later criticized for not making sure that everyone else was off before taking to the water himself. The men dived into the sea and swam for the rafts but, because of oil in the water, they had become fouled and were quite slippery making it very difficult for survivors to board them.

The abandonment was both hurried and disorderly, which was later attributed at least in part to the fact that, while more than 50 per cent of the crew were new on departure from Genoa, no boat drills had been held since the ship left Melilli. Some of them climbed down a pilot ladder on the port side, others simply jumped overboard, and some slid down mooring lines that were hanging over the stern. The master was one of the latter, and said that he did so by way of example to encourage others to leave the doomed vessel.

Although the crew of *Mycene* would probably not have thought of themselves as fortunate luck had not entirely deserted them. When *Mycene* exploded the Spanish refrigerated cargo ship *Sierra Luna* and the Dutch freighter *Aludra* were both within sight. The master and nine other crew members were picked up by the former vessel and Captain Sormirio had enough presence of mind to ask the Dutch master how many survivors he had picked up. The answer was sixteen, which left five unaccounted for. Three men were then seen on the stern of *Mycene* and *Aludra* moved in and picked them up.

At the time of the explosion the chief, first and third assistant engineers were all in the engine room. It was obvious that something drastic had occurred but just what was a matter of conjecture since there was no response to a call to the bridge. The chief stopped the main engine and switched the electrical load to two diesel alternators and then sent the third assistant topside to find out what was going on. When the third assistant did not return the chief followed him and found him on the stern by himself. Together the two slid down one of the mooring lines and swam to one of the nearby liferafts, at which point the chief passed out and did not regain consciousness until taken aboard the Spanish ship.

The first assistant had stayed below with the chief and also left with him though by a separate route. He went first to the bridge and then to the officers' mess, both of which were a shambles. He then descended to the deck on the port side where he met three crew members. The first assistant found a lifebelt which he put on and he suggested to the others that they jump over the side. As they apparently had no lifejackets they thought less of that idea than he did, and when he did so they refused to follow. These three were the ones later seen standing on the stern and rescued by the Dutch ship.

The first assistant spent from two to three hours in the water before he was seen by chance just as *Aludra* was preparing to depart, after an agreement had been reached with the *Sierra Luna* that she would stand by to continue the search for those still missing.

With the rescue of the first assistant there was only the bosun still unaccounted for, and as he had been seen in the vicinity of the explosion just before it had occurred there seemed little likelihood he had survived. The Spanish ship, however, continued to search the area. The stern section of the VLCC was still afloat but was settling lower in the water, and about 1530 it suddenly capsized and quickly sank. Two hours later the master of *Sierra Luna* called off the search for the bosun and left the scene.[16]

The master was charged, understandably, with negligence. He admitted at the investigation that he had read the 'operating instructions for the master' prepared by Mr Caforio, which give clear and explicit instructions for the procedures to be carried out in loading, discharging and cleaning tanks. In these instructions it clearly states: 'If the inert gas plant has to be taken out of service for any reason specific instructions are to be requested from the technical office.' He was also censured for failing to see to the safety of his crew before abandoning ship himself, and for sailing from Genoa without the required three mates on board. His Liberian licence was suspended for three years dating from the loss of *Mycene* with the further proviso that he must attend an approved resident course in COW and IGS procedures. The chief mate, Mr Spadavecchia, received a two-year suspension subject to the same proviso, and the chief engineer, Mr Salvitore Vaudo, was censured for 'failing to bring his professional influence to bear to ensure that the inert gas system was operated on this final voyage.'

The owners were also found guilty of failing to provide the vessel with the required three mates on departure from Genoa, and for failing to see that proper tank cleaning procedures were 'established and carried out'. Note was also made that they had knowingly employed a chief officer without experience or training in the use of inert gas or tank cleaning.

The Board also noted with disapproval the practice of using a crewing agent for supplying officers and crew. Counsel for the Republic of Liberia further made a concluding statement in which he 'expressed the concern of his administration as to the role of marine insurance in casualties such as this one.' In a post-hearing submission he remarked: 'the existence of readily available insurance compensation would appear to insulate owners and operators to some degree from the financial consequences of a relaxed attitude toward safety at sea. . . .'[17]

It would be instructive and certainly very interesting if an analysis could be made of just what financial impact the loss of this vessel, and similar losses, had upon those who owned her. Were they better off financially after the loss than before?

Betelgeuse

The French tanker *Betelgeuse* was built in 1968 for the French oil company Total. At the time her deadweight tonnage of 121,432 placed her among the largest vessels of the day. During the following decade she and her sister ships saw hard usage, and as the demand for oil increased larger and larger tankers were designed and built to meet that demand. A decade later *Betelgeuse* was no longer considered large as tankers go. VLCCs of over 250,000 tons were now common and the first of the ULCCs of up to half a million tons were in service. Ships like *Betelgeuse* were not as economical to run as when they were first built, and to try to make ends meet those responsible for her operation spent no more than the bare minimum on her maintenance. Indeed, it was later concluded that they spent not even this. It was afterwards estimated that the wastage of the steel plating in the ballast tanks was in the order of 40 per cent. To compound the problem excessive stress was frequently imposed on the vessel's hull through incorrect ballasting.[21]

The tribunal convened to investigate the casualty concluded: 'On the night of the disaster the structure was abnormally, seriously and significantly wasted due to corrosion, and that wastage was particularly marked in way of the permanent ballast tanks. An important cause of the excessive corrosion was Total's decision not to renew the cathodic protection in the permanent ballast tanks and/or its failure to have the tanks coated with a protective coating.' The report went on to note Total's failure to renew seriously wasted longitudinals when the vessel was in dry dock in 1977 and the defective nature of some of the welding in some of the longitudinals that were renewed.[22]

The owners were aware of the advanced state of deterioration of *Betelgeuse*; her sister ship, *Cassiopee*, had sailed from Bantry Bay for the breaker's yard only a few hours before the catastrophe. Essential repairs had not been carried out simply because the ship was also due to be sold. A number of crew changes were made on the last voyage, including a new master and mate at Vigo, and although it should have been evident to an experienced seaman that the ship was in an advanced state of decay the owners offered no word of caution to the master with respect to avoiding stress in ballasting because of the vessel's weakened condition. It is understandable though hardly excusable in that it would have been a curious and embarrassing admission on the part of Total, that they were asking the master and his crew to embark on a voyage in a vessel of questionable seaworthiness. Indeed, so careful were those in charge of expenses that they didn't even supply the ship with a stress calculator which would have simplified any ballasting problems.

Betelgeuse finished loading a cargo of 115,000 tons of crude at Ras Tanura in the Persian Gulf during the early morning hours of 24 November 1978 and sailed for the port of Leixoes, Portugal, with an intermediate stop at Sines, south of Lisbon, to lighten the vessel. Bad weather frustrated the first plan and the sinking of a ship in the entrance to the second prevented entry at Leixoes. She was then ordered to proceed to the Gulf oil terminal at Whiddy Island in Bantry Bay, Ireland, for final discharge, and she arrived there on 4 January 1979 but did not berth until two days later. Prior to that, however, she made a stop at Vigo where crew changes were made including a new master, Captain Roger Hamono and Chief Officer René Bazin.

Discharge of the parcel of heavy crude (about 75,000 tons) commenced late on 6 November and was completed on the following day at 1800. Ballasting of the permanent wing ballast tanks began almost immediately thereafter, following the discharge of the parcel of Arabian heavy crude but before the discharge of the Arabian light crude. The investigating tribunal concluded that ballasting had either been completed or nearly completed at the time of the explosion.[23]

The practice of commencing ballasting on tankers before discharge is completed is common, but it entails risks that are often not fully appreciated by those who indulge in this questionable activity. While it is a relatively simple matter to calculate the stress after a loading or discharging operation has been completed it is a much more complicated affair to estimate accurately the stress during the operation; and where weights (cargo or ballast) are simultaneously being added and removed the calculation is doubly difficult (and subject to error). Although experienced ship's officers are aware, or should be aware, of the dangers of an uneven distribution of weights aboard ship it is not a problem that they frequently encounter. Moreover, where it does occur it rarely leads immediately to such serious consequences as were experienced here. The officers of *Betelgeuse* were apparently aware of the stress problems and of their inability to accurately assess them with the information available.[24] However, they were obviously not sufficiently aware of all of the ramifications of the problem or they would not have accepted the risks that led to the destruction of their ship and the loss of all aboard her.

During the lifetime of a vessel its hull may occasionally be subject to stresses that exceed designed limits. Because these limits allow for a certain foreseeable wastage these instances pass unremarked at the time, but as the vessel nears the end of its useful life the built-in safety factor formerly obtaining (allowances for wastage) becomes degraded. The effect of such stressing is cumulative and eventually the overloading of the ship's main hull girder, done once too often, may cause it to fail – as happened here. To use a loose but useful analogy it is somewhat like an individual breathing carbon monoxide. He suffers no noticeable ill-effects at once, but over time the cumulative effects of the intake of this poison can prove fatal.

On *Betelgeuse* the practice of starting ballasting before discharge had been completed was pursued in the interests of expediency. The vessel had no 'loadicator' (a computer that allows quick and easy calculation of stress moments) so the master and his chief officer had to fall back on the use of the 'Conditions de Chargement', a booklet supplied by the ship's builders for such calculations. Calculations of stress moments are so complicated and tedious that it was established that this was not a practical alternative and 'it was not the practice to consult the "Conditions" for ballasting operations.'[25]

The pilot that berthed the vessel, Captain Daly, discussed the cargo distribution with Captain Hamono and pointed out to him that due to the prevailing southwesterly winds to which Bantry Bay was exposed it would be necessary to begin ballasting before the discharge had been completed in order to make the vessel less susceptible to the effects of sea and swell both during cargo operations and during undocking afterwards. Normally the ballast taken aboard was about

30 per cent of deadweight but conditions at Bantry Bay were not normal, and it was intended to take on more than this amount, which of course would increase the stress.[26]

The tribunal concluded that the PBTs (permanent ballast tanks) began to be ballasted at about 1130 on the 7th and that at the time of the explosion they had only been filled to sea-level and not yet topped up. The ballasting of the centre tanks began at 1835, and at the time of the explosion the number two and five centre tanks had been filled to about 90 per cent of their capacity though it may have been slightly more than that.[27]

In the event, the tribunal concluded that the stresses set up by the ballasting exceeded the critical buckling range in some of the deck and side-shell longitudinals in the PBTs. The failure of these longitudinal members led to a weakening of the deck and side-shell plating, leading to their buckling, followed by progressive failure of the hull in the way of frame 77½ in number four PBT.

This buckling caused gas from either or both the number three wing tanks and the number four centre tanks to enter the PBTs. Although the gas may have been initially over-rich it became diluted when mixed with the air in the PBTs creating an explosive mixture. Sparks from the tearing of the steel ignited the mixture causing the initial explosions, which led to failure of the bottom plating and associated strength members, and the fracture of the hull. This led to the escape of large quantities of oil on both sides of the vessel, which was ignited by subsequent explosions.[28] It should be noted that *Betelgeuse* was not equipped with an IGS. The failure of the main hull girder also fractured the ship's fire lines thus forestalling any effective fire-fighting measures on the ship.

According to a number of independent witnesses, not long after 0030 on the 8th a small fire was observed just forward of the ship's manifold in way of the PBTs. The fire continued to grow in size over the next few minutes with flames enveloped in heavy black smoke. A number of minor explosions were heard during this time and then at about 0040 the fire suddenly swept across the vessel and within seconds the ship was enveloped in smoke and flame.[29] It was probably at this time that the hull failure reached its climax causing some of the cargo to spill into the sea and ignite.

The fire continued to increase in intensity during the next ten minutes or so attended by further explosions. Then at approximately 0050 a much bigger explosion was heard and felt, resulting in a dramatic increase in the intensity of the fire. The blaze was clearly out of control by now and, at a time fixed by several witnesses at between 0106 and 0108, a final massive explosion occurred splitting the hull of *Betelgeuse* just aft of the bulkhead separating the number five and six tanks. Had the ship been equipped with an IGS and had these tanks been inerted this last and fatal explosion would almost certainly have been prevented.[30]

Little is known about what transpired aboard *Betelgeuse* during this time since none of those aboard survived. All of the crew, including the wife of the ship's baker, two visitors, the shore crew on the jetty and the ship's pilot (a total of fifty), perished in the disaster. The vessel was berthed starboard side to alongside an isolated jetty located some 400 yards offshore of the northwestern shore of Whiddy Island. She was made fast to the jetty with mooring lines on bollards on the dolphins (mooring dolphins are reinforced piles driven into the sea bed fitted with mooring hooks and bollards) at each extremity of the jetty supplemented by spring lines. The control tower or platform through which the discharge was controlled was located on the centre of the jetty abreast of the number four tanks of the ship.

When the fire first broke out it would normally have been noticed almost immediately by the Gulf terminal dispatcher in the control tower, Mr John Connolly. Unfortunately he had left his post moment-arily, most probably to get something to eat,[31] and probably did not return until about 0045. On discovering the fire on the ship, which had now broken in half allowing oil to escape into the water and ignite, he activated the fire pumps and attempted but failed to close the emergency block valves. He then called, in quick succession, the operations manager Mr William Flynn; the launch *Donemark* on VHF channel 14 saying, 'Go to the jetty – we have a fire'; the duty tug *Bantry Bay*, passing a similar message; Mr John Downey, the pump-man on duty in the power-house ashore, telling him, 'The ship is on fire – do what you can to help'; and Mrs Catherine Desmond, the Whiddy Island postmistress. Connolly then made a second call to the *Donemark* saying, 'Go as fast as you can, Bruce, to dolphin 22 to take the lads off.' A second call to *Bantry Bay* followed, 'Are you coming? She has broken her back. She is on fire all over.' He also talked on a walkie-talkie to the duty pilot on the ship, Captain Warner, and Mr Kingston the pollution control officer on the jetty.

While he was making these calls he activated the fire pumps at Ascon Jetty and attempted to close the emergency block valves to cut off the flow of oil from the vessel. Shortly after 0050 Mr Kingston called enquiring about the *Donemark* and Connolly told him 'she is on her way'. Not long after the pollution control officer called for the last time saying, 'quick, John, quick'. At about the same time, and before the major explosion between 0106 and 0108, Captain Warner called Mr Connolly from the poop deck of *Betelgeuse*, where he had retreated with three or four of the crew saying, 'I'm going over. Ask the boats to be on the lookout for us.'

By this time the fire had gained such headway that it is unlikely it could have been checked, though had there been rescue craft on the scene many, if not all, of those lost might have been saved. The burning oil was drifting from the centre of the vessel from whence it was escaping in a roughly southeasterly direction at an angle of between 35 to 45 degrees to the line of the jetty. During this time, prior to the explosion at about 0050, the flames were not yet as high as the jetty, according to the pumpman John Downey. Some three to four minutes later when he had returned to his station in the control room in the power-house (he had driven to Ascon Jetty about a quarter of a mile away to check to see that the fire pumps were working), the fire was raging out of control with flames 200–300 feet high. He judged that by then it would 'have required a miracle to save anyone on the jetty.'[32]

The *Donemark* left Ascon Jetty as soon as her acting coxswain, Bruce Tessyman, received Connolly's call at about 0048 and arrived in the vicinity about ten minutes later. The tug *Bantry Bay* was alerted about 0050 and responded with commendable dispatch. Due to her greater distance from the scene, however, she did not arrive until about 0110. Meanwhile the *Snave*, a sister boat to *Donemark*, had also arrived, but all were too late to do anything other than witness the development of the tragedy and search for bodies.

Most of the crew of *Betelgeuse* were apparently given sufficient warning of the fire to put on their clothes before attempting to escape. Although the crew and officers were well trained in emergency procedures there was apparently too little time for anything effective to be done, particularly with the rupture of the fire mains. By the time they reached the open deck it had probably reached the stage of every man for himself, and they either jumped over the side or attempted to reach the seeming safety of dolphin 22 about a hundred yards astern. Only a handful of the crew (apparently those on watch) succeeded in reaching this 'point of refuge', and they all died as a result of burns and the force of the explosion. They were joined there by the 'shore gang' on the jetty. The rest apparently died in the water from drowning though only about half of the bodies were recovered.

The root cause of the disaster was the failure of Total's management to maintain the ship's hull because of economic considerations. Their penny-pinching also resulted in denying the ship's personnel the 'luxury' of a loadicator, which meant that the master and his chief officer were unable to determine with any degree of accuracy the dangerous stress to which their ballasting plans subjected the vessel. A further complication was that both of these key officers were strangers to the vessel having just joined in Vigo a couple of days before. They had little or no idea of the seriously weakened condition of *Betelgeuse*, which might have alerted them to the need to pay particular attention to stress considerations. The responsibility of the owners in this affair is clear and gross, but the owners of the terminal, Gulf Oil, must share an appreciable amount of the blame for what happened after the casualty occurred. Here too measures were adopted for the sake of economy that had a disastrous effect on safety.

Over the years a number of modifications to the fire-fighting system were made to improve it, but three 'had the effect of downgrading it'. The original system had provided for the fire mains to be permanently pressurized, but in 1970 this was changed so that the intervention of the dispatcher in the control tower was required to activate them. The pre-mixed foam system on the jetty was also modified at that time so it ceased to be an automatic one. A year later the remote control button for the system was disconnected.

The operational plan originally devised had made adequate provision for evacuation of jetty personnel in case of an emergency. This plan was later downgraded, particularly the change in the mooring position of the standby tug and failure to provide adequate escape facilities (there was no means of direct access from the jetty to the shore). Maintenance of fire-fighting equipment also suffered from shortsighted economic policies.

However, even with all these organizational and operational defects the loss of life could have been substantially reduced, or even eliminated, had the dispatcher employed by Gulf Oil not been absent from his post when the fire started. It was never established just where he was in those critical first few minutes, but it was accepted by the tribunal that he was not at his post.

The Board was convinced that the evidence given by the dispatcher was fabricated, but it was never established just why he adopted this line.[33] It is, of course, understandable that he didn't want to admit to being absent from his post, as the delay in giving the alarm that stemmed from this most likely contributed to the deaths of friends and acquaintances; but while this consideration may (or may not) have induced him to offer this distorted version of events initially, it is likely that the interests of his employers provided a powerful inducement to persist in a story that was so patently at variance with the testimony of other disinterested witnesses and known facts. While the dispatcher may have had personal reasons for initially concocting a story about the original circumstances of the disaster, four of his colleagues and two senior Gulf personnel had no such personal motive for supporting his version of events.[34]

The tribunal concluded:

> The management of Gulf . . . had a duty to ascertain the truth of
> what had happened on the night of the disaster. They very
> inadequately fulfilled that duty. They were made aware of the
> existence of independent witnesses whose testimony conflicted
> with that of their employees, but they did not approach the
> Gardai [police] to ascertain their names. The legal advisers of
> other interested parties had made their own separate enquiries
> and had obtained the names of others who had seen the disaster
> and had obtained statements from them. Gulf made no such
> enquiries. They did not even take the trouble to contact their own
> employee, Mr O'Leary, whom they knew on 11 January was in a
> position to give important evidence as to the time the disaster
> occurred. Instead of gathering as much information as they could,
> they contented themselves with the statements they obtained from
> their employees, and took active steps to ensure that this evidence
> – which was highly favourable to their own financial interests –
> was not weakened in any way by any official inquiries. They were
> highly selective in the sources from which they obtained their
> information, and were anything but assiduous in seeking out the
> truth of the events of the disaster.[35]

Since the *Betelgeuse* disaster the terminal at Whiddy Island has ceased to be used as an oil terminal. One of the main results of this and other disasters recounted in these pages appears to be a move-ment among the traditional owners to reduce the size of their fleets and rely more on chartered vessels to meet their needs. Although the more responsible operators take considerable care in choosing those they patronize, this practice means that those who before were most careful and responsible in the operation of ships have less control and responsibility in this area, and that is a development that all those with a concern for marine safety must deplore.

6

Collisions

The ancient Greek historian Thucydides proclaimed, perhaps with tongue in cheek, that 'a collision at sea can ruin your whole day'. The Greek ships that Thucydides was familiar with were minuscule compared to the average ship today, let alone the mammoth tankers, and it seems reasonable to assume that collisions between ships in the fourth century BC were not the threat to life and livelihood they are today. A modern day collision between ships can result in the loss of hundreds of lives and millions of pounds, and the unfortunate masters may have their careers ruined and even suffer imprisonment.[1]

Before the introduction of steam propulsion collisions did not ordinarily result in serious and costly damage. Vessels were occasionally sunk, but the ships were small and the total value of vessel and cargo rarely exceeded £10,000. This was a large sum in those days (the equivalent of about £1 million today), but not so great as to bankrupt the underwriters. The introduction of steel in the construction of ships, not long after steam propulsion began to be widely used, saw a rapid increase in the size and value of both ships and cargo.

Steam propulsion enabled vessels to steer straight courses so that traffic tended to become concentrated along the shortest routes. Speed also increased, and as ships were no longer at the mercy of the wind for their progress scheduled sailings and arrivals became practical. Competition became more and more intense, and all of the above factors made collisions between ships a greater hazard. Although rules for the prevention of collisions have existed for several centuries they had no statutory basis. In 1846 the Marine Division of the Department of Trade conducted an inquiry into collisions, and in 1850 the Mercantile Marine Act was passed by Parliament in the first attempt to regulate such inquiries. So acute became the problem that the first standard 'traffic rules for ships', or 'rules of the road', were adopted in 1863 by Great Britain and France. Similar rules were adopted in the United States in 1864 and other maritime nations soon followed suit. Finally an international conference to deal with the matter was held in Washington in 1889 where international rules were formulated.[2]

The greatly increased incidence of collisions, involving greater degrees of damage as a result of heavier vessels travelling at higher speeds, and the escalation of losses, which ensued as more expensive ships and more valuable cargoes became the norm moved shipowners and their underwriters to begin to seek redress by bringing suit against the owner of the other vessel. This greatly increased the financial risk of marine ventures, and shipowners sought to minimize their liability through new laws.

Limitation of liability legislation had been passed in Great Britain in the latter part of the eighteenth century and copied by most other major maritime nations in the form of statutes designed, amongst other things, to protect the shipowner from ruin in the case of honest mistakes made by those to whom he entrusted his vessels. The increased risk arising from collision claims stimulated shipowners to have ever greater recourse to the protection afforded by these laws. In recent years owners who do not like to take their chances with the courts have chosen to further limit their liability by setting up single-ship companies as well as disguising their ownership in order further to discourage litigation.

Of all marine casualties collisions are the most common and costly (in total). They ordinarily pose no great threat to the environment, though occasionally substantial loss of life can result. It is rare, however, for a ship suffering a collision to sink so rapidly that those aboard are unable to get off. We have seen, however, in the case of the *European Gateway* that ro-ro vessels are particularly vulnerable to collision and capsize. Should such a vessel suffer such damage in deeper water, her vehicle deck would fill rapidly, followed quickly by capsizing. Under such circumstances it seems unlikely that there would be many survivors. *The Herald of Free Enterprise* was not a victim of collision, but that catastrophe offers a vivid example of what might happen to a ro-ro ferry whose hull was ruptured in collision with another vessel: had she been in only a few fathoms more water she would have turned turtle, trapping almost all the crew and passengers inside her hull.

The good news is that the masters and watch officers of the ro-ro passenger ferries in north European services are, almost without exception, highly competent seamen fully alert to the operational hazards they face. The bad news is that none of these flawed vessels have been taken out of service because of their faulty design, and that new ships have been, and are being built, with the same inherent defects.

Andrea Doria–Stockholm

Probably the most notorious collision of modern times is that which took place between *Andrea Doria* and *Stockholm* off Nantucket lightship in the summer of 1956. There was much speculation in the press at the time about which vessel was at fault, but it was immediately apparent to knowledgeable mariners that both vessels were to blame.[3]

Andrea Doria was bound from Genoa to New York with a full complement of passengers. It had been a normal and uneventful crossing, and few if any of the passengers felt any cause for alarm when they heard the ship's whistle begin to sound a single long (about five seconds) blast every two minutes on the afternoon before arrival. *Andrea Doria* had encountered fog, a frequent hazard in those waters in the summer months. The ship was then about 150 miles east of Nantucket lightship as Captain Piero Calamai took up his station on the bridge.

The essence of the master's job is the safe navigation of the vessel he commands: to see that she collides with no hazard floating on the sea (other ships, ice, derelicts, etc.), or the sea bed, or with rocks beneath the surface. Unfortunately the pressure on the master of a transatlantic liner to maintain schedule was intense. Captain Calamai was no doubt well-aware of his responsibilities for the safety of his ship and the people aboard it, but he was almost certainly even more conscious of the immediate cost of delay. He had the engines put on 'standby', which resulted in an insignificant reduction in speed, but with a functioning radar he felt justified in pressing on at full speed.

Legal precedents (the interpretations in the courts of what the law actually means in practice) at that time still upheld the old pre-radar view that a ship in restricted visibility must be able to stop in half the distance of visibility. This stance was perhaps meaningful in those places where ships were forced to congregate in narrow waterways, but it was completely unrealistic to expect vessels on the open sea to abide by such a restriction.

With the advent of radar practical seamen soon came to realize that on the open sea, radar, properly used, allowed one to keep one's distance from another ship thus preventing the development of close quarters. Unfortunately many who are in charge of a bridge watch are indifferent seamen, and they believe that mere detection of the presence of an approaching vessel is adequate. Others are simply stubborn, and expect the other ship to keep out of the way. Changing course to avoid the close approach of another vessel creates a delay. It may also be construed as timidity, so for a variety of insufficient reasons mariners (a mariner is not necessarily a seaman in the true, professional, sense of the term) allow the development of the close quarters that is the inevitable prelude to every collision.

The Swedish liner *Stockholm* had sailed from New York shortly before noon the same day. The ship was bound for the Baltic and the 1948 SOLAS (Safety of Life at Sea) treaty, of which Sweden was a signatory, prescribed that eastbound vessels should take a track 20 miles to the south of Nantucket lightship. The treaty, however, was not legally binding, and Captain Gunnar Nordenson, *Stockholm*'s hard-bitten master, stubbornly refused to take a route that added almost 40 miles to his journey. He laid down a course from the departure point just south of Ambrose lightship, which marked the entrance to the port of New York, of 087° true. If that course was made good *Stockholm* would pass one mile south of Nantucket lightship, the same point for which *Andrea Doria* was steering.

At 2000 Johan-Ernst Carstens, the 23-year-old third mate, relieved the first officer. Captain Nordenson had come up to personally instruct his young third officer as to how to conduct his watch on the approach to Nantucket. He cautioned him about keeping a sharp lookout for approaching traffic and the possibility of fog. When he left the bridge about 2140 the weather was clear, and the lightship was about 43 miles off bearing approximately 085°. At 2230 Carstens told the quartermaster to steer 2° to the right to compensate for a northerly current set. Twenty minutes later he again altered 2° more to starboard as *Stockholm* continued to set to the north. It was then, according to later testimony, that he first discovered a blip on his radar screen about 12 miles off slightly to port.

On the *Andrea Doria* the presence of the *Stockholm* was discovered five minutes earlier. The second officer later claimed he first noticed the reflection of *Stockholm* on his radar scope at a distance of 17 miles about 4° on the starboard bow. He also testified that from the swiftness of the rate of closing he realized that the approaching vessel was eastbound, although that is questionable as no attempt was made to plot. He further claimed that he estimated that *Stockholm* would pass about a mile to starboard. Although Captain Calamai felt some disquiet at the approach of this other vessel he continued on at full speed. (Full speed was a bit over 23 knots; when the engines were placed on standby speed was reduced by slightly over a knot.)

Aboard *Stockholm* Carstens began to plot the progress of *Andrea Doria*, but he apparently didn't feel it necessary to notify Captain Nordenson. He claimed that when he began the plot the target on the scope was 10 miles off about 2° on the port bow, and when the distance had closed to 6 miles the bearing had opened to 4°. He calculated from these ranges and bearings that the other ship would pass about three quarters of a mile to port.

Clearly the testimony of the two ships is in conflict, and as the Bial plotter (a plastic disk that fitted over the radar scope, and on which the plot was made), which Carstens used to plot was never produced both accounts must be treated with reservation. In any event both ships continued on into a developing close-quarters situation.

As the distance between the ships closed Carsten began to feel uneasy at his inability to see the approaching vessel visually. It apparently didn't seem to occur to him that the other ship might be masked by fog, though Captain Nordenson had specifically warned him of that possibility. It was also Captain Nordenson's policy not to pass within one mile of another vessel on the open sea.

Carstens was also probably concerned about *Stockholm*'s set to the north by the current. The lightship marked the southern extremity of the Nantucket Shoals. If he continued on he would pass it by less than the distance stipulated by Captain Nordenson. To turn to port to increase the CPA (closest point of approach), particularly as he could not see the other vessel, was an unseamanlike manoeuvre. (The Collision Avoidance Rules prescribe that when two vessels are meeting end on, or nearly so, that each shall alter course to starboard in order to keep clear of the other. The crossing rule also provides that the vessel required by the rules to manoeuvre – the ship on the port side – shall alter course to starboard. The courts have uniformly condemned course changes to port, except *in extremis*, as unseamanlike when collision has resulted.)

Carstens later claimed that the lights of *Andrea Doria* were first sighted to port, and that he then ordered a course change of 20° to starboard to increase the passing distance. What is more likely is that he ordered the course change to starboard before he sighted the lights of the Italian ship.

Aboard *Andrea Doria* Captain Calamai was also experiencing concern about the developing close approach of *Stockholm*. When the distance closed to about 3½ miles he ordered a course change of 4° to port to increase the passing distance. This was a very questionable measure. Turns to port to avoid an oncoming vessel are now specifically warned against by the rules. Although vessels meeting at sea frequently pass starboard to starboard, the rules recommend a port-to-port passage where the closest point of approach to starboard is deemed inadequate.

As the distance decreased to 2 miles *Andrea Doria* started to emerge from the fog enveloping her. To the horror of all on her bridge *Stockholm* was seen on the starboard bow crossing from starboard to port. Calamai immediately ordered hard left rudder, but before that could take appreciable effect the bow of *Stockholm* sliced into the starboard side of the Italian liner just forward of the bridge at a speed of almost 19 knots.

Andrea Doria lurched to port under the impact, but as the sea poured into her hull through the wedge shaped hole in her side the stricken vessel began to heel to starboard. Subsequent efforts by the engineers to counter the list by fuel and ballast transfers were hampered by flooding of compartments containing the pumps. It was soon apparent that the wound was fatal, and Calamai sent out an SOS. This is a heavily trafficked area, and rescue ships began shortly to arrive on the scene. *Stockholm* launched her own boats, and the French liner *Île de France* bound for Europe reversed her course and took off the major portion of the passengers and crew.

As the collision happened in international waters it was outside the jurisdiction of US authorities. Many of the passengers, however, were American citizens, as was the case in the *Titanic* disaster. This was the first major marine casualty to be exposed to television coverage, and public interest and outrage ran high. How could two modern passenger liners equipped with the latest navigational equipment including radar collide? Public ignorance about this affair was, not surprisingly, as great as the interest, and the investigation carried out by the lawyers representing the Italian and Swedish owners did little to enlighten the curious. It revolved mainly around the question of who was telling the truth, the Swedish third mate or the Italian captain. The question of why each allowed the other to approach so close was never asked. The lawyers eventually decided that their clients' interests could not be furthered by a court action, and the underwriters were left to absorb the losses.

Several positive developments did, however, result from the inquiry and debate about the causes of the *Andrea Doria–Stockholm* collision. The need for communication between vessels approaching one another was obvious, a need for which this collision, and that related earlier in chapter 2 between *European Gateway* and *Speedlink Vanguard*, supply ample illustration. VHF radio communication between ships by means of walkie-talkies had been in use in inland waters of the United States and on the Great Lakes for several years. It had proven to be an invaluable adjunct to the use of radar enabling those in charge of the navigation to discover the intentions of the other.

In 1972 the United States Congress passed a law that, among other things, required all vessels over 300 gross tons navigating the inland waters of the United States to be equipped with VHF radio. Prior to this time few vessels engaged in international trade were so equipped. The immediate effect of the law was to see a rapid upsurge in the number of ocean-going ships equipped with VHF. In spite of the fact that it was now possible for vessels so equipped to use VHF for anti-collision purposes that was not done. Seamen are very reluctant to initiate change, and though they were already accustomed to pilots using VHF in American waters they were reluctant to follow this lead. They used VHF to alert the pilot boat of their approach to the pilot station, but after the pilot was disembarked on the way out the VHF was turned off until approaching the next pilot station.

During the next few years a few adventurous souls tried to make contact with approaching vessels on the high seas, but the attempt was rarely successful. Aside from the novelty of the equipment there were, unfortunately, several major drawbacks to its use. English is widely accepted as the lingua franca of the sea but many mariners speak it only haltingly if at all. The most serious obstacle to the effective use of VHF for anti-collision purposes is, however, the difficulty of identification of the vessel with whom you wish to speak. In pilotage waters one can usually identify oneself by means of reference to a geographical point or navigational aid. On the high seas, particularly in the most congested areas where it is of the most potential use, the presence of more than one vessel in the area can easily lead to confusion. None the less, when employed with intelligence VHF can be used with success.

The collision also served to highlight the necessity for radar plotting when vessels are approaching one another. The Collision Avoidance Rules were later amended to encourage the use of plotting or equivalent systematic observation. Radar observer courses were developed where radar plotting was taught, and proficiency in this technique became a requirement for those actively employed in the profession.

None the less, in the two decades following the *Andrea Doria–Stockholm* collision, ships continued to collide with alarming frequency, and the phrase 'radar assisted collision' began to be used increasingly in official reports and investigations. Radar gave many mariners a sense of false security, and though it came to be widely recognized that radar plotting was an essential element in the effective use of radar, far too many mariners were inadequately trained. In December 1977 a collision occurred off the Cape of Good Hope between two sister ships (VLCCs) belonging to the same company that dramatically illustrated the use, or misuse, of radar that leads to collision.

Venpet–Venoil

The VLCCs *Venpet* and *Venoil* belonged to the Bethlehem Steel Company and were employed in the carriage of crude oil between ports in the Persian Gulf and Point Tupper, Nova Scotia. Although Bethlehem Steel had for some years operated a fleet of vessels under the American flag, they like so many others had decided that their vessels could be more economically managed under Liberian registry. They later decided that operating ships was an unprofitable adjunct to their main business and disposed of their vessels, a decision to some extent influenced by their experience with *Venpet* and *Venoil*.

The ships were built by Bethlehem Steel in Japan in the early 1970s and placed under long term charter to Gulf Oil. Crewing arrangements were conducted by Marine Transport Lines, another US company who employed Taiwanese Chinese in both licensed and unlicensed capacities. *Venoil* had loaded 307,045 long tons of heavy Iranian crude at Kharg Island and was eastbound en route to Point Tupper. *Venpet* was in ballast westbound. Both vessels were aware that they would pass each other somewhere off the South African coast, and there was widespread speculation that the ships had in fact arranged to pass so close in order to exchange gossip over the VHF. The Liberian board of investigation found no basis for the allegation,[4] and the circumstances attending the incident do not favour such a hypothesis.

Venoil sailed from Kharg Island on 2 December 1977. Captain Shing-Pao Zia had just assumed command after some three weeks as 'trainee master'. On the morning of 16 December about 0630 the vessel passed Cape St Francis about 12 miles off in compliance with South African regulations requiring loaded tankers to keep a minimum distance of 12 miles off the coast. The master visited the bridge briefly at about 0650 before going down for breakfast. The weather was fine with good visibility and a course was set of 267°.

The second mate was relieved by the third officer shortly before 0800. The visibility had stated to deteriorate with occasional fog patches. Fog signals were being sounded, but no ships were in sight though the second mate said he had passed a vessel some time earlier. The radar was on the 24-mile scale and there was nothing showing ahead.

The master returned to the bridge shortly thereafter. He checked the distance to Capetown and calculated his ETA off that port. *Venoil* was to rendezvous with a helicopter to pick up ship's mail and other documents. He then went to his cabin to prepare the mail and returned about 0830 to verify his ETA. While there he glanced at the radar and saw an echo ahead 2–3 ° on the port bow about 22 miles off. This was the *Venpet*. The visibility at the time was estimated to be from 6 to 7 miles with patchy fog. The ship was making her maximum speed of 13.5 knots. The third mate made no attempt to plot the progress of the approaching vessel, but he estimated that she was on a roughly parallel course and would pass about half a mile off to port when abeam.[5] The master then went back to his cabin apparently satisfied with the third mate's evaluation.

Shortly after 0900 Captain Zia again returned to the bridge. He looked at the radar and saw that the echo of the approaching ship was now some 13 miles about 3–4 ° on the port bow. If this was accurate it would indicate that the other ship would have passed 'safely' down the port side. He estimated the distance off when abeam to be 0.7 of a mile, though without plotting this would be no more than a guess. About ten minutes later *Venoil* ran into dense fog, which persisted until after the collision. It was so thick the third officer said he could barely see the bow. He now switched the range of the radar to 12 miles and instructed the A.B. to steer the vessel by hand. In spite of this dramatic decrease in visibility neither the master nor his watch officer considered it advisable to post a lookout or to take the elementary precaution of placing the engines on stand by. Although another ship was approaching on a course on which she would pass less than a mile off it apparently did not occur to the master that he should make a substantial alteration of course to starboard to increase the passing distance or order a drastic reduction in speed.

In way of excuse the master later testified that the chief engineer told him that an hour's notice was required to reduce to manoeuvring speed. In point of fact steam turbines can be slowed easily and quickly, and if the master believed they could not then he had no option but to make a bold alteration to starboard to keep well clear of the approaching vessel. So little did Captain Zia appreciate the danger to his vessel and his responsibilities that after taking another look at the radar scope he then went below to consult with the radio operator about the coming rendezvous with the helicopter off Cape-town. When the board expressed some doubt about the wisdom of this move the master admitted in retrospect that if he felt it necessary to leave the bridge at this time he should have summoned the chief officer to relieve him. Instead the master went to the chief mate's room where he found the radio officer, and joined them for a cup of tea and conversation. He was still there when the ships collided.

Venpet had left Point Tupper on the evening of 19 November in ballast. The loss of *Berge Istra* two years before had seemingly made an impression on those who managed the Bethlehem Steel Company ships. Both *Venpet* and *Venoil* were equipped with inert gas systems and they were in use at the time of the collision. It was probably this that prevented an even more disastrous conclusion. *Venpet*'s long voyage across the North and South Atlantic was uneventful. She experienced some minor trouble with her radio transmitter, but this was repaired by two technicians flown out from Capetown via helicopter. A more annoying problem, and one not readily fixed, was the fact that she had been outfitted with two identical ten-centimetre (the wave length of the radar signals) radar sets, probably because it was cheaper. If both sets were put in operation together they tended to interfere with one another. Moreover, the number two set, which was in operation at the time of the collision was subject to a defect that caused it to produce false targets.

Venpet arrived off the Cape of Good Hope about noon on 15 December. Various courses were steered as she rounded Cape Agulhas until just before midnight when course was changed to 085° to make good a course of 084°. She had by now passed to the north of the Alphard Banks in order to put into Durban to disembark the two technicians that had boarded off Capetown, and was unfortunately steering a course almost directly oppposed to that of vessels rounding the Cape from the east.

Shortly before 0800 the third officer relieved the second mate. There was no traffic in the vicinity at the time and the visibility was good. The vessel was on automatic steering with an A.B. on the bridge acting as lookout. The third mate fixed the ship's position at half-hourly intervals using either the Decca navigator or radar. (The Decca navigator is an electronic short range – 250 miles – navigational system of great accuracy that grew out of war-time developments. Special charts with Decca overlays are needed for its use. It requires a special receiver aboard ship from which readings from adjacent stations allow the navigator to plot his position.) He checked the radar intermittently, and just before 0900 he noticed three targets on the scope. One was a westbound cargo ship just passing, which he sighted visually at a distance of about a mile and a half. The second, which was *Venoil*, was dead ahead at a distance of about 13 miles. The third was further off on *Venoil*'s port quarter.

Visibility must have been considerably restricted by this time since he did not apparently see the ship abeam until it was little more than a mile off. According to his testimony later he said visibility became restricted at 09.10 with patchy fog. *Venoil* was now some 7 miles off about 3–5° on the starboard bow. He later claimed that he now noticed a few 'spots' on the scope 1–1½ miles away on the starboard bow. Because of their ill-defined nature he at first suspected that they were false targets, but he finally concluded that they were probably fishing vessels.

The fog had become even thicker as the third mate made no visual sightings. In spite of this he took none of the precautions dictated by good seamanship other than to have the A.B. put the ship in manual steering. He did not place the engines on stand by, post a lookout, sound fog signals or begin plotting on the radar, nor did he inform the master of the deteriorated visibility. He did, however, order a course change of 5° to port on the unfounded assumption that the vessel he was meeting was on a reciprocal course and would pass on his starboard side. His objective in doing this was to achieve a greater passing distance.

Not long after this the master, Chung-Ming Sun, appeared on the bridge. He later said the visibility at this time was only about 50 yards. As he looked at the radar scope he claimed he saw a target 4 miles off 10–15° on the starboard bow. He also noticed several 'spots' about a mile distant broad on the starboard bow. The third mate told him that the 'spots' were fishing vessels, and the vessel approaching was on a reciprocal course and would pass about a mile off to starboard. He had also altered course another 5° to port.

The master was apparently satisfied with the situation and, in spite of the fact that another vessel was approaching close on his starboard side in thick fog, he went into the chart room to calculate *Venpet*'s ETA at Durban. The third officer testified that he took another look at the radar several minutes later and observed the other ship about 2½ miles away with the bearing increasing. This indicated to him, so he later claimed, that the vessels would pass safely, and he went into the chart room where Captain Sun was working at the chart.

After Captain Zia left the bridge of *Venoil* the third mate began to feel a little uncomfortable about the passing distance, and decided to increase it by ordering the helmsman to steer 272°. After some five minutes on this course he saw it was not having the desired effect, and the other ship had apparently altered to port towards *Venoil*. He ordered the A.B. to come right another 5° to 278°. The other ship continued to close, however, and the third officer ordered 'Starboard 15.' As *Venoil* started to swing to starboard he saw what he later described as a 'red wall' just ahead and to starboard. He ordered 'midships' just before the bow of *Venoil* stuck *Venpet* on her starboard side aft. The anchor of *Venoil*, which was housed on a horizontal platform protruding from the bow, sliced into the side of the other ship like a 'giant can-opener', tearing open her hull plating from her number five cargo tank all the way back to the engine room.

The *Venoil*'s number one cargo tank and forward bunker tank, (only the cargo tanks were outfitted with IGS) were also ruptured in the collision and, as the two giant vessels recoiled under the blow, the heavy crude spewed out of the *Venoil*'s tanks, igniting from the sparks generated by the collision. The sea between the two ships immediately burst into flame enveloping the bridge of *Venpet*.

On *Venpet* both the master and the third mate were in the chart room when their ship collided with *Venoil*.[6] By the time they got back to the wheelhouse the starboard side was enveloped in flame. The lifeboat on that side was also threatened by the fire, and the master and third mate left the bridge to try to control it. The rest of the deck crew under the chief officer were fighting the fire on the decks below. Fire had also broken out in the engine room, and it was soon raging out of control. A helicopter appeared on the scene about 10.00 and advised the master on the VHF to abandon his ship.

The abandon ship signal was sounded on the whistle and the port lifeboat was launched. All forty-three of the crew (including the two technicians) were successfully evacuated, and when the fog lifted not long thereafter a British vessel, *Clan Menzies*, was seen stopped about two miles off. All of the crew except the master and five others were taken aboard. The lifeboat with the master and five volunteers returned to the *Venpet* in hopes of reboarding her when the fire subsided.

After several hours the third mate was able to scramble up the ladder, but Captain Sun, attempting to follow, was struck on the head by the block of a lifeboat fall and fell into the sea. He was quickly pulled out, and the third mate reported that the fire was still burning too fiercely to control. Several hours later the salvage tug *Smit Lloyd 109* arrived on the scene. The third mate and second engineer had both sustained injuries and were taken aboard the tug for treatment. At the request of Captain Sun a brief but unsuccessful attempt was made to bring the fire under control, but not long thereafter the bosun succeeded in boarding and put a ladder over the port side which was now the lee one.

A helicopter arrived between 1900 and 2000 carrying an American Bureau of Shipping official representing the owners. The chief engineer and chief officer climbed back aboard, but as the master attempted to follow he was again struck on the head by a swinging block and fell back into the boat. He was then taken aboard the tug and treated for his injuries. Under the instructions of the ABS representative the tug resumed her efforts to extinguish the fire. Not long after midnight they finally succeeded, and preparations were put in hand to take the ship in tow.

*

Both vessels suffered major damage and some 26,000 tons of oil spilled into the sea from *Venoil*, much of it consumed by fire. Had not both ships been equipped with IGS the losses would almost certainly have been much greater. It is quite possible that both vessels would have been wrecked by explosion, with attendant heavy loss of life.

The Board of Investigation took note of the possibility that the VHF might have been used to advantage in this case, particularly in light of the fact that each watch officer chose to alter course to achieve a greater passing distance.[7]

The conduct of both masters was severely censured. The captain of *Venoil* had his licence suspended for twelve months while that of *Venpet*'s master was suspended for eighteen. The Board went on to question the role of the owners in this affair. It was noted that numerous instructions and documents had been issued to masters relating to the safe navigation of the ships under their command. What is abundantly clear, however, is that the instructions and advice had either been ignored or misunderstood.

The Board went on to say:

> Owners cannot wash their hands of responsibility for safe navigation of their vessels merely by issuing written instructions. They owe a positive duty to exercise all reasonable care to see that their instructions are in fact carried out. It might have been expected that the owners would submit evidence to the Board from one of their principal officers to deal with this question. Had such a witness been called, the Board would have wished to have answers to a number of penetrating questions. For instance, what steps, if any, were taken by the owners to assure themselves *that their masters and officers, though licensed, really did possess sufficient capability?* . . . [Emphasis supplied].[8]

The Board went on to ask what steps the owners had taken to ensure that their officers and masters were proficient in the use of radar, and that the standing orders, which they had furnished for guidance were in fact observed. The Board observed that the answers to these questions had been provided by the conduct of the individuals involved. The Board was particularly critical of the way the masters were prepared for their commands. Captain Zia had assumed command of *Venoil* on 2 December after little more than three weeks as a 'trainee master'. He had never before previously commanded a VLCC and the IGS, Decca navigator and radars were all new to him. They concluded that his training had been 'pitifully inadequate', and 'In light of the cumulative effect of the foregoing criticisms the board can only say that it is by no means satisfied that the owners of the two vessels fully carried out their duty to exercise all reasonable care to see that their vessels were safely navigated. They too must share some degree of responsibility for this collision.'[9]

Aegean Captain–Atlantic Empress

The collision of the two VLCCs *Aegean Captain* and *Atlantic Empress* off the island of Tobago in the West Indies in the summer of 1979 was not the first collision between such ships, but it was undeniably the worst. The 78,000 ton Liberian flag *Pacific Glory* and the 95,000 ton Liberian vessel *Allegro* collided off the Isle of Wight in October 1970. Failure to keep a proper lookout, including the use of radar, was a salient feature of this casualty. Then, as just described, in 1977 the VLCCs *Venpet* and *Venoil* collided in fog off the South African coast. The collision off Tobago, however, had the dubious distinction of causing the destruction of the largest vessel ever lost from a marine casualty. It furthermore established a record for pollution. The 279,000 long tons of crude oil was the most ever let loose on the environment from a tanker.[10]

Aegean Captain was 210,257 tons deadweight carrying a cargo of about 200,500 long tons of crude loaded at Curaçao and Bonaire bound for Singapore. She was owned by a company registered in Liberia and flew that flag, but she was operated and managed in Piraeus. Her officers and most of the crew were citizens of Greece.

Atlantic Empress was somewhat larger, being 292,666 dwt, and was bound from the Persian Gulf to Beaumont, Texas. *Aegean Captain* was equipped with an IGS which was in operation at the time of the casualty and almost certainly prevented her destruction. *Atlantic Empress* was not so equipped and was probably lost as a consequence. She flew the Greek flag though her owners claimed Liberia as their base.

Aegean Captain had sailed from Bonaire on 17 July, and at 17.10 on the 19th had reached a position about 8 miles north of Little Tobago Island from where course was altered to 122°. The master, Captain Ioannis A. Zissakis, was on the bridge at this time but went below shortly afterwards. He returned about half an hour later before leaving once again at approximately 18.15. The visibility at the time was good though nightfall was approaching. The vessel was under the control of an automatic pilot and the adjusted speed was about 14 knots.

The 34-year-old chief officer, who had first obtained a licence in 1974, had served aboard *Aegean Captain* for the past two years. An unlicenced second mate was on watch with him and an able seaman was on the bridge as lookout. The ship was equipped with two three-centimetre radars one of which was in operation. At about 18.30 the second mate obtained a position by means of a radar distance and bearing, and then altered course 1–2° to starboard. The radar was on the 24-mile scale and it was noticed about this time that a rain squall was showing on the scope at about 12 miles some 20–40° on the port bow. The A.B. was now permitted to go below for a coffee break, which normally meant he would be gone for approximately thirty minutes.

The wind, which had been moderate, now increased to about 30 knots. Not long thereafter, at about 1835,[11] the vessel entered the rain squall showing on the radar on the port bow. The rain interference on the radar scope now extended clear across the screen on the 12-mile scale and for about 5 miles ahead.[12] The chief officer later testified that he adjusted the rain clutter knob to reduce the interference, but he saw no indication of any target within the rain. The rain, which was originally light to moderate, became very heavy after about ten minutes and visibility was reduced to not much more than a mile.

The situation aboard *Atlantic Empress* cannot be described with as much accuracy as the vessel and all her records (except for the engine room log) were lost. The master, Captain Paschalis Chatzipetros, also suffered severe burns which prevented him attending the first hearing, and he subsequently refused to appear at the second. A landfall had just been made after a long trek across the South Atlantic from the Cape of Good Hope. At around 1730 the master went below for dinner but returned shortly before six to fix the vessel's position.

The *Atlantic Empress* also had two radars, a three-centimetre and a ten-centimetre. The former was located in the wheelhouse while the latter was in the chart room. According to the testimony of the A.B. on watch the three-centimetre was in use, but the captain claimed he turned on the other radar when he came up in order to measure the distance off Tobago. The *Atlantic Empress* was making about 15 knots.

The watch officer on *Atlantic Empress* was in fact the radio operator. The vessel's normal complement including three watch-standing second officers as well as a chief officer who stood no watch. Prior to the vessel's call at an English port in May one of the second officers had asked to leave the vessel. The owners, for reasons not given, chose not to send a relief but allowed or instructed the master to use the radio officer as a 'replacement'.[13] This gentleman had apparently stood deck watches on other vessels in the fleet and supposedly had some knowledge of navigation and was 'familiar with the rules of the road'.

The question that immediately arises is that if this questionable practice was to be allowed, then why was the radio operator not assigned to the 8–12 watch where the master would be best able to exercise supervision over his activities? The answer was that the radio officer was to double as both deck watch-stander and radio operator, and only the 4–8 watch would allow that. His normal watch hours in the latter capacity were from 0800 to 1200 and 1300 to 1700. The small overlap of watch-keeping hours was accommodated by allowing him to leave the bridge when necessary to attend to his duties as radio operator.

The owners' disregard for traditional manning practices and requirements was further demonstrated by their failure to provide a relief on the ship's arrival at the next port in the Persian Gulf in spite of their promise to do so. A replacement was sent, however, for an assistant steward.

Even if the radio operator had been fully qualified as a deck officer, the practice adopted would have been unacceptable since he was required to stand watches totalling fifteen hours each day. While this may have been no overriding consideration in respect to his radio watch, where he would be sitting and perhaps even dozing in his chair, it would be completely unacceptable as regards his bridge watch. If he kept a normally active watch during these hours the question of fatigue affecting his capacity to keep an effective lookout is raised and, indeed, the collision was due to his failure to keep an effective lookout. The situation was further complicated by the fact that he had allowed the seaman on watch with him to go below for a break just as the vessel began to enter the rain squall where visibility was reduced. The master arrived on the bridge shortly thereafter.

To make matters even worse the radio officer was known to be a heavy drinker, and according to the testimony of several witnesses was under the influence of alcohol on the day in question. In addition the investigation revealed that he may also have suffered from defective eyesight.[14] The Board of Investigation summed up the situation:

> It is an arresting fact that a laden VLCC with a large crew and female and infant supernumeraries on board should be proceeding into the dusk in the charge of an uncertified watchkeeper, a radio officer who was being paid to double as a deck officer, who was known to be a habitual drunkard and who on this occasion was affected by alcohol recently taken in the opinion of the able seaman who stood the watch with him.[15]

One half hour before *Aegean Captain* entered the fringes of the rain squall the ships should have been less than 15 miles apart. The *Aegean Captain* at this time had not yet encountered any rain, and did not do so for about another five minutes. Had a good lookout been kept at this time it seems possible that one or both of the vessels might have discovered the presence of the other before *Aegean Captain* was hidden from view by heavy rain. That possibility aside it seems almost certain that had either of these vessels been keeping an adequate radar lookout the other would have been discovered before the squall engulfed *Aegean Captain*.

When the master of *Atlantic Empress* came to the bridge shortly before 19.00 he claims he remonstrated with the radio officer for letting the A.B. go below, but he did not insist that he be recalled. The ship was now entering the outer extremity of the squall. In spite of the fact that the vessel was about to encounter heavy rain no concentrated attempt was made to see what, if anything, was in that squall. It was then suddenly, out of the mist and rain, that the lights of *Aegean Captain* were seen about two points on the port bow. The distance between the ships was little more than a mile. Attempts were apparently made to avoid collision, but at the speeds the vessels were travelling collision was unavoidable. At about four minutes past seven the bow of *Aegean Captain* struck *Atlantic Empress* on her port side in the way of the number three wing tank at an angle of about 30 degrees. The master of *Aegean Captain* rushed to the bridge to find his fore deck swept by fire. The engines were stopped and he ordered the two watch officers to go below to prepare the fire-fighting equipment and ready the port lifeboat for launching. The fire was spreading rapidly, and it quickly became apparent that the lives of all would be endangered if they remained aboard. He instructed the radio operator to send a distress message and preparations were made to abandon ship. He and the chief officer made a last desperate attempt to check the advance of the fire by means of the foam monitors on deck, but that proved fruitless. The ship was abandoned in an orderly fashion using the port lifeboat and an inflatable raft. The electrician fell into the sea in attempting to board the lifeboat and was lost. All of the other crew members escaped.

The collision had ruptured the shell plating of *Aegean Captain* in the way of the port number one wing tank allowing 14,000 tons of crude to either ignite or escape into the sea. On the following day after the vessels had drifted apart the master and some of his crew returned aboard the ship, and together with the crew of the salvage tug *Oceanic* finally succeeded in extinguishing the fire. The damaged vessel was subsequently towed into Curaçao where the rest of her cargo was discharged, but the ship was ultimately declared a constructive total loss.

Aboard *Atlantic Empress* things did not go so smoothly. The lack of an IGS allowed the fire to spread much more rapidly. The damage was apparently more severe and several tanks were ruptured. An attempt was made to combat the blaze but was quickly abandoned when thick smoke interfered. Safety was not a matter of high priority aboard *Atlantic Empress* as the watch-keeping arrangements suggested. There had been no fire and emergency drills held for several months[16] though Greek law, in conformity with international custom, prescribed that weekly drills be held. The equipment was apparently likewise neglected, which led to tragic consequences when the ship was abandoned.

There was apparently also a lack of firm leadership aboard this unfortunate vessel, and as the fire swept aft terror amongst the crew members led to panic. As a consequence of the lack of training crew members thought that the sounding of the emergency signal following the collision had been the signal to abandon ship. Escape was the only thought, but as their training in abandon ship procedures had been perfunctory the attempt to launch the port lifeboat was bungled. There were no officers present to supervise the operation. The ship still had some way on her, and when the boat became waterborne the falls could not be released because the releasing gear had seized up. The boat began to ship water and some of its occupants were swept into the sea. Efforts to launch the port liferaft were similarly unsuccessful. The result was a heavy loss of life. Twenty-six of the forty-two aboard *Atlantic Empress* were drowned.

The Board of Investigation felt that Captain Zissakis had on the whole behaved creditably, but he was criticized for failing to instruct his watch officers in the performance of their duties.[17] The Board concluded that the chief officer bore the heaviest responsibility for what happened to *Aegean Captain*. One of the Board felt his certificate should be suspended,[18] but the others took a more lenient view. The harshest punishment was reserved for Captain Chatzipetros. When he refused to attend the reconvening of the Board in September 1980 his licence was revoked.[19] The radio officer who doubled as second mate did not survive, so the Board was saved the perplexing duty of dealing with his dereliction.

The Board refrained from directing any criticism towards the owners of these vessels or those responsible for the operation of the ships. Apparently the Bureau of Maritime Affairs of Liberia had circumscribed the scope of the investigation because only one of the vessels involved was under Liberian registry. They, however, took note of:

> the reluctance of shipowners to produce evidence relating to management of their vessels when there is pending civil litigation in which that evidence may be crucially important. None the less, as our previous recommendation implies, all shipowners and managers bear a heavy responsibility for ensuring the safe navigation of vessels in their care. Investigations that concentrate attention on the conduct of watchkeepers but exclude examination of the conduct of shipowners and managers may reveal less than the whole truth and may hamper the primary aim of all investigations, namely to prevent future casualties.[20]

7

Stranding

Of all ship casualties strandings have the most potential for damage to the environment. They are also the most preventable of all marine disasters, so one would expect that especially today they would be the rarest of such incidents. Unfortunately that is not the case and they are only exceeded in their frequency by collisions.

Human error is widely credited with being responsible for the vast majority of marine casualties, and nowhere is that more true than in the case of strandings. Even where mechanical failure disables a vessel, as in the case of *Amoco Cadiz* to be described shortly, misjudgement, not the failure of a pump or electrical circuit is often the root cause. In the case of *Amoco Cadiz* the real cause of the stranding was not the break in an oil line that disabled the steering gear, or the master's delay in summoning help, but the decision to build the ship with an inadequate steering system.

The *Torrey Canyon*

When *Torrey Canyon* impaled herself on the Seven Stones in the Scilly Isles while bound for Milford Haven in March 1967 the world was rudely introduced to the true cost of transportation of oil in the new supertankers. *Torrey Canyon* was a mere 118,285 deadweight tons, which today is no more than a medium size. In 1967 she was the thirteenth largest vessel afloat.

The 119,328 tons of oil she spewed into the ocean, much of which eventually found its way on to the beaches of Cornwall and Brittany, was many times larger than any previous spill. Before *Torrey Canyon*, tanker groundings and the pollution attending them rated no more than a passing comment in the newspapers. The wreck of *Torrey Canyon* dominated the news for days and left a lasting imprint.

*

Torrey Canyon loaded a full cargo of crude at Mena al Ahmadi in the Persian Gulf during the latter part of February before sailing for Milford Haven via the Cape of Good Hope. She flew the Liberian flag and was owned by the Barracuda Tanker Company of Bermuda, a subsidiary of the Union Oil Company of Los Angeles, California. The crew was Italian[1] and the ship was under charter to British Petroleum. The passage round the Cape and up the African coast through the Canary Islands was uneventful. On the afternoon of 14 March the vessel passed between Tenerife and Grand Canary Island from where a course of 018° was set. If that course had been made good *Torrey Canyon* would have passed 5 miles to the west of the Scilly Isles. Unfortunately no allowance was made for wind or the effect of current, and when a landfall was finally made early on 18 March the ship was found to be substantially to the east of the dead reckoning position.

Captain Pastrengo Rugiati was a very experienced officer having served as master since 1952. He had been in command of *Torrey Canyon* for several years. His wife had recently been in poor health, and it had been more than a year since his last vacation, which added to the stress. To complicate matters his relationship with his chief officer was marred by ill feeling. After the vessel cleared the Canary Islands the ship's agents in Milford Haven had advised the master that unless the vessel could make the evening tide at the port on the 18th she would have to wait until the 24th before she could enter. Captain Rugiati was hence somewhat anxious to prevent any avoidable delay.

At about 0630 on the morning of the 18th the chief officer, who had assumed the watch at 0400, picked up the first reflection of the Scilly Isles on the radar. The land should have been on the starboard bow, but the islands showing on the scope were to port. It was obvious that the vessel had been set appreciably to the east, and the chief officer adjusted course to the left sufficient to pass the prescribed distance off to the west. He then notified the master of his action. 'Who told you to make that decision?' was Captain Rugiati's curt response. He next asked the mate if the ship would clear the islands to port on the original course, and on being told they would he brusquely told the mate to 'Go back to the original course.'

The master arrived on the bridge about half an hour later and · assumed the conn. The chief officer's original assessment of the position was inaccurate. The vessel was in fact not quite as far to the east as he originally estimated, and the course of 018° put the Seven Stones dead ahead. Unaccountably Captain Rugiati made no comment on this and stubbornly held to his original course. The simple and safe step would have been to alter course slightly to the right so as to leave the Seven Stones to port. Instead the master chose to keep to the course of 018° until the Seven Stones were little more than a couple of miles off before altering course to port to pass between them and the rest of the Scilly Isles.

Contrary to accepted safe practice Captain Rugiati instructed the third officer, who relieved the chief mate shortly before 0800, to engage the automatic pilot as the vessel approached the Seven Stones. The situation had become further complicated by the presence of fishing vessels as the ship neared the place to alter course. Common prudence dictates that whenever a vessel approaches a point where it may be necessary to manoeuvre the ship should be steered by hand; yet at this critical juncture the master did the reverse. It was not until the *Torrey Canyon* had almost reached the point at which course was to be changed that Captain Rugiati directed that the vessel be switched to hand steering. In the event the able seaman assigned to act as helmsman was unfamiliar with the switching mechanism. A delay of over a minute resulted, and by the time helm was actually applied it was too late and *Torrey Canyon* struck the outcroppings of Pollard Rock, the westernmost of the Seven Stones, at her full speed of almost 16 knots.

Shortly after nine o'clock the man on watch on the Seven Stones lightship saw the *Torrey Canyon* steaming north heading straight for the rocks. He gave the alarm and warning rockets were fired at 0910, and the international code signal 'JD', meaning 'You are standing [heading] into danger' was hoisted. Three more rockets were fired during the ensuing interval until the ship grounded.

There was understandable public indignation about why a vessel with such a horrific potential for damage to the environment could be so negligently navigated. The British government also was the target of much criticism for failing to have anticipated such an event and provided for its actualization. There were official investigations by both the British and Liberian governments.

Unfortunately for Captain Rugiati his ship had grounded just after high water, and there was no hope of getting *Torrey Canyon* off without help. He sent off a 'Mayday' over the radio-telephone asking for immediate assistance. The response was almost instantaneous. The salvage tug *Utrecht*, owned by the Dutch salvage firm of Wijsmuller, was nearby in Mounts Bay and quickly picked up her anchor. Several other vessels in the vicinity responded, and Land's End radio station alerted the St Mary's lifeboat before calling for helicopters from Culdrose, the naval air station at Land's End.

The *Utrecht* was the first to arrive and the lifeboat put two salvage specialists aboard *Torrey Canyon*. The weather had meanwhile freshened making it impossible for the tug to go alongside. Plans were made to try to pull the ship off at the next high water that evening. Meanwhile the crew started pumping cargo over the side to lighten the vessel. The weather continued to deteriorate, and the big tanker rolled and pounded on the rocks on which she lay. By evening over 5000 tons of crude had escaped (or been pumped over the side), and the British authorities realized they were faced with pollution on a scale never before experienced. Spills from previous casualties in the British Isles had not exceeded 10,000 tons. There was more than ten times that amount aboard *Torrey Canyon*.

The first attempt to pull the stricken ship off not long after nine that evening was unsuccessful. The crew spent a miserable and apprehensive night with the stench of crude oil in their nostrils. From the beginning the smell was distinctly noticeable as far as 3 miles downwind. A week later it could be smelt as far away as the western slopes of Dartmoor and at Torquay. At dawn *Torrey Canyon* had an 8 degree starboard list and her deck was awash forward; so serious had the situation become that fourteen of her crew were taken off by the St Mary's lifeboat.

During the next eight days four separate attempts were made to pull the tanker off. On the fourth day after the stranding an explosion in the engine room injured seven men. One later died. This at first raised fears that an even bigger explosion might follow and everyone was taken off. *Torrey Canyon* was now officially abandoned. Work was cautiously resumed the following day, and the remaining cargo in the tanks was covered by a layer of foam to reduce the risk of fire and explosion.

The weather, which had turned fine after the gale blew itself out on Sunday the 19th, now threatened to worsen. The tides, however, were increasingly favourable with a rise of over 20 feet predicted for the day after Easter, the 26th. The freshening westerly wind drove the first of the oil ashore at Sennen on the Cornish coast at midnight on Good Friday, giving rise to speculation that the British government might try to destroy the ship and her cargo by bombing in an attempt to halt the spread of the oil.

Late Saturday afternoon three tugs made fast, and began their pull at 1740 shortly before high noon. *Torrey Canyon* moved but would not come off. She seemed to be jammed amidships, and it was believed that a large rock had penetrated her hull just forward of the bridge. The wind continued to increase and by Sunday morning was blowing at almost gale force. None the less, four tugs were made fast for another attempt on the afternoon tide. With the increasing sea it was hoped that the ship might float free on a rising swell. Unfortunately the cable connecting the two largest tugs parted under the strain. At 1945 *Torrey Canyon* broke in two just aft of the bridge.

Oil now poured forth from previously intact tanks. Then on Monday evening the forward half of the ship fractured leaving the vessel in three pieces. The following morning Wijsmuller informed the solicitors for Union Oil that they were abandoning the salvage operation.

The British government now decided to destroy the wreck and set fire to its cargo. 'Buccaneer' strike aircraft of the Royal Navy swept in at 500 miles an hour at an altitude of 2500 feet dropping forty 1000-pound bombs. About three quarters hit their target setting the hulk afire. During the next several days bombs, napalm and rockets caused further fires destroying a large part of the oil remaining in the wreck. Unfortunately some 50,000 tons of oil had already escaped, and the huge slick fouled over 100 miles of Cornwall's beaches from Newquay on the north coast to the Lizard on the south. The pollution of Brittany's coast in France was almost as great, stretching from just east of Brignogan almost to St Malo. The entire coast of Guernsey, except for the eastern shore, was also heavily affected. By the end of April remnants of the oil had reached the Hook of Holland.[2]

Tens of thousands of sea birds died from contamination, and uncountable numbers of creatures of the sea perished. The cost to the underwriters has been estimated at about £10 million,[3] which is a mere trifle compared to the incalculable damage to the environment. The British government talked for a while about placing navigational restrictions on large tankers, but commercial considerations prevailed and little was done.

Argo Merchant

Argo Merchant was built in Hamburg in 1953 and christened *Arcturus*, and since then she had undergone several name changes under different owners. In early December 1976 when she sailed from Puerto La Cruz in Venezuela she was owned by the Thebes Shipping Company whose principals were some 'New York Greeks', as the Liberian Board of Investigation later characterized them. To say the ship had seen better days would be a charitable description of her condition. She had a record of almost one hundred casualties including a number of engine failures. On two occasions she had to be towed into port. She was a typical 'sub-standard tanker',[4] and what is remarkable is that she had sailed so many miles without finding an earlier resting place.

After leaving Puerto La Cruz *Argo Merchant* took a normal course up through the Caribbean. After clearing the Mona Passage a course was set for Boston via Cape Hatteras. A landfall was made late on 12 December southeast of Diamond Shoal light. A position was established using a radar distance and an RDF bearing, and a course of 040° true and gyro (see appendix 10), 054° magnetic, was laid down for Nantucket lightship. About five hours later at 04.00 on the 13th the gyro heading was altered to 036° to allow 4° leeway for the force 5 northwesterly wind.

By that afternoon the wind had reputedly generated a sea of sufficient size to necessitate a reduction in speed to about half that normally made. The noon position the following day based on celestial navigation showed *Argo Merchant* to be about 4 miles to the west of the plotted track. The course made good from the previous day's noon position was about 035°. That afternoon the wind backed to the southwest, which put it just about dead astern. In spite of the fact that the ship was to the west of the plotted course line, and the wind was no longer on the port bow but astern, no adjustment was made to the course. The explanation later offered was that while there was no longer need for leeway to offset the effect of the wind, there was now need for a correction for an easterly current set. The current sets in this area are weak and shifting.

However, this was not the sum of the casual attention given to the course steered. The course originally laid down from the position off Diamond Shoal was 040° true and gyro. The magnetic heading on that course was 054°. The variation at that time was 8° giving an apparent deviation of 6°. Two days later when the variation had increased to 14° the magnetic compass read 047°. The deviation should not have been affected noticeably by the 4° adjustment to port so the magnetic heading should have been 056°, yet the magnetic compass read 9° less than that indicating that the gyro had developed a substantial error. This discrepancy was apparently ignored, at least for the time being.

When the chief officer returned to the bridge from supper at about 1800 he noticed that *Argo Merchant* was yawing more than usual. He checked the gyro steering compass repeater and saw that it was fluctuating 7–8° on each side of the course. He notified the master who ordered that the ship be steered by the magnetic compass which read 047° before the malfunction. The fact that the magnetic compass heading had decreased during the past two days in spite of increasing variation was disregarded.

As further evidence of the slipshod manner in which *Argo Merchant* was navigated, no attempt had been made during the past two days to check the gyro compass error by means of an azimuth (a compass bearing of a heavenly body used to calculate compass error). Admittedly this routine navigation chore was not as easily accomplished on *Argo Merchant* as on most vessels. There were no gyro repeaters on the bridge wings, and the one on the flying bridge had not been operational for over a year. There was a centre line compass repeater in the wheelhouse, but it could be used for azimuths only if the sun or other heavenly body was forward of the beam and low down. The alternative was to use the inoperative repeater on the flying bridge as a dummy compass or pelorus, a procedure so awkward and requiring such skill that it was probably beyond the meagre talents found on *Argo Merchant*.

For the remainder of the chief mate's watch and up until midnight the course of 047° magnetic was held in spite of the fact that the variation was increasing as the ship steamed north. The master, however, left orders to steer 050° magnetic at 2400. The second mate, who took over the watch at midnight, estimated that the ship should be abeam of the lightship between 0330 and 0400. *Argo Merchant* was actually abeam of the Nantucket lightship a few minutes after three, but she was about 20 miles to the west of her dead reckoning position.

Apparently the master felt he could rely on the radar to pick up the lightship, and that may have led him to neglect other more rudimentary aids to navigation. *Argo Merchant* admittedly lacked sophisticated navigation equipment for fixing the ship's position, such as 'Loran', but she did have a functioning RDF and an echo sounder. The hundred fathom curve runs in a roughly east to west direction about 45 miles southwest of Nantucket lightship. The ship was making a little more than 9 knots at this time so she would have crossed the hundred fathom curve at around ten that evening. A diligent and prudent navigator would have turned on the echo sounder at least an hour before the anticipated time of crossing the curve. An RDF bearing taken at the time of crossing the curve should have given a position of sufficient accuracy to reveal the westerly set of *Argo Merchant*. The bearing of the lightship could then have been checked frequently with appropriate adjustments to the course until it was sighted visually.

This rudimentary precaution was not attempted. The master left word to have him called at 0100, and he later claimed that he made several atempts during the second mate's watch to take RDF bearings. The RDF on Nantucket lightship is a powerful one with a listed range of 200 miles. The second mate offered no corroborating testimony to support this claim. After the chief officer came on watch at 0400 (about an hour after *Argo Merchant* had actually passed the lightship) both he and the master claimed that they actually obtained RDF bearings of the lightship ahead. So preposterous did this claim appear that the Board of Investigation accused them of lying. What seems more likely is that the bearing they obtained was a reciprocal,[5] and it was not ahead but astern.

Perhaps the reason for neglecting the RDF was that it was made more difficult to use due to the failure of the gyro compass. Without a gyro compass and its repeaters (the RDF set was equipped with one) it was necessary to use the inoperative repeater as a dummy compass. This transforms a simple procedure into a clumsy and complicated operation. It should not, however, deter an assiduous navigator. In any event all reliance was apparently placed on the radar, and only after that device failed them[6] did they turn to more basic means of navigation.

The echo sounder was turned on belatedly towards the end of the second mate's watch. It showed depths of between fifteen and twenty fathoms, substantially less than the soundings should have been if *Argo Merchant* was making good her intended course or close to it.

This strongly suggested that the ship was substantially to the west, probably inside the lightship.

Everyone was now feeling very uneasy. The second mate, though he had been relieved, had stayed on to assist. They were lost, and the prudent thing to have done at this point was to anchor until daybreak and ascertain the ship's position by star sights. However, although the master did not try to hide his concern he was not willing to make so bald-faced an admission of his ineptitude. He was also probably concerned about making the tide at Boston, and the embarrassing explanation he would have to offer if he missed it due to slowing or stopping his ship. He chose instead to continue on and trust to luck which was about to run out. The chief mate later testified that he urged the captain to 'do something', and claimed if he had been in command he would have turned the ship around. In desperation he tried to take a round of star sights at 0530 even though sunrise was an hour and a half away. The result only added to the confusion. At about 0600 *Argo Merchant* grounded on Fishing Rip Shoal 30 miles due north of Nantucket lightship.

In spite of everything the master of *Argo Merchant* had almost struck lucky. Had the vessel been perhaps a ship length further east she would have barely cleared the shoal and passed into deeper water. It was soon evident that *Argo Merchant* was hard aground and unlikely to get off unaided. The vessel's agents in New York were contacted but demonstrated no great sense of urgency. Over twenty-four hours elapsed before any action was taken, and that was confined to hiring divers to examine the hull. No attempt was made to hire tugs or lighters to lighten the ship and attempt to refloat her. The weather eventually made the decision for them when it worsened as expected. *Argo Merchant* subsequently broke up and spilled her cargo of almost 28,000 tons of crude into the fishing grounds off Cape Cod. Fortunately the prevailing westerly winds carried the oil out into the broad reaches of the Atlantic.

Amoco Cadiz

Almost eleven years to the day that *Torrey Canyon* set her record for the worst oil spill in history, the 228,513 deadweight ton VLCC *Amoco Cadiz* smashed that record when she drove ashore on the rocks of Portsall on the Brittany coast. Close to a quarter of a million tons, almost four times the amount of crude oil carried by *Torrey Canyon*, spilled on to the beaches of Brittany and beyond. Although the direct cost of the spill was initially estimated at only $100 million the claims ultimately rose to over $2 billion. This did not include the damage to the environment and its creatures, which was incalculable.

Amoco Cadiz was built in Spain in 1974, flew the Liberian flag, was owned in the United States, and was crewed by Italians. In addition to her master *Amoco Cadiz* had a crew of forty-one. She had loaded a full cargo of Iranian crude in the Gulf during the middle of February. Too big to pass through the Suez Canal, she had come via the Cape of Good Hope. Most of the passage had been made in balmy summer breezes, but from the time she rounded Cape Villano on the northwest tip of Spain she was buffeted by gales.

Amoco Cadiz approached the traffic separation scheme off Ushant at breakfast time on 16 March in a strong southwesterly gale. At around 0600 some drums on deck came adrift and the master, Pasquale Bardari, altered course to 270° for upwards of an hour while they were secured. Speed was reduced, but when course was finally resumed the vessel was actually in the southern approaches to the southbound lane. At 0726 the chief officer entered a position in the deck log showing the vessel 15 miles from Point de Creach on Ushant on a bearing of 079°, which placed the *Amoco Cadiz* squarely in the middle of the southbound traffic lane. The course at this time was apparently 037°, but after the third mate relieved the mate just before 0800 the movements of the ship became difficult to trace.

The Board of Investigation later described the third mate's testimony as 'very muddled'. The master himself admitted that the vessel's navigation was 'not very precise', an embarrassing admission under the circumstances. The Board observed: 'The impression left . . . is that none of the officers concerned during this period was paying attention to what was going on. . . .'[7]

When the third mate assumed the watch just before 0800 *Amoco Cadiz* was on the verge of entering the traffic separation scheme through the separation zone, an entry forbidden by the rules pertaining to such schemes. A variety of courses were seemingly steered before the ship reached a position from which she could proceed normally, which was at about 0845. The course steered from that point was apparently 045°.

Amoco Cadiz continued on that course for the next hour until at 09.46 the steering gear failed. Captain Bardari had no way of knowing how serious the problem was at this point. His initial response was to order the engines stopped and have the two black balls that indicate 'Not under command' hoisted at the yardarm. He also broadcast a warning on the VHF to warn other shipping in the vicinity of his predicament. The ship was just emerging from the northern end of the separation scheme and, though it was quite possible that the fault could be quickly found and repaired, the master had to be concerned at his plight: he was in a fully loaded VLCC 'not under command' in a full gale blowing down on a lee shore.

Steering gear failures are by no means uncommon, and as often as not require not much more than the replacement of a blown fuse to put things right. None the less, if the failure of *Amoco Cadiz*'s steering gear proved to be irreparable no time was to be lost in calling for assistance. In a situation such as this the master must not feel constrained to act on his own. The prudent course would have been to contact the nearest shore station and inform the local authorities that *Amoco Cadiz* was experiencing difficulty with her steering gear and hoped to have it fixed shortly, and, as a precaution, the master should also have asked to be put in touch with salvage tugs in the vicinity in case assistance was required.

Owners, however, wish or demand to be involved in any salvage operation from the outset. On the face of it this is not an unreasonable position. The ship and its cargo, for whom they are responsible, may be worth many millions of dollars. In the case of the *Amoco Cadiz* the ship was valued at $50 million and the cargo at almost half that. Should the master accept a tow from a salvage tug the owner is faced with all the uncertainty of a salvage award. This is an area in which many owners and those who act for them may have had no direct experience. Salvage is an unknown quantity. The owner understandably regards the ship as his private property, and his first consideration is to protect his investment. In such a situation the master will not deal directly with the owner, who in any event is rarely a single individual today. He will report to an owner's representative, who is an employee like himself, usually a marine superintendent or manager. The last thing this individual wants is to be faced with an unpredictable situation that may result in large claims or costs. The simplest solution, and the one the owner's representative is most familiar with when a ship breaks down and needs assistance, is to hire a tug on a fixed contract.

There is ordinarily nothing wrong with this approach since when ships break down and need a tow they are usually not in such a desperate situation. More often than not they will be miles from land and only occasionally experiencing bad weather. It is rare that a ship will be in need of immediate assistance to keep her off the rocks. It is even more rare for that ship to be a threat to anyone else. If the ship is lost it is a matter for the underwriters. A few crewmen may be drowned, but more often than not they will hail from some remote village in the Philippines or Malaysia. Nothing to get excited about. This is not to say that all shipowners and those who represent them are callous. The best are sometimes like a big family, and the marine superintendent and his staff may be bound by ties of friendship to many in the fleet. However, that is becoming increasingly rare as the old names in the industry disappear or are swallowed by a conglomerate, and more often than not today the owner's representative knows little or nothing about those who man the ships. He does not want to have to answer awkward questions asked by his superiors. If a ship is lost he will not be blamed for the mistakes made by the master, and the underwriters will absorb the loss. Exposure to the vagaries of a salvage arbitration is therefore not an attractive option.

At the time *Amoco Cadiz* experienced the failure of her steering gear the German salvage tug *Pacific* owned by the Hamburg salvage firm of Bugsier, was some 15 miles away in the Chenal du Four, inside Ushant, heading for the Dover Strait to assist another tug in towing an oil rig. At 1125 her radio operator had intercepted a VHF message: '*Amoco Cadiz* to all ships. Our position 8 miles north of Ushant. We have complete fallout of gear. Please keep clear.'[8] Captain Hartmut Weinert, *Pacific*'s skipper, told the radio operator to make contact and offer assistance on the basis of Lloyd's 'open form', which contains a 'no cure, no pay' clause, meaning that unless the salvor succeeds in saving the property at risk he receives nothing.* If he does succeed the compensation will be decided by an impartial arbitrator.

Captain Bardari was trying to contact his immediate superior in Chicago over 4000 miles away. His response to this offer was simply to 'stand by'. He wasn't prepared to bind himself with a salvage agreement without the prior approval of his principals. Valuable minutes were lost by this prevarication, but Captain Weinert wasn't

---

* Since the *Amoco Cadiz* disaster provision has been made for compensation to salvors, sufficient to cover their expenses, in cases where the vessel at risk poses a potential threat to the environment.

to be put off. He altered course for the stricken ship and repeated his offer.

By now Bardari knew he was in a poor position to bargain. The chief engineer had confirmed that the steering gear was beyond repair, but his propulsion system was intact and the distraught skipper still clung to the hope that he could get the German to accept a towing contract. It was a vain hope in any event, but when *Pacific* reached the scene about 1220 the Italian master was still unready to accept a tow on the basis of Lloyd's open form. He appeared to feel he was being victimized.

Captain Weinert was in no doubt. If he didn't get a line aboard the disabled tanker shortly the whole argument would become academic. Even while he was negotiating with Captain Bardari he and his crew were manoeuvring into position to get a line aboard. This was done by means of a Konsberg gun, which was both more efficient and safer than rockets or the traditional heaving line. With seas breaking over the bow it was no simple matter, but skill and determination saw them through. About an hour after the tug arrived on the scene the towing hawser was fast and *Pacific* began to pull the bow of *Amoco Cadiz* up into the wind.

With the wind out of the northwest the stricken tanker had assumed a heading of about south-southwest with the wind on the starboard quarter. It was Weinert's intent to pull the ship's head to port and tow her up into the Channel, hopefully into the shelter of Lyme Bay east of Torquay. At first the plan seemed to work. The bow of the huge tanker began to swing slowly to port, but no sooner were spirits raised than they were dashed. After swinging only a few degrees the ship would move no more. *Pacific* was simply not up to the job. The only hope now was to keep *Amoco Cadiz* off the rocks until a bigger and more powerful Bugsier tug, *Simson*, could arrive later that evening.[9]

Amoco Cadiz was now a little less than 6 miles off the rocky Brittany coast, and now that the tug was fast it was time to settle the terms. *Pacific* was pulling almost at right angles to the heading of *Amoco Cadiz*, and it appeared to Captain Bardari that after the initial attempt to swing the bow to port that the tug had stopped pulling. Perhaps, he reasoned, the German tug captain was seeking to emphasize the vulnerability of the immobilized VLCC. The heavy towing cable hung in a pronounced bight, but the tug was in fact pulling at 80 per cent of her maximum power. After the initial unsuccessful attempt to swing the heavy loaded tanker Weinert eased off a bit on his engines. He didn't want to risk overloading the towing line. Unknown to those aboard *Amoco Cadiz* he was waiting for *Simson*, when together they could commence the tow.

In the meantime a series of acrimonious exchanges took place between the German and the Italian masters. Most of the actual talking for *Amoco Cadiz*, however, was done by Mr Lesley Maynard, a Maritime Safety Services specialist who had joined the vessel off Las Palmas by helicopter to instruct the crew in fire-fighting techniques and other safety matters. The customary form of agreement in such a situation is that spelled out in Lloyd's open form, which set out the normal and equitable terms that Captain Weinert was accustomed to work under, summed up in the 'no cure, no pay' clause, and he found Captain Bardari's stubborn insistence on a flat rate towage contract unreasonable and unrealistic. *Amoco Cadiz* was drifting helpless on to a rocky coast under the influence of a driving gale. This, to him, was a clear case of salvage.

The Italian skipper, like most other seamen in his predicament, had no previous experience in negotiating a contract for assistance under such pressing need. He did not view his situation in the same way as it was seen from the bridge of the salvage tug. True enough, he could not steer his vessel, but his engines were intact. All he wanted from the German was to point his ship in a direction away from the French coast so he could use his engines to propel his ship in the desired direction. Surely such a simple service did not warrant a potentially exorbitant claim for salvage, but was a matter to be paid for at a fixed rate – and that was a matter to be arranged between his principals and Weinert's employers.

The captain of *Pacific* was beginning to lose his patience, and he pointed out ominously (at least that was the way Bardari interpreted it) that he. (Captain Bardari) was hardly in a position to bargain. 'Captain, you are in a very bad position.' Weinert recalled saying later. 'You have a very big ship. The weather condition is the same, very bad, and we must have Lloyd's open form. You accept it. Please you accept it.'[10] The German captain meant this as a bald statement of fact, the Italian took it as a threat. Bardari continued to resist, still trying to contact the marine operations manager, Captain Phillips, in Chicago. Finally, at about 1545, he got through. Captain Phillips quickly recognized that *Amoco Cadiz* was in dire straits and gave his approval. Fifteen minutes later everything changed. The heavy steel chain towing link parted where it passed through the chock when both vessels rose on the crest of succeeding waves, and then fell off away from one another.

Both masters felt a mixture of frustration and anger, but neither could afford indulgence. *Pacific*'s crew almost immediately began hauling in the parted hawser and at the same time prepared a replacement. On *Amoco Cadiz*, Bardari first rang 'Slow astern' on his engines, followed by 'Half' and then 'Full'. The forbidding rocky coast of Brittany was clearly visible little more than 6 miles away. The fatal drift was slowed but not completely overcome. The effect of the engines going astern also caused the stern to swing directly into the wind. *Amoco Cadiz* was now heading about 130° pointing straight at the closest part of the Breton shore. The ship was now drifting northeastward, almost directly parallel to the coast.

Captain Weinert took fresh stock of the situation. He had been unable to budge the ship when he had her fast by the bow, and the resulting heavy strain finally parted the hawser. He decided now to make fast by the stern. He radioed *Amoco Cadiz* word of his intention and also informed her of the expected arrival of *Simson* about midnight. Bardari was cheered by the news of further help on its way, but he didn't like the idea of making the tug fast astern. It meant he would have to stop his engines, and they seemed his best hope at this point of staying clear of the rocky shore.

However, unless he wanted to dispense with *Pacific*'s help he had no choice. He stopped his engines just after 1900, with the Roches de Portsall less than 4 miles distant. Weinert now eased his big tug as close as he dared to the heavily pitching stern of the big ship before firing a line across. Time after time the line either fell short or was torn out of the seamen's hands as they struggled to heave it aboard. Bardari looked on helplessly and impatiently from the wing of the bridge. The distance off the coast narrowed inexorably. With the engines stopped *Amoco Cadiz* had slowly swung broadside to the wind again, adding to the difficulties of making fast aft.

After an hour Bardari felt he had to do something. He had earlier given orders to prepare the port anchor in case of need. With seas breaking over the starboard bow it was deemed too dangerous to do the same with the one on that side. He gave the order to the second mate on the bow to drop the anchor. Though it may have delayed a final reckoning for a few minutes it was a futile gesture. The anchors of VLCCs are huge, weighing almost 50,000 pounds each; in proportion to the size of the ship, however, they are minute. (On a 14,000 deadweight ton freighter, an average size thirty years ago, an anchor would weigh about 8000 pounds – approximately 0.6 pounds per deadweight ton. The ratio for *Amoco Cadiz* had dwindled to 0.2.) They are effective enough for normal anchoring in moderate weather, but for this kind of work they are totally inadequate. The chain took a heavy strain, but when the French navy later recovered the anchor both flukes (the blades that dig in and give the anchor its holding power) had been torn off.

The ship was now only 1.3 miles off the rocks of Portsall. Only a couple of minutes after the anchor was dropped a line was finally put aboard. Twenty minutes later the tanker's crew started to make the hawser fast. Shortly before 2100 Bardari informed the tug to start pulling. At 2104 *Amoco Cadiz* grounded aft almost exactly at high water. It was the end.

The grim-faced Italian master acted promptly to minimize the risk of an explosion. The cargo was a relatively volatile type of crude oil, and the captain of *Amoco Cadiz* had already warned the engine room to be ready to respond immediately should the ship strike the rocks. He now gave the order and within moments the ship was dead. Not a light was showing. Unfortunately that left no power to work the radio transmitters. Some of the crew tried sending out Mayday calls over portable radios, but their range was limited to line of sight. Lesley Maynard found a sheltered spot to windward where the crude oil fumes were least and fired the ship's distress rockets.

Captain Bardari had meanwhile given orders to muster the crew on the bridge. Although the hull was holed the ship was still moving in the seaway. Then she struck again aft about 2130. The engine room began to flood, there was the sound of an explosion in the engine room and flames shot out of the stack. But to everyone's amazement nothing else followed. The port lifeboat was prepared for launching, a prospect none could have viewed with enthusiasm, but they were saved from that frightful challenge when the sea swept the boat away.

Pacific had meanwhile been pulling away hopelessly until her second hawser parted at 2212. Although Weinert and his crew clung to the hope that when *Simson* arrived they still might get the battered tanker off, it was obvious that the plight of those aboard *Amoco Cadiz* was desperate and immediate. A call was sent out for help and was quickly answered by the French navy. The first helicopter arrived about midnight and the last of the crew, except for Bardari and Maynard, were lifted off at 0145. Their decision to stay was gallant but futile. They were in danger of being overcome by the heavy fumes from the spilling cargo, and about four in the morning Maynard saw what he at first thought were lightning flashes. There wasn't, however, a cloud in the sky, and he realized then that the flashes were generated by the ripping of the plating of *Amoco Cadiz*. The ship was breaking up. The time for any further heroics was past, and he fired the last of the flares. *Pacific* passed the word on to the French, and at 0510 a navy helicopter lifted off the two weary men.

*

During the first few weeks approximately 64,000 tons of crude came ashore spreading along some 40 miles of shoreline. The drift of the oil was at first easterly under the influence of the prevailing westerly winds. In early April, however, a reversal of winds caused the oil to move in the opposite direction, creating pollution as far southwest as Pointe du Raz just beyond Brest, and by that time almost 200 miles of beach had been contaminated.[11]

The combination of strong winds and exceptionally high tides exposed the coast of Brittany to catastrophic pollution. It extended to Pointe du Raz almost 80 miles to the south and west, and nearly 125 miles to the east at Paimpol. The amount of oil spilled was 223,000 metric tons, or over four times that which escaped from the *Torrey Canyon*. Although tankers, including some VLCCs, continued to suffer casualties with monotonous and disturbing frequency during the next decade some thought perhaps the lessons had finally been learned. There were no further catastrophic spills until on a dark night on 23 March 1989 a modern, well-found, superbly equipped VLCC belonging to the oil company Exxon, and skippered by one of Exxon's most talented young masters, slipped her moorings in Valdez, Alaska and sailed down the channel into Prince William Sound bound for a port in California on a routine voyage.

Exxon Valdez

When the VLCC *Exxon Valdez* stranded on Bligh Reef on 24 March 1989 spilling almost 250,000 barrels of North Slope Crude into the pristine waters of Prince William Sound, Alaska the public outrage generated in the United States was enormous. This dwarfed all previous spills in United States waters, yet it ranked only tenth on a world-wide scale. It was only an eighth of the size of the *Aegean Captain–Atlantic Empress* spill, and a seventh of that of the *Amoco Cadiz*.

After the discovery of the North Slope oil field in 1968 a consortium (Alyeska) of eight companies (Sohio Pipeline Company, British Petroleum Pipelines Inc., Exxon Pipeline Co., Mobil Alaska Pipeline Co., Union Alaska Pipeline Co., Phillips Petroleum Co., and Amerada Hess Corp.) was formed to exploit the find. Getting the oil out of the frozen Alaskan soil was just one of a number of tasks of daunting proportions, the least of which was overcoming the opposition of environmentalists. The problem of transporting it to market was equally difficult and even more contentious. The preferred solution was via a pipeline direct to refineries in the Midwest, most of which would pass through Canada. But the Canadians could not be persuaded that this was in their interest. In 1973 it was finally decided to lay a pipeline from the North Slope fields to Valdez in southern Alaska in the northern reaches of Prince William Sound. From there VLCCs would carry it to refineries in the United States. The Alyeska Pipeline Service Company was formed by the consortium, and was given the responsibility for the construction and operation of the pipeline and the terminal at Valdez.[12]

Exxon Valdez is a 211,469 dwt VLCC built in 1986 and equipped to a very high standard. At the time of the casualty she had a crew of twenty (*Amoco Cadiz* had a crew of forty-two) which included a master, chief, second and third mates and six A.B.s. The master, 32-year-old Joseph Hazelwood, had served in command for ten years and in *Exxon Valdez* since 1987. He had made many trips into Valdez aboard Exxon vessels.

On the evening of the accident *Exxon Valdez* was scheduled to sail at 2100, and promptly at that time the deck crew went to their undocking stations. The lines were cast off, the vessel manoeuvred clear of her berth, and under the conn of *Valdez* pilot Ed Murphy *Exxon Valdez* proceeded through the Valdez Narrows and down the Valdez Arm channel. The third mate was the watch officer.

Gregory Cousins, the 38-year-old third mate, was first employed as A.B. by Exxon in 1980. He impressed his superiors by his diligence and industry, and in 1985 was promoted to third mate. He proved to be a dependable, competent officer, and was highly regarded by those he worked for, including Hazelwood[13] with whom he had sailed previously. Hazelwood apparently thought well enough of Cousins to request his assignment to the *Exxon Valdez*. In an evaluation report dated 12 January, 1988 Hazelwood rated Cousins as having 'excellent navigational skills' but 'only average knowledge of ship handling characteristics.'[14]

The waters of Prince William Sound through which *Exxon Valdez* proceeded after leaving her berth in Valdez are federally regulated pilotage waters.[15] The most difficult part of the pilotage is the first twenty miles or so, and Pilot Murphy remained on the bridge directing the vessel's navigation through the Valdez Arm traffic lanes until she came abeam of Rocky Point. He disembarked there at 2324. At 2325 Captain Hazelwood contacted the USCG Vessel Traffic Control (VTC) reporting that the pilot had disembarked, and he was now increasing to sea speed.

After dropping the pilot Captain Hazelwood found the normal route, as defined by the Traffic Separation Scheme, (see appendix: 8) blocked by a belt of ice composed of small bergs (which can be the size of a house) known as bergy bits, growlers (so-called because of the noise they make as they bob up and down in the sea), which may be as big as a room, together with smaller pieces. After first checking with the USCG Vessel Traffic Control Center to make sure there was no inbound traffic, Hazelwood announced his intention to go around the ice to the east.

Cousins had left the bridge to see the pilot off. He then helped the lookout to pull the pilot ladder back aboard and stow it. This took him about ten to twelve minutes. During that time the master was alone on the bridge except for the able seaman acting as helmsman.

Hazelwood first changed course to 200° not long after the pilot departed, but after several minutes he found ice further to the east showing on the radar and hauled further to the left to 180° to clear it. After the helmsman had steadied on this course Hazelwood ordered him to switch to automatic steering (autopilot).

Cousins returned to the bridge shortly before this change and Hazelwood instructed him to fix the ship's position, which he did at 2339. It was Hazelwood's intention to hold this heading until he cleared the ice just below Busby Island, when course would be altered to the southwest to take the ship between the ice and Bligh Reef about two miles south of Busby Island. This would require careful navigation, but Hazelwood apparently had no qualms in adopting this course. In fact he seemingly regarded the evolution as so simple he planned to leave it to the third mate once Cousins had the chance to get his bearings.

Hazelwood explained to Cousins what he wanted to do. They were approaching Busby Island to port, and would pass it just over a mile off. After the island was abeam and the ice was cleared to starboard, Hazelwood told the third mate he 'should start coming back into the lanes.'[16] After explaining his plan Hazelwood asked Cousins if he felt comfortable with the situation. Cousins said he did, and the master then went below to do some paperwork.

Exxon Valdez was coming abeam of the light on Busby Island, and Cousins' attention was directed towards fixing the ship's position at this point. At 2355 the light was abeam and Able Seaman Kagan relieved the helmsman. Kagan had been employed by Exxon for thirteen years, mostly as a messman. When his job was phased out several years earlier he was given an ordinary seaman's job. This is an entry rating requiring no experience, no skill, no qualifications of any kind. Kagan performed satisfactorily in that position, but as Exxon, along with almost everyone else, continued to reduce the size of their crews, the ordinary seamen were made redundant. Kagan, however, was able to obtain an able seaman's document. Because of his length of service with Exxon he was given an A.B.'s berth. Nine evaluation reports during the preceding three years agreed that while Kagan's performance of menial tasks was satisfactory, he had difficulty carrying out more demanding duties. The most recent evaluation report noted that he 'lacks the necessary skills to do the A.B.'s job.' Second Mate LeCain, who would normally have relieved Cousins at midnight (Cousins had agreed to a late relief because LeCain's off duty rest period had been interrupted by the undocking operation), had planned to have Kagan take the second wheel watch since he was ' "nervous" at the prospect of being helmsman in Prince William Sound.'[16]

When the helm was relieved the A.B. going off duty reported to the third mate giving the course steered, and informing him that the autopilot was engaged. Cousins was apparently surprised at this, since it was normally the practice to steer by hand in confined waters. Sometime later he told Kagan to switch back to hand steering.

The change of watch occurred just as *Exxon Valdez* reached the point where Hazelwood had told Cousins to change course, but for some unaccountable reason the turn was delayed for another six minutes. Cousins was understandably concerned about keeping clear of the ice and this is perhaps the most likely explanation for the holdup, but there may also have been some confusion about the switch back to hand steering. The ship was making about 12 knots at this time, and whatever the reason for the delay she had reached a position about 1.2 miles south of the position Hazelwood had told Cousins to begin to 'turn back into the lanes.' Bligh Reef was then just under a mile off almost dead ahead.

Cousins claims he first ordered 10° right rudder at 0000 with ice still close aboard to starboard. According to the course recorder chart there was no movement of the ship's heading until a minute later.[18] Cousins then called Hazelwood on the phone and reported that he had started the turn. He did not, however, tell the master that the ship had run over a mile past the point where he had been ordered to change course. Hazelwood apparently assumed that the Third Mate was carrying out his orders, and that Bligh Reef therefore posed no threat.

At 0002 the ship had only swung 10° to the right (190°), so Cousins ordered the rudder angle increased to 20°. As he looked at the radar scope he could see that the ship had still not moved perceptibly to the right of her original path. According to the manoevring diagram posted on the bridge of *Exxon Valdez* the ship would advance .3 of a mile, after the helm was put hard over (35° rudder), before the ship would start to move appreciably to the right of her original path (in this case 180°). If less helm was applied the vessel would move an even greater distance ahead before entering her turn. Cousins now ordered hard right rudder. He estimated that this order was given about 0004. The ship's swing now began to accelerate, and at 0005 the heading had reached 234°. At 0006 it had reached 247°.

Cousins had apparently (probably at, or not long after, the first helm order of 10° right) told Kagan that the course would be between 235° and 245°.[18] Kagan now presumably tried to check the ship's swing in anticipation of an order to steady on the new course. In any event the course recorder shows an interruption of the turn. The turn then resumes and Cousins telephoned the captain saying, 'I think we are in serious trouble.' Almost immediately thereafter the first of a series of sharp jolts was felt. The time was 0007, and *Exxon Valdez* was hard aground on Bligh Reef.

*

Hazelwood was one of Exxon's most highly regarded masters. Only ten years after graduation from the New York State Maritime College he was appointed to command of the *Exxon Philadelphia*, a vessel in the California to Valdez service. At the age of 32 he was the youngest skipper in Exxon's American fleet. Like many other seafaring men, Hazelwood also liked a drink or, more accurately, several drinks.

Hazelwood had a few drinks ashore that afternoon and early evening. How many is unknown, but enough for the odour to be detectable by the pilot.[19] It was also noticeable to the USCG officers who boarded *Exxon Valdez* about three hours after the grounding. The media shortly uncovered the fact that Hazelwood had two convictions for drunken driving, and had undergone treatment for alcohol rehabilitation in 1985. From there it became a simple exercise in charging Hazelwood with 'drunken driving' of his ship, a charge the public could readily understand.

Alcohol can impair an individual's judgement, as anyone can testify who has seen a person, almost too intoxicated to stand, insist he can drive. It certainly affects reflexes, which are critical in driving an automobile. Hazelwood's reflexes were not a factor in what happened here. His judgement was, but whether it was impaired significantly by the alcohol he had earlier consumed is impossible to determine.

Most knowledgeable observers would agree that in those matters leading directly to the accident Hazelwood made several decisions that, at least in retrospect, were highly questionable. It is the usual practice after dropping the pilot to increase to sea speed almost immediately, as Hazelwood did. If there are any hazards to navigation in the immediate vicinity – particularly at night – such as other ships approaching the pilot station or shoals or other dangers such as ice, it would be prudent to proceed cautiously, adjusting speed as circumstances warrant before increasing to maximum speed.

This is a procedure that is perhaps more widely followed in theory than in practice, but it is the prudent course. While the prudent ship operator will not criticize a master who follows such prudent practice (if it comes to his attention, which is unlikely), it is practically unheard of for those to whom the master reports to check to see that he takes no undue risks. It is left to his good judgement, which ordinarily should be sufficient. In the situation in which Hazelwood found himself the decision to give the order 'load program up' (a computer program which regulates the build up to maximum speed) was perhaps understandable however questionable.

If Hazelwood planned to leave Cousins alone on the bridge to make the course change, it would have been advisable to have reduced speed substantially to allow more time for Cousins to execute the manoevre and so reduce the chance of error. But if Hazelwood had thought that necessary, he would probably not have left the bridge. He had been in and out of Valdez so many times, however, that he may have become complacent.

The decision to engage the autopilot while the ship was in confined waters has also been criticized. The recommended practice, though widely disregarded, is to have the vessel steered by hand whenever in pilotage waters or in a situation where it might be necessary to change course to avoid nearby ships or a navigational hazard (see Appendix 9). The question here, however, is not so much why the autopilot was engaged, as why was a helmsman of known inadequacy allowed to take the wheel in this situation? The further question of why Cousins was not informed of the switch to autopilot may have been no more than an oversight.

The biggest question, however, and one for which no satisfactory answer has been offered, is why did Hazelwood leave Cousins in such a position? A clue was offered in a television interview shortly after Hazelwood's acquittal on criminal mischief charges. When confronted with that question he made reference to the 'hands-on' approach followed by some masters, and implied he favoured allowing his watch officers more latitude and responsibility in the conduct of their watches.

Hazelwood reportedly modelled himself after 'old-time captains', and it was – and still is, though probably less so – the practice of some highly competent ship masters to practice a 'hands-off' policy of bridge management. The hands-off approach, which is the one Hazelwood seemingly favoured, allows the watch officer wide latitude in conning the vessel. The advantage of this approach is that it encourages and even demands that the watch officer – in this case Cousins – exercise a high degree of initiative in carrying out his duties. Given competent watch officers, which Hazelwood believed Cousins to be, the hands-off approach has definite advantages. It has no rival as a means of confidence building. It also provides a range and depth of experience that an officer will otherwise not ordinarily be exposed to until he is appointed to command. A further significant advantage is the morale building factor. Competent people usually perform best with a minimum of supervision. This demonstration of confidence in the watch officer's ability to perform at a high level is the sincerest form of flattery. This apparently was Hazelwood's style of operation, and it explains to a great degree the devotion and loyalty he apparently inspired in many of his subordinate officers.

There are, of course, masters who follow what seems to be a hands-off approach, but avoid or neglect the bridge because of their inadequacy or incapacity. No one has suggested that Hazelwood was one of the former, and while it is debatable whether or not his judgement was impaired by drink it has not been suggested that he was incapable at the time of conning the vessel himself. Indeed, the common view is that the accident would not have happened if he had stayed on the bridge.

Having said all this, the reason why Hazelwood made these 'mistakes' was perhaps not because his judgement was impaired by alcohol, but (as a highly respected colleague of mine observed recently) because his own talents were so considerable he could not visualize how an officer as competent as he thought Cousins to be would have any problem in such a simple (as Hazelwood saw it) situation. The presence of ice and the proximity of the reef, however, made the situation far from simple. Hazelwood's apparent failure to recognize this casts some doubt about the quality of his judgement, at least in this instance.

*

Whatever the merits of a hands-off style of bridge management, and they are considerable, today's circumstances require more constraint in its practice. On vessels carrying toxic or highly dangerous cargoes the master must take every reasonable precaution in the operation of his ship if he is to avoid not just censure, but the prospect of severe penalties including imprisonment.

The magnitude of the risks involved in the operation of such vessels is so great that procedures and practices that might be acceptable on other less hazardous ships may be questionable on an *Exxon Valdez*. Whenever such a vessel is in a situation where a mistake or miscalculation by the officer at the conn could place the ship in immediate jeopardy, another officer should be present to monitor the conning officer's performance.

This has been the traditional role of the master when a pilot is at the conn. When the master assumes the conn the monitoring role falls on the watch officer. This has always been a less than satisfactory arrangement for the obvious reason that while the master should have no inhibition in questioning the intentions or activity of a pilot, the converse is not true when the master assumes the conn with the watch officer in the monitoring position.

One way this problem could be resolved is by making the chief officer the navigating officer, with responsibility for pilotage in those situations (such as Prince William Sound) where for some reason pilotage is unavailable. This would entail a major restructuring of operating duties and responsibilities, but it would restore the master to his proper role of overseer. It would also give the chief officer much needed preparation for the day he is promoted to command. To be truly effective this would require that the chief officer be restored to non-watchstanding status, and the re-employment of another deck officer.

The plain truth of the matter is that masters today are subject to far too many distractions and pressures that can erode their capacity to make command decisions. The master's job should essentially be confined to overseeing a routine of which he is the author. I do not suggest that he should be the sole author. The routine should be the product of consultation with his colleagues, subordinates and employer. He should have no duties, only responsibilities. Those immediately below him, specifically his watchstanders, should be qualified and competent – and he should have full confidence in their capacity and judgement – to perform their routine duties without his intervention. When something occurs that falls outside the routine the master then steps in to provide the necessary guidance. In the days before the traditional maritime nations lost their pre-eminent position, this was the norm in most of the best companies.

At the Annual General Meeting of the Nautical Institute in London in 1985 three distinguished figures on the international maritime scene, Mr J. D. Davis, chairman of the International Maritime Forum, Mr Lars Lindfelt, managing director of the Swedish P & I Club, and Mr J. C. S. Horrocks, secretary-general of the International Chamber of Shipping, were invited to offer their views on the theme, 'Can International Shipping Be Self-Regulating?'[20]

Mr Lindfelt had some very interesting and thought-provoking things to say about classification societies. He pointed out that 'classification societies were once formed by underwriters to help in getting certain safety standards applied. . . . In the good old days, underwriters could rely on the fact that the ship was classed, but I state that this is no longer so.' He complained that the classification societies, whose original function was to assist the underwriters in minimizing risks, had developed an almost incestuous (not his term) relationship with the owners whereby information that could be invaluable to an underwriter in assessing a particular risk, was regarded as privileged, much like that between a lawyer and his client.

He suggested that if the original co-operative relationship between underwriters and classification societies was restored the underwriters could more accurately gauge risks and assess corresponding premiums. Unfortunately, he observed, 'classification societies have succeeded in placing themselves in an isolated world of their own. When you try to co-operate with them, you get the same dreamlike feeling as if you were driving against one-way traffic. You meet a lot of obstacles.'

Mr Davis had earlier addressed the problems of over-tonnaging, and its depressing affect on freight rates. He pointed out that in 1972 when oil was selling for two dollars a barrel, the cost of transporting it was about a third of the selling price. When the price rose to nearly thirty dollars in 1985 the freight had only risen to about a dollar. Had freight rates followed inflation they should at least have doubled. Instead the rise was less than half that. He suggested that the 'objective should be to raise freight rates rather than reduce operating costs.' He did not suggest how that could be done, but his proposal illuminated one of the major reasons for the depression of safety standards.

Individuals and companies engaged in international trade have rarely been supporters of legislation or government policies designed to shield shipowners from the effects of unrestricted competition.[21] The general public, the consumer, cares no more, and knows less about the subject. As has been reiterated several times in the preceding pages, measures and policies designed to improve ship safety add to the shipowner's cost of doing business. How many importers enquire about the safety record of the vessel booked to carry their goods? How many of the ultimate purchasers of the goods know or care? The name of the game is free trade, and that means shipping with whomever will carry it cheapest.

Competition amongst tanker owners is a somewhat different case.

The oil companies (see appendix 10) have for many years owned and operated their own fleets, which are usually employed in carrying the oil of the parent company. The major companies have their shipping operations split up into a number of different companies which serve different markets and areas. These companies are often operated as separate entities with their own objectives and policies, as is the Exxon Shipping Company, which operates vessels exclusively in the American domestic trade. These companies do not ordinarily compete in the usual sense with the fleets of other oil companies, but they are none the less responsive to competitive pressures.

The independent shipowner who registers his ship in Panama, Cyprus or whatever registry is most convenient, and cheapest, will usually be able to offer the lowest freight rates because he is subject to almost none of the restrictions, and added costs, that his competitor flying a traditional flag is burdened with. The cost of insuring his ship will perhaps be marginally higher, but because of the difficulty underwriters have in assessing the risk accurately his premium will often be substantially less than it should be.

The shipowner, required by the law of his flag, to purchase and maintain expensive safety equipment, pays wages that may be two or three times that of his competitor whose ship is registered under the flag of a more 'sympathetic' regime, and abide by laws that add substantially to his operating expenses, finds it increasingly difficult to compete. In his attempt to reduce his costs under these circumstances he has, among other things, sought to utilize his sea-going personnel more effectively.[22]

Some successes have been achieved by the elimination of restrictive work practices. Automation has helped to reduce the number of personnel needed, particularly in the engine and stewards department. Unfortunately the drive to cut costs through manning reductions has come to be seen almost as a criterion of efficient management. These manning cuts in the beginning eliminated some fat. Further cuts may have tightened up the muscle a bit. Finally the sinew came under threat, and on some ships today the term skeletal might be appropriate as a description of the manning scale.

Though automation has reduced the work load in some cases, the need to maintain and service faulty and insufficiently proven equipment has actually increased it in others. Where crew cuts were not attended by a corresponding reduction in the work needed to safely operate the ship, the work required of those remaining naturally increased. Some of this additional work has been compensated for by overtime payments, but some has not. To fatigue has been added stress and resentment, with an attendant detrimental impact on efficiency and safety.[23]

Ships represent a long-term investment, but they tend to be operated for short-term profit. The obsession with *the bottom line* that infects the thinking of so many today, is probably responsible for many of the accidents conveniently labelled 'human error'. When a captain or his third mate makes a mistake because he is suffering from fatigue this undeniably fits into the 'human error' category. That the ship they are employed on has only half the crew she had when she was built ten years earlier is ignored.

An accountant, or someone relying on his advice and concerned only with monetary costs, can easily see how profits can be smartly increased if thirty people can be used to do the work that formerly required forty. And if thirty succeed in getting the ship successfully from port to port, perhaps twenty will do. Legal manning scales are based upon the absolute minimum number of people that a compliant government bureau or agency estimates can do the job.

There is a difference, however, between the smallest number of people who can be induced to man a vessel, and the number required for her safe operation under all reasonable circumstances. As anyone who has followed the sea for many years can testify, you can go a long way on luck. Fatigue is not a constant threat. Unfortunately it is most likely to be felt after a short stay in port, but the pilot has usually had sufficient rest. Once the vessel gets beyond the pilot station everyone can *normally* relax. The master can turn in, the autopilot can be engaged. The mate on watch may even be able to doze (this is not a recommendation, but an observation of what might happen) if the captain is sleeping. The people on inbound ships will probably be alert and give you a wide berth. After a good night's rest everyone is right as rain. If fog sets in, or the vessel is bound down a treacherous coast, or a gale springs up and the mate is called out with the watch below (off duty) to secure some loose gear on deck (which interferes with their rest), a little more luck may be needed. It would help, of course, if the mate didn't stand a watch, but that would require a higher level of manning.

A lot of attention is being given these days to the effect on the atmosphere of burning hydrocarbons in huge quantities, and the

225

damage done to the ozone layer by the use of fluorocarbons. Consumers are becoming progressively more critical of industries and corporations who indulge in practices that damage our environment. Perhaps it is time we give more thought to the threat to our environment posed by the careless and reckless operation of ships using our ports.

Concepts such as the 'right of free passage' and 'freedom of the seas' need to be tempered by the recognitition that insistence on rights without an acceptance of corresponding responsibilities often leads to infringement of the rights of others. If we allow a shipowner the right to use our ports, we have the right to expect he will operate his ship in a manner which will minimize the hazards of that venture. The vessel must not only be competently manned, but sufficiently manned so that fatigue does not erode the judgment on which competence is based. In commenting on the wreck of an under-manned Greek vessel in attempting to enter the Columbia river in Oregon in bad weather without a pilot the American judge quoted the opinion of a colleague a half-century earlier. 'It is a matter of common knowledge that safety in anything which requires human effort depends, in the last analysis, on the human being. A weary man is infinitely more dangerous than a defective pipe or an obscured light, because he is unfit to discover the unfitness of the inanimate object.'[24]

When it came time for Mr Horricks to respond to the question, 'Can international shipping be self-regulating?' he agreed with both Mr Davis and Mr Lindfelt that the answer was a qualified 'yes.' He was understandably distrustful of unilateral attempts by governments at regulation, and he expressed no more confidence in the altruism of shipping companies. He thought that the Port State Control (see Appendix 11) programme had 'been remarkably successful' in curbing the worst excesses of sub-standard shipowners. One was left, however, with the impression that he believed that the industry and its ancillary services were doing a rather better job than they were generally credited with.

My own answer to the question, 'Can international shipping be self-regulating?' is 'Perhaps, but not without some help.' It was appropriate that this question was posed by the Nautical Institute, because that organization is admirably equipped to offer just the sort of help needed.

What the international shipping industry seems incapable of doing is coming to grips with the manning problem. It is obvious that the shipowner is not always the best judge of how his ship should be manned if the interests of safety are to be accorded their rightful place. His attitude to safe manning is too often coloured by the standards of his competitors. Government agencies, who are entrusted to regulate such things, are too vulnerable to political and commercial pressures to be trusted in such a delicate matter.

The underwriters, except for a few such as Lars Lindfelt, decline to become involved in such a contentious affair. They maintain that their expertise lies in the assessment of risk, though it would seem that they could benefit from some help in this matter.

The classification societies, who in effect give a guarantee of the physical soundness – seaworthiness – of the ship, are themselves vulnerable to commercial pressures that might render suspect their further involvement in matters of safety beyond their present brief.

The ship's master, who is best placed to make a judgement, (relying on the technical advice of his classification society surveyor) on the seaworthiness of his ship (which includes its manning), must unfortunately be disqualified because he is beholden to his employers for his job. The responsible shipowner will usually defer to the master's judgement if he declines to take his ship to sea because of a defect in her equipment, or because of the severity of the weather, or perhaps even because he and his officers are in need of rest. A master, however, who refused to sail because he was dissatisfied with the prescribed (by his employer) manning level of his ship would soon be confronted by his relief.

Minimum manning standards only encourage a shipowner to reduce the number of his crew as near to that figure as possible. What is needed are optimum manning standards where safe operation is the guide. Competition as a means of securing the lowest freight rates for the consumer (shipper/importer) is all very well as long as all the players (shipowners) observe the same rules. When some players make their own rules, as some registries allow, then there arises a need to right the imbalance.

Ships are currently classed by classification societies as regards the standard of their construction, machinery and equipment. Underwriters, as Lars Lindfelt pointed out, rely upon this classification as a means of gauging the risk involved in issuing a policy for hull insurance, though he apparently feels that the mere fact of classification is an insufficient recommendation. Mr Lindfelt, along with others, has suggested that the classification societies should certify not only the ship but the owners.[25]

There is certainly a need for some regulation of owners. Whether there is a seafaring equivalent of Gresham's Law where the bad tends to drive out the good, there is considerable evidence that good shipowners are finding it increasingly difficult to compete. Whether the classification societies, however, are the best qualified for the job is debatable. The simplest and surest means of judging the fitness of an owner, I submit, is by the quality and adequacy of the manning of his ships.

The people best qualified to pass judgement on the adequacy of the manning and competence of the master and crew are those who have faced the problems and risks themselves and not been found wanting, and are not subject to the necessity to please an employer. The Nautical Institute (perhaps in co-operation with similar bodies elsewhere), I suggest, has the people, the experience, and the will – I believe – to address that problem.

Conclusion

What are the lessons to be learned from these casualties? Perhaps the most common and persistent factor is the neglect of safety considerations by almost all of those concerned. Captain Smith knew the danger of proceeding at high speed at night in the presence of icebergs, but prior to the loss of *Titanic* it was an accepted practice. Bruce Ismay's unwillingness to provide an adequate number of lifeboats was unchallenged by any government regulation. The failure to conduct proper emergency drills and the resistance to the use of inert gas systems in the carriage of oil cargoes is yet more evidence of this neglect. The desire to economize where the vessel was approaching the end of its useful life led those responsible for such decisions to turn a blind eye to the need for essential repairs aboard *Marine Electric* and the French tanker *Betelgeuse*. The laudable but misguided wish of those in charge of *Berge Istra* and her sister ship *Berge Vanga* to expedite repair work, led them to ignore safe working practices, probably causing the destruction of those vessels. The sacrifice of safety to economic expediency is further demonstrated in the use of ro-ro ferries in the carriage of passengers. In the recent capsizing of the *Herald of Free Enterprise* in the entrance to the port of Zeebrugge the disregard of safety measures was so shocking that criminal charges have been brought against those involved.[1]

It is a commonplace in the shipping industry that while everyone is willing to talk about safety few are willing to do anything about it.[2] A familiar explanation is that while the implementation of safety measures and provision of equipment adds directly to the cost of operating a ship no compensating advantage can be directly attributed to such expense. Indeed, the immediate result of installing safety equipment aboard a ship is an increase in the insurance premiums since it will cost that much more to replace the vessel in the event of her loss.

While we can see in retrospect how neglect of safety procedures and practices can produce the most horrific results, that is only clear after the event. It is not merely that the owners and operators are unenthusiastic in trumpeting the virtues of safety, the masters and those who serve under them are often equally bored by drills and safety procedures that appear to interfere with their job. Experience can of course provide a corrective, assuming one survives the experience. It seemingly requires a *Titanic*, a *Morro Castle*, an *Andrea Doria*, a *Torrey Canyon*, a *Herald of Free Enterprise* or an *Exxon Valdez* to remind us that we neglect prudence at our peril.

If the people who sail ships and those who employ them share a lack of urgency about this critical matter then the prospects for improvement seem slim. In an atmosphere where short-term economic considerations prevail there seems to be no practical alternative to instituting regulation to enforce the measures needed for protection of the public interest. Unfortunately the national regulatory agencies such as the USCG and the British Department of Transport are prone to suffer from the 'locking the barn door after the horse has bolted' syndrome. This is not to suggest that their efforts are entirely futile, but in a context where changes are occurring at an escalating pace action, rather than reaction, is needed.

While regulatory bodies may help effect an improvement in safety standards the chief hope must lie with those whose lives and livelihood are directly involved. Ships' masters are not disinterested in safety, but by and large they are not encouraged to spend much effort or money in pursuit of its elusive benefits. The best of them, however, know only too well that safety and efficiency are inextricably intertwined. One of the key aspects of the master's job is the evaluation of risk, and determination of the best way to minimize it. The safe completion of the voyage is the common goal of all, owner,[3] captain, crew and passengers. It should thus be in everyone's interest to avoid any practice or procedure that might interfere with this process.

Modern communications systems make it possible for the ship's master to contact his home office at any hour of the day or night. This can be an invaluable aid in supplying him with technical support or advice in arriving at a sound decision in an emergency, but it also allows shore staff to interfere (see appendix 12). It has become an accepted strategy by many of the new breed of ship owners and operators to hire masters of limited capacity who, by and large, merely act as a conduit for orders passed from ashore. The flaw in this arrangement, however, is that men who are willing to accept such a truncated command role are unlikely to have much taste for, or ability to make, hard decisions. When an emergency suddenly develops in the middle of the night, which calls for immediate action and may involve the survival of the ship and its crew, the master may hesitate and prevaricate with predictably disastrous results.

As long as the underwriters are prepared to cover the risks of such imprudence at a reasonable rate, such policies may result in a short-term competitive advantage. Whether they provide an acceptable foundation from the standpoint of providing efficient (which includes minimal risk to the public) ocean transport is questionable. Such an operating philosophy may be well suited to dealing with the routine problems of ship operation, but it suffers from potentially fatal flaws when an emergency interrupts the routine. There can be no substitute for quality manning if the pursuit of private profit at public expense is to be avoided. Efficient operation in the sense that the term is used here requires not only seamen of high calibre, but management policies that allow them to function with a minimum of interference (see appendix 13.)

One of the major obstacles to accomplishment of this desideratum is the increasing reliance on casual employment of key personnel. The casualty suffered by *Mycene* demonstrated clearly the disastrous consequences of such policies. Mutual confidence and trust are essential to efficient performance, which can best be achieved through continuity of association, and while that in itself is not enough, as we saw with the *Morro Castle*, we can hardly deny its necessity.

The inescapable conclusion is that prevailing arrangements on board ships flying flags of the so-called 'free world' are often woefully inadequate from the standpoint of safety, particularly when that nation has no substantial maritime tradition. There is a temptation in the marine industry to look to the airline industry for guidance in the area of regulation. There is no question but that safety imposes itself upon the operation of aircraft in a manner that those mariners interested in the promotion of safety might well envy, but in looking for an example it might be more pertinent to consider what has happened in the airline industry in the United States after almost a decade of deregulation. Many seem to feel that airline deregulation has led to deteriorating standards of safety along with higher costs to the consumer. Can it be then that the public might benefit from more rather than less regulation of the maritime industry?

Aside from the costs of administration and bureaucratic inefficiency it is doubtful that this would be a profitable road to follow. The accepted and natural vehicle for international regulation of marine affairs is IMO and other allied international bodies. While IMO has achieved some notable successes in regulation, such as the many traffic separation schemes it has encouraged and approved, the type of improvements needed might make it a less effective vehicle for change.

If safety in operating ships is to be improved it will probably be best achieved by convincing those who operate ships that safety is good business. Unfortunately as was noted earlier, there is little incentive for the individual shipowner to institute innovations that will inevitably increase his operating costs without any certainty of future benefits. In such case the imposition of safety measures through international treaty is perhaps the only means of achieving worth-while progress, though a promising exception to this is the initiative recently shown by underwriters in granting a reduced premium to vessels equipped with inert gas systems. To impose specific safety measures through a national regulatory agency may only result in penalizing those least likely to offend.[4]

Finally, the key figure in any attempt to enhance shipboard safety standards is, of course, the man, or woman, in command. Up until shortly after the First World War underwriters took into account the casualty record of the master in arriving at the insurance premium charged. This sensible practice was abandoned for administrative reasons, and it became the practice to rely on the fleet record of the owner. In effect this is a reflection of the average performance of all the masters in the fleet.

A return to such a system could go some way towards encouraging the employment of masters with a proven record of competent service, but it would be unfair to 'put all the eggs in the master's basket' without giving him some say in the appointment of those who would help him carry out his task. This would entail some drastic restruc-turing of the way of choosing masters and their officers and crew, and there will be no attempt made here to explore that path.[5] However, unless the degradation of safety standards aboard ships throughout the 'free world' is to continue unchecked the implementation of radical changes in the way ships are now manned is a pressing necessity.[6] Without this, increased pressures for regulation of a unilateral kind, such as followed the *Amoco Cadiz* and *Argo Merchant* strandings and will almost certainly follow the accident to the *Exxon Valdez*, is an unwelcome likelihood.

Glossary

A.B.: Able seaman.

ABAFT: Aft of.

ALLEYWAY: Passageway or corridor.

AZIMUTH: A compass bearing of a heavenly body used to calculate compass error.

BIGHT: A sag in a rope or line.

BITS: Twin steel posts around which mooring lines are made fast.

BULKHEADS: Steel walls.

CABLE: 100 fathoms or 600 feet.

CHIPPY: A nickname for the carpenter.

COMPARTMENT: A space enclosed by bulkheads.

CONN: Control.

CONDENSER: A type of pump that converts steam into water by cooling it with sea water.

COUNTER: Overhang of a ship's stern.

CQ: A morse signal meaning 'Attention all ships'.

CQD: As above, but signalling greater urgency.

CW: Continuous wave wireless transmission, Morse code.

DECCA: A short range electronic navigational system.

DOGS: A metal device similar to a butterfly nut, used to tighten a door or port against a gasket to make it watertight.

DONKEYMAN: An engine department rating.

ENGINE-ROOM TELEGRAPH: A signalling device for transmitting engine orders from the bridge to the engine room.

FIDLEY: The enclosed space surrounding the stack exhaust.

FLYING BRIDGE: Above the wheelhouse.

FO'C'SLE HEAD: The forward part of the ship from the stem to the beginning of the first cargo compartment. Was originally used for crew quarters, hence, forecastle or fo'c'sle.

GREASER: Oiler, an engine department rating responsible for lubricating machinery.

GUNWALE: Upper edge of a boat's side.

HOT WORK: Welding or cutting with an acetylene torch.

IMO: International Maritime Organization.

JACOB'S LADDER: A rope ladder with wooden rungs.

LONGITUDINAL: A term used to denote a strength member (a steel beam) running fore and aft.

LEEWAY: Correction applied to a course to offset the displacement effect of wind.

LINE: A length of rope.

MONITORS: Fixed fire nozzles.

OBO: Ship designed to carry either oil or ore cargoes.

ON LINE: In operation.

PORT SIDE: Left side of ship facing forward.

RADIO SHACK: Radio room, the place where the radio equipment is located.

RHUMB LINE: A straight line drawn on a chart as opposed to a curved great circle line.

SCANTLINGS: Structural members.

SCUPPER: A drain.

SEA PAINTER: A line used to secure a lifeboat to the ship.

SHELL: The side or envelope of the ship's hull.

SMOKE HELMET: Fresh air breathing apparatus.

SOLAS: Safety of Life at Sea.

SPARKS: A nickname for the radio officer.

SPRING LINE: A mooring line leading in the opposite direction to the head and stern lines.

TRIM: The difference between the draught forward and aft.

VHF: Very high frequency.

WATERTIGHT DOOR: A steel door that when closed makes a compartment watertight.

Appendices

1: MARCONI

In the early days of wireless telegraphy the operators of the ship stations were actually employees of the owners of the station and were assigned to vessels by these employers, as is witnessed by the fact that Phillips had served aboard both of White Star's competitor Cunard's chief vessels, *Mauretania* and *Lusitania*, not long before his assignment to *Oceanic* from which he was transferred to *Titanic*. As they were therefore not properly 'members of the family' they were often treated as intruders and interlopers by the ship's officers. They did not mess with the officers and, regarded with disdain if not scorn, they were less likely to share the sense of loyalty to the vessel felt by the rest of the ship's crew.

2: STABILITY

It is commonly believed, even by many seamen, that the cause of vessels foundering is due to an initial loss of reserve buoyancy, which is the amount of intact watertight capacity below the vessel's main deck. It is extremely rare for a vessel to suffer such initial damage, so the widespread belief that *Titanic* was 'unsinkable' was not as misconceived as is commonly supposed. What ordinarily happens when vessels founder is that they first lose stability (the ability to float upright and on a comparatively even keel) with a resulting list, which then submerges openings in intact compartments, which leads to progressive flooding and ultimate sinking.

In order to remain afloat a vessel must satisfy three basic conditions. She must not only possess positive transverse stability, which keeps her from assuming a list, but her longitudinal stability, which determines her trim (difference in draught fore and aft), must be sufficient to keep her main deck from submerging at the extremities and so allow entry of water through openings (hatches, vents, etc.) that would not normally be submerged. Lastly, she must possess more intact reserve buoyancy than her displacement.

Normally an undamaged vessel will float upright with a slight trim by the stern. In this condition her intact buoyancy will be divided into two equal halves separated by a horizontal plane that intersects the centre of gravity of the vessel and the centre of buoyancy, which is the geometrical centre of the volume of the submerged portion of the vessel. In order to remain normally afloat her displacement forward of this dividing plane must be equal to the displacement aft, and the sum of the two equal halves will equal the total displacement at any given time. At different conditions of loading and consumption of fuel and water this plane will shift slightly so as to give an equal displacement on each side.

When the ship suffers damage such that her hull is ruptured and loss of buoyancy ensues, the centre of gravity will remain the same except for the effects of displacement of the cargo and internal members of the vessel in the flooded compartment. This displacement of the centre of gravity will ordinarily be slight, but the loss of buoyant capacity represented by the external volume of the flooded compartment will usually result in a substantial shift of the centre of buoyancy of the ship away from the point of damage. The vessel will thus trim markedly towards the damage, as her intact compartments on the damaged end submerge deeper in order to make up for the loss of displacement in the flooded space. This loss will roughly equal the underwater displacement volume of the flooded compartment or compartments, minus the displacement volume of the cargo in these compartments and the displacement of the structural part of the vessel in the damaged spaces.

When the damage on one end of this longitudinal dividing displacement plane (LDDP) results in the loss of more than one half of the original intact displacement (as happened in the case of *Titanic*), the vessel will attempt to assume an angle of flotation corresponding to the new conditions, i.e., she will attempt to float 'end up', so to speak. The new position of the LDDP will shift dramatically away from the damaged end (aft in the case of *Titanic*). In such a state of temporary equilibrium the fore part (or aft as the case may be) of the damaged vessel will become completely submerged and the intact compartments in the portion of the hull forward of the new position of the

LDDP will begin to flood through the hatches, vents and other openings unable to withstand this submerged pressure, or incapable of being effectively closed. At this new angle of flotation the pressure on the foremost bulkhead of the most forward intact compartment will almost certainly exceed its designed capacity. The vessel in this new position will thus remain poised for a moment before the bulkhead collapses under the pressure, and then the succeeding intact watertight bulkheads will quickly collapse under the impact of the rapid ingress of water as the vessel begins her plunge to the bottom.

Alternatively, as shall be seen in some of the other cases in this book, the loss of transverse stability will cause the vessel to list to the point where her deck edge on the low side will become submerged and her intact compartment will progressively flood as vents, ports and other openings come under water until all reserve buoyancy is lost and the vessel sinks. This is often a much more leisurely process and the vessel may remain afloat on her side for some hours, such as was the case with *Andrea Doria* following her collision with *Stockholm*.[1] Before this happens a shift of cargo may occur due to the vessel's extreme list causing her to turn turtle. In this case the vessel may remain afloat indefinitely upside down.

3: AUTO-ALARM

Ships are now equipped with an auto-alarm receiver which is activated by a series of dashes sent out prior to the transmission of a distress signal. The auto-alarm is turned on when the radio operator is off watch. This signal, when received by the auto-alarm, causes an alarm bell to sound in the radio officer's quarters and on the bridge thereby alerting the operator to the distress signal.

4: CLASSIFICATION SOCIETIES

Although there is no legal requirement that a ship be classed, the need for the owner to prove that his ship is seaworthy in order to obtain insurance makes the practice almost universal. Over the years the courts have come to accept that a hull and machinery certificate issued by a recognized classification society is prima-facie evidence of a vessel's seaworthiness in respect to its hull and machinery. The choice of classification society rests with the owner, however, and while the standards of classification societies tend to be more or less identical the rigour with which they adhere to these standards can be less than uniform. A society that insists too strongly that a shipowner carry out a repair in order for his ship to remain in class may find that the shipowner will turn to another society for classification.

Marshall Meek, a well-known and highly respected British naval architect, and his associates point out that '. . . it is a fact that owners sometimes switch from one classification society to another from preference – and it could be to obtain easier approval of safety features. One can detect too, a certain competition for business between societies, which are commercial bodies, which some would say ill becomes safety authorities. . . .'[2]

Moreover, when a switch is made from one classification society to another the ship's record is not passed from one society to another, which could encourage neglect and oversight of deficiencies.

Safety standards are themselves largely set by the classification societies. As the owners are the clients of the classification societies, the latter are sometimes subject to competitive pressures that can lead to a relaxation of their own rules. During the boom in shipbuilding in the 1960s one of the major classification societies tried to increase their market share by relaxing specifications for new vessels, viz., the degree of thickness of steel plates and other less stringent design features, with respect to their safety. The other classification societies reluctantly followed suit. The lowered standards, however, created unforeseen problems resulting in modification of the new rules. The damage to international standards, however, was done.[3]

Michael Grey, the former editor of the international shipping weekly *Fairplay*, related some time ago in the weekly 'Lookout' column of that magazine the experience of a potential purchaser of a tanker. The gentleman in question had the opportunity to inspect the vessel and found her in a shocking state of repair. Perhaps remembering what had happened to *Betelgeuse* and *Marine Electric* he somewhat naively felt the classification society involved should be appraised of the facts. His answer was a letter from their solicitors threatening him with legal proceedings for defamation.

The idea, however, that mere compliance with existing governmental and existing classification society rules is the final word in the design and construction of ships is only accurate to a point. The courts will almost always defer to the judgement of such authorities, but 'they have the authority in themselves to decide in any particular case what standard ought to apply.'[4]

5: METACENTRIC HEIGHT

GM, or metacentric height, is the measure of a vessel's stability or resistance to inclination. The theory behind this is involved and no attempt will be made here to explain it fully. It is dependent in large degree, however, on the area of the water-plane at which the vessel is floating. Hence when the stability is eroded by free surface to a negative value the vessel must list in order to increase the area of the water-plane to restore a state of stable equilibrium. At that point, however, the vessel will have zero GM, or very close to it, and will have very little resistance to heeling. Once the vessel heels, or lists, to the point where the deck edge of the highest enclosed deck is submerged, the area of the water-plane will begin to decrease with a further list and the ship will capsize.

The determination of ship stability in its simplest sense is a matter of calculation of the centre of gravity of the vessel and other weights it carries, of which its cargo, fuel and water are the major items. This figure, known as KG, is then subtracted from the metacentric height, known as KM, to give the figure GM, which is the measure of the vessel's stability at that displacement. The calculation of KM is indeed a complicated process understood by few seamen, and it need not concern us here. It varies with the ship's displacement as measured by her draught. The values for it are supplied by the shipbuilder in a stability booklet compiled by them. Also given are minimum values of GM required for all situations of loading from a light ship state, when the ship has no cargo, to its fully loaded condition. These minimum values are based upon the loss of GM which would occur if the vessel suffered damage resulting in flooding of her single largest compartment.

The GM a vessel has on any particular occasion is also a measure of her ability to resist heeling or rolling in a seaway. If she has a large GM she will have greater resistance to wave motion that causes her to roll, but once she starts to move her motion in the seaway will be quicker and more uncomfortable. This is known as stiffness, and the quicker or shorter the rolling period of a vessel, the greater the stress on the vessel and her cargo and the more likelihood of the cargo shifting.

6: AMVER

This system, which is voluntary but provided free of charge to all who wish to participate, enables the USCG AMVER facility in New

York to keep track of participating vessels through a computer. When a vessel leaves from a port she simply sends a message to the USCG giving her departure time from the port, her anticipated speed, the route she intends to follow, and her expected ETA (estimated time of arrival) at her destination. She is also asked to update her position if she deviates from her anticipated progress by more than 25 miles during the voyage. The computer can thus track the progress of the vessel during her voyage and predict her position at any given time with a fair degree of accuracy.

7: COMPASS COURSES

The course steered is the gyro compass course. Gyro compasses are normally quite accurate having little or no error. If there is no error the gyro and true courses are the same. The magnetic compass today is now a backup compass in case the gyro compass fails. Its heading will often differ substantially by a predictable amount from the gyro heading. This results from the fact that the magnetic pole is in northern Canada, about 900 miles south of the true pole. This is called variation, and it varies from zero to over twenty degrees depending upon the observer's position on the earth's surface. The other element of magnetic compass error is called deviation. It is caused by the magnetic field of the ship itself. It will vary according to the heading of the ship, but ordinarily it does not exceed about ten degrees.

8: TRAFFIC SEPARATION SCHEMES

The first traffic separation scheme was set up in the Dover Strait in the late 1960s under the guidance of The Royal Institute of Navigation. Since that time they have proliferated around the globe. They are normally situated in international waters and are approved by the International Maritime Organization (IMO) in London.

The purpose of the TSS is to separate the inbound from the outbond traffic in much the same manner that automobile traffic is separated on a motorway. Separation schemes are *not*, however, designed to prevent accidents such as that which happened to the *Exxon Valdez*, though they obviously have to provide a safe route for the vessels that pass through them. The TSS will not necessarily be the most direct route, since it is designed for all vessels and all conditions and thus must be a compromise.

Where the TSS is set up in national waters, as was the one in Price William Sound, there will often be a Vessel Traffic Control (VTC) station associated with it to monitor the movements of vessels, and in some cases actually control traffic. This was not a function of the VTC in Prince William Sound.

9: AUTOPILOTS

The reasons why the use of the autopilot is not recommended in confined waters or during periods of reduced visibility, are to a degree based upon inherent defects and inadequacies of such systems. Until fairly recently autopilots, of which the Sperry Mark XIV and the Kelvin Hughes were typical, switching from auto to manual steering was awkward and could take several seconds or more. The switching arrangements, even on the same make and model, could be different on different ships. This was ordinarily of no consequence where the individuals involved were familiar with the vessel and its equipment, but particularly as crew changes became more freqent the possibility of delay and confusion in switching from auto to manual steering increased.

These older systems were also composed of two separate elements. The transmission of steering signals in autopilot mode, via the application of helm (e.g. ten degrees right rudder) to the steering engine that moves the rudder, was accomplished electrically. The manual steering system was hydraulic. The manual steering systems tended to be less prone to failure, which was a further reason for preference in situations where another vessel or shoal water was in close proximity.

Replacement of electrical components by electronic circuitry have greatly increased the reliability of the new steering systems. Hydraulic steering systems have all but been abandoned in the construction of new ships. The transmission of helm orders to the rudder is now the same for both manual and autopilot systems. Dependability is no longer an issue on most ships built in the last twenty years or so. Ease of switching between auto and hand steering, with a steering system such as that found on *Exxon Valdez*, should not be a problem (that it may have been a problem in this case is a different problem).

The main objection to the use of the autopiolt is in traffic situations

where the near approach of another ship may require an instantan-
ious response to avoid collision, (see my *Collisions*, chapter Twelve,
Cockcroft, pp. 40–41, 217, and Mankkabady, p. 52), and when a
vessel is proceeding along a narrow channel (usually in pilotage
waters) where frequent course changes are necessary.

There is also a further objection to the use of the autopilot that
receives little recognition, though it has no direct bearing upon the
case at hand. Because autopilots are now so reliable and capable of
steering a better course than any helmsman they tend to be used
whenever conditions permit. Many masters of vessels flying flags of
the traditional maritime nations insisted, because of the limitations,
technical and otherwise, of automatic steering systems, that their
vessels be steered by hand during hours of darkness, reduced visibility, and in areas where there was a high risk of collision or grounding.
This ultra conservative posture tended to become the standard by
which the courts judged the propriety of its use. It came to be known
in the jargon of maritime law as 'the ordinary practice of seamen.'

With the advent of greatly improved autopilots, however, this
attitude had come to be regarded as outmoded by many seamen and
those who hire them. The courts, however, change their opinions
much less readily. As infractions of the courts' view of 'the ordinary
practice of seamen,' based upon past experience, can expose the
established shipowner to horrendous penalties, those responsible for
the operation of his ships must adopt policies in accordance with the
current legal concept of the 'the ordinary practice of seamen.'

10: OIL COMPANIES

The oil companies are in a fundamentally different position from
most other shipowners. They do not compete with other shipowners
for cargoes. The cargoes they carry are usually their own. Their
business is not the transportation of cargo for profit. They own ships
in order to transport their oil efficiently.

Oil companies have traditionally maintained fleets only sufficient
to meet their needs at the bottom of the economic cycle. They depend
on the charter market to carry the surplus in good times. This is not
to say that their ship operations are immune from market generated
pressures. If operating expenses for company owned ships rise too
high the option to replace them with chartered vessels will become

more attractive. There is, however, probably no well defined point which dictates a switch to this option.

11: PORT STATE CONTROL

Because of the problems associated with sub-standard ships the Port State Control system was set up in E.E.C. countries to conduct spot checks on vessels in E.E.C. ports to see that these ships confirm to international standards in respect to safety and navigational equipment, manning and certification. Vessels found to have significant defects can be subject to detention until such defects are rectified.

12: SHIP-TO-SHORE COMMUNICATIONS

Since the introduction of wireless telegraphy it has been an almost universal policy of shipowners to require their masters to report details of all ship casualties as soon as feasible after their occurrence. Until the adoption of modern communications systems this was done by wireless telegraphy. Now that direct telephone links are common between ship and shore masters are directed to establish phone contact at the earliest possible moment. It thus happens that except in the case of a collision the master will often be in phone contact with his immediate superior ashore during the development of the emergency. This can be a source of considerable distraction at a time when the utmost concentration is required. Much time can be wasted in trying to explain the situation to the person ashore, and even under the best of circumstances the description may lead to misunderstanding and misconception. Not infrequently it will interfere with decisions being taken and even lead to mistakes, a notorious example of this being the delay in asking for tug assistance in the stranding of the *Amoco Cadiz*.[5]

13: DECENTRALIZED SHIP MANAGEMENT

While the introduction of sophisticated communications equipment aboard ship in the 1970s allowed ship operators to exercise highly centralized control over their ships it also allowed the converse. Some owners in Scandinavia and elsewhere in northern Europe decided to use these advanced communications systems to embark on an experiment in decentralized ship management. The evolvement of ship management staff ashore had originally come about for a variety of reasons, but not least of these was the fact that many operational decisions could not be made aboard ship because the master lacked the necessary information. With a satellite link the master now could access that information, and so the idea was to return the management of these affairs to those on the scene.[6] Great care was taken in the choice of masters and other senior officers, and some impressive results were obtained.[7] At the time long-term employment contracts were the norm on many northwest European ships. In the study *Effective Manning of the US Merchant Fleet*, the authors remarked:

> . . . European ship operators are interested in long-term contracts with seafarers because of the employment stability that they bring. The operators are convinced that longer association between seafarer and ship, and among crews, results in greater operating efficiency. . . . Also, as the size of vessel crews diminishes, the quality of the crew and crew organization become more important.[8]

Unfortunately cut-throat competition has driven many of these operators from the industry, and many of those who are left have chosen to adopt the easier course of adopting the policies of their competitors. Casual employment is becoming increasingly common, and employers are seeking to cut their manning costs to the bone with scant regard for safe practice.

Decentralized ship management schemes require high calibre personnel with an independent cast of mind; the willingness to accept responsibility is probably to a considerable degree dependent upon this latter quality. The most favourable conditions for the implementation of such a scheme are likely to be found in those companies where there exists a large degree of continuity of employment; where the officers and ratings are 'home-grown', so to speak. It is only under such conditions that the owner is likely to have enough confidence in his masters and other officers to entrust them with such a high level of responsibility. Except for the fleets of some of the oil companies these conditions are found only on ships flying the flags of traditional maritime nations, and even there the situation is rapidly deteriorating.

Many years ago when serving as a young chief officer under an extremely able master of Norwegian descent he told me that he had chosen to spend the major portion of his career in the Far East and

Australian services since this gave him the greatest freedom from interference from the head office in New York. He also gave me the widest possible latitude in running the ship under his command. Although these views and practices were perhaps not typical they were not uncommon, and I believe they were typical among the best masters.

In early 1981 I had a conversation with the late Captain R. K. N. Emden, then commanding officer of the UK coast guard station at St Margaret's Bay in the Dover Strait, concerning the resistance of ship's masters to taking advice. He remarked that he found the young masters today much less resistant to direction than those with a more traditional background. I believe this is due in large part to the fact that modern shipboard communications expose them to advice and direction from ashore much more readily today than several decades earlier. There is simply less opportunity for independent decision making, and that, I suggest, bodes ill for the future.

Notes

Introduction

1. Boswell's *Life* vol. 1, p. 348.
2. The conflict in the chief officer's duties was brought to the attention of the Townsend-Thoresen director responsible for vessel operations, J. K. Develin, by Captain Hackett, senior master of *The Herald of Free Enterprise*, in a memorandum of 21 August 1982 (*Report of Court 8074*, London, HMSO, p. 11). Cf. also p. 5.
   '. . . immediately loading was complete the chief officer felt under pressure to leave G deck to go to his station on the bridge.' The pressure put on the vessel's personnel to sail at the first possible moment is also exemplified by an internal memorandum sent to assistant managers in the port of Zeebrugge by the operations manager there in August 1986: '. . . put pressure on the first officer if you don't think he is moving fast enough. . . . Let's put the record straight, sailing late out of Zeebrugge isn't on. It's fifteen minutes early for us.'
3. If a shipowner spends $100,000 on a safety feature, which by any reasonable standard should reduce the ship's exposure to risk (providing it is properly used), usually the underwriter will simply increase the insurance premium by an amount sufficient to cover the additional cost of the vessel and its equipment. It was only recently that any exception to this practice was made. The loss of such ships as *Berge Istra*, *Berge Vanga* and *Mycene*, due to lack of or failure to use an inert gas system (see page 160), led underwriters to offer a premium reduction to those owners who equipped their ships with such a system (see Hodgson's *Lloyd's of London*, Harmondsworth, Penguin, 1986, pp. 157–8). Underwriters almost without exception steadfastly maintain that safety is no part of their business, or to put it another way, 'there is no such thing as a bad risk: only a bad rate' (*Ibid.*, pp. 153–4).
4. See F. M. van Poelgeest, 'Sub-Standard Tankers', Rotterdam, Netherlands Maritime Institute, 1978, pp. 1, 25–7.
5. Some of the former British Dominions might also be included. I am ignoring the Soviet bloc nations and also China. They form a separate category in that they are not unqualified victims of market pressures.
6. The 'old-fashioned' owner with an operating philosophy steeped in tradition is on the verge of extinction. The family-owned or controlled companies that were dominant in the major maritime nations until recently have been all but supplanted by consortia and conglomerates. See Tony Lane, *Grey Dawn Breaking*, Manchester, Manchester University Press, 1986, pp. 12–16.

1: The Loss of *Titanic*

1. See Roy Anderson, *White Star*, Prescot, (Lancashire), T. Stephenson & Sons, 1964, pp. 97–8. Cf. also Geoffrey Marcus, *The Maiden Voyage*, London, Allen & Unwin, 1969, pp. 207, 211; and Michael Davie, *The Titanic: The Full Story of a Tragedy*, London,

The Bodley Head, 1986, pp. 9–12. Davie contends that though Morgan talked Ismay into taking ostensible control of White Star, the responsible decisions were ultimately made by Morgan.

2. See Senate Documents 463, US Congress, 1912, vol. 28, pp. 170, 199; cf. also Wilton J. Oldham, *The Ismay Line*, Liverpool, published by *The Journal of Commerce*, 1961, p. 172.

3. See K. C. Barnaby, *Some Ship Disasters and their Causes*, London, Hutchinson, 1968, pp. 95–8; cf. also *Ocean Liners of the Past: The White Star Triple Screw Liners Olympic and Titanic*, London, 1970, Patrick Stevens, pp. 152–4. This contains a reproduction of the special issue of the *Shipbuilder* of 1911, which was devoted to the two vessels. See also Anderson, pp. 109–110.

4. Charles Herbert Lightoller, *Titanic and Other Ships*, London, Ivor Nicholson & Watson, 1935, p. 214.

5. Quoted from Marcus, p. 39.

6. See HMSO's *Formal Investigation into the Loss of the Titanic*, London, 1912, p. 431 (referred to as *British Inquiry*).

7. Lightoller, p. 218.

8. Marcus, p. 82.

9. *British Inquiry*, pp. 520–1, 716; cf. also Conrad, Joseph, *Some Aspects of the Admirable Inquiry into the Loss of the Titanic*, London, 1919, pp. 29–39.

10. Lightoller, p. 219.

11. Contrary to popular legend it was *Olympic* rather than *Titanic* that occupied the limelight at the time of their construction. See *Ocean Liners of the Past*, p. 152.

12. Cf. R. A. Cahill, *Strandings and their Causes*, London, Fairplay Publications, 1985, pp. 21, 91, 124.

13. Marcus, p. 123.

14. *Ibid.*, p. 44. Cf. also J. P. Eaton & C. A. Haas, *Titanic Destination Disaster – the Legends and the Reality*, Wellingborough, Patrick Stevens, 1987, p. 89.

15. *British Inquiry*, pp. 734, 739–40, but cf. Oldham, p. 187.

16. Davie has suggested that Captain Smith was perhaps less careful of risk than most (p. 29).

17. Marcus, p. 58; cf. also *British Inquiry*, p. 855.

18. It was not uncommon, but by no means a universal practice, to supply lookouts with binoculars on some passenger ships. They were carried aboard *Olympic*, but Second Officer Lightoller was one of those who was less than enthusiastic about the practice. See Senate Documents 463, vol. 40, 'Loss of the Steamship *Titanic*', pp. 38, 80; cf. also *British Inquiry*, pp. 290, 307–8, 532, 618, 627; and *Ocean Liners of the Past*, p. 147: 'the use of binoculars by lookout men is not recommended'.

19. Senate Document 463, vol. 40, p. 41.

20. See Barnaby, p. 121; but cf. also Conrad's comments in *Some Reflections Seamanlike and Otherwise on the Loss of the Titanic*, published by *The English Review II*, 1912, pp. 16–20, and *British Inquiry*, pp. 485, 725–6, 765.

21. See Eaton & Haas, p. 147.

22. Quoted from Marcus, p. 80.

23. *Ocean Liners of the Past*, p. 26.

24. Senate Documents 463, vol. 28, p. 28. Captain Rostron's knowledge of stability seems somewhat sketchy.

25. Lord, Walter *A Night to Remember*, Harmondsworth, Penguin, 1976, p. 73; cf. also *British Inquiry*, p. 740.

26. *British Inquiry*, p. 697. The CQ call was then the international distress call. The SOS call now used had only recently been proposed, and it was in fact used by Phillips later at the suggestion of his assistant. This was the first known use of the SOS call.

27. See Brian Elliot, 'Where Exactly Did *Titanic* Sink?', *Safety at Sea International*, June 1980, p. 28. Elliot calculated that *Titanic* was about 8 miles ESE of the accepted

position and that the distance of *Carpathia* from the scene was about 49 rather than 58 miles. He pointed out that for *Carpathia* to have reached the speed attributed to her she would have had to develop almost three quarters more horsepower than she did at her normal cruising speed. Dr Robert Ballard in *The Discovery of the Titanic*, (Toronto, Madison Press Books, 1987, p. 199) says that *Titanic* was roughly 13.5 miles ESE of her reported position, which places the *Californian* no more than 21 miles to the NNW. Dr Ballard gives the position of the wreck as 49°56'54"N, 41°43'35"W.

28. *British Inquiry*, p. 697.
29. Senate Document 463, vol. 28, p. 426.
30. *Ibid.*, vol. 40, 'Loss of the Steamship *Titanic*', p. 53; cf. also *British Inquiry*, p. 761.
31. Senate Document 463, vol. 40, p. 28.
32. *Ibid.*, p. 206.
33. *British Inquiry*, pp. 690–2, 703, 704, 772, 776–7, 780–1, 794.
34. Marcus, p. 205.
35. *Ibid.*, p. 254.
36. See note 27.
37. *British Inquiry*, p. 311; cf. also Lightoller, p. 225.
38. See Marcus, pp. 264–74; cf. also *British Inquiry*, p. 741.
39. Quoted in Marcus, pp. 290–1.
40. Conrad, *Some Aspects*, p. 31; cf. also Marcus, p. 315, and *British Inquiry*, pp. 739, 767.
41. Lightoller, p. 257; cf. also the remarks of Conrad, *ibid.*, pp. 14–18. At the time it was said in the *Ottawa Evening Citizen* that 'The *Titanic* has been advertised as an "Express-train boat" which would leave and arrive on schedule, and with whose operation "nothing would interfere".' Quoted in Marcus, p. 205.
42. See Anderson, p. 126.

2: The Ro-Ro: An Unsafe Design

1. In 1947 the cross-channel ferry *Dinard* entered service, but she was a conversion. In 1955 the *Rigoletto* and *Traviata* of the Wallensia Line opened a car ferry service in the Baltic. In 1959 the *Princess of Tasmania* opened a service between Melbourne and Tasmania, and in 1962 the *Aramonia* began trading between Wellington and Picton. See Report of the Ro-Ro 76 Proceedings International Conference on Marine Transport Using Roll-on, Roll-off Methods. See C. L. Sauerbier, *Marine Cargo Operations*, New York, Chapman and Hall, 1964, pp. 506–8. The term 'roll-on, roll-off' was apparently coined by the US Army Transportation Corps, who pioneered the concept. See R. P. Holubowicz (ed.), *Progress in Marine Cargo Handling*, Cornell Maritime Press, vol. 3, p. 97.
3. *Report of the Ministry of Transport Inquiry into the Loss of the Motorship Princess Victoria and Findings of the Court*, Liverpool, Charles Birchall & Sons Ltd., 1953, p. 11. The Portpatrick station apparently logged this at 0932 (p. 42).
4. *Ibid.*, p. 50.
5. *Ibid.*, p. 33–5, 39–40, 45.
6. *Ibid.*, p. 72.
7. *Ibid.*, p. 11.
8. See *ibid.*, p. 42–4 for a discussion of this; also p. 49.
9. *Ibid.*, p. 13.
10. *Ibid.*, p. 40.
11. A later count listed 176 aboard, see *ibid.*, p. 56.
12. See *ibid.*, p. 66; cf. also p. 26.
13. *Ibid.*, p. 57–8.
14. The marine superintendent for the Scottish Region made the remarkable observation that 'if a ship developed a 10 degree list on passage it would not be very serious. . . .', which casts some doubt upon that gentleman's appreciation of the matter at issue here (*ibid.*, p. 60).

15. *Ibid.*, p. 106.
16. *Ibid.*, p. 100.
17. *Ibid.*, p. 108.
18. Marine accident report, *Foundering Loss of the Ro-Ro Passenger Ship Zenobia at the Roads of Lanarca, Cyprus on 7 June 1980*, p. 39–40.
19. *Ibid.*, p. 28.
20. *Ibid.*, p. 30.
21. *Report of Court 8072*, London, HMSO, pp. 12–13.
22. see R. A. Cahill, 'The Use of VHF Radio to Reduce Uncertainty in Marine Encounters', published in *The Journal of Navigation*, the Royal Institute of Navigation, May 1979, p. 259.
23. At a meeting of the Royal Institute of Naval Architects held on 17 April 1985 in London a paper was presented by J. R. Spouge entitled 'The Technical Investigation of the Sinking of the Ro-Ro Ferry *European Gateway*', London, 1985. The paper was, as its title indicated, devoted mainly to the technical aspects of the sinking, and particularly the development of the theory of transient asymmetric flooding. The majority of comments both verbal and written by the naval architects and other interested parties were directed towards that topic, but the comments of Mr Marshall Meek and Mr R. Adams, who are both prominent members of that profession, are revealing of the concern that some of them feel. After commenting on the paper they say: 'The safety of a ship in conditions of flooding whether by collision or grounding depends on (a) adequate compartmentation to contain the water entering the ship; and (b) adequate freeboard, i.e., all openings through which water may enter once the ship begins to sink or heel must remain sufficiently high above the waterline. Modern ro-ro ships like the *European Gateway* and many others are inadequate in both respects and the *European Gateway* incident proved it. It can no longer be theory or supposition. There have, of course, been several other cases which have not had the same publicity nor have they perhaps been so "near home".
    'It is instructive to consider why we have arrived at such a point in the development of ships. It is no secret that not a few naval architects have similar concerns but little is done to correct the current state of affairs. We believe it has something to do with the fact that the early ro-ros were small, short-sea vessels, where it would have been a severe limitation on their economic success to have added requirements for bulkheads or extra freeboard. From that starting point the commercial pressures which have been particularly compelling in forcing designers towards more cost effective ships, led towards rapidly increasing size of ro-ros. But the same leniency was extended towards compartmentation. And with every addition to the active world fleet of ro-ros it has become more and more difficult for designers who are concerned about the position to voice a caution or a protest. Shipbuilders will design to whatever the law allows. Shipowners' technical staff know where their monthly pay packet comes from and keep quiet; and so the unsatisfactory position continues from year to year until an event such as described in this paper occurs. The author says we should heed the lesson being taught from the accident. Instead we hear murmurings that statistics show that ro-ros are not really so much worse than other ship types, and if they are then why is IMO (International Maritime Organization) or somebody not acting!' (p. 63). See also *Report of Court 8072*, p. 26.
24. *Report of Court 8072*, p. 26, para. 16.7.
25. *Ibid.*, para. 18.1
26. M. Meek, W. R. Brown and K. G. Fulford, 'A Shipbuilder's View of Safety', paper given at the Marine Safety Conference, University of Glasgow, Department of Naval Architecture and Ocean Engineering, 1983, p. 21–2.
27. Cf. *ibid.*, p. 4.
28. See *ibid.*, p. 23.
29. *Ibid.*

30. *Ibid.*, p. 24.
31. *Ibid.*, p. 25.
32. *Ibid.* Cf. also C. J. Parker, *'The Herald of Free Enterprise'*, an article in *Seaways*, September 1987.
33. See C. J. Parker, *'The Herald of Free Enterprise* (Part 2)' *Seaways*, October 1987. Cf. also B. E. K. Gilmour, 'A Management System Towards Improving the Safety of Passenger Ro-Ro Ferries', also published in *Seaways*, May 1989.
34. See 'Ro-Ro Fear Brings Call for Design Changes', *Lloyd's List*, 22 January 1980. See also remarks of Mr R. Adams (Ocean Fleets Liverpool) on ro-ro dangers in the Ro-Ro 76 Proceedings Report, p. 122. See also the comments of Michael Grey in *Fairplay*, 19 March 1987, p. 3, and 12 March 1987, pp. 10–11; and 'The Nautical Institute on Passenger Ro-Ro Safety and Vulnerability', *Seaways*, May 1988.

3: Foundering

1. *The New York Times*, 11 January 1952, p. 3.
2. *Ibid.*, 12 January, p. 6.
3. *Ibid.*, 9 January, p. 1.
4. *Ibid.*, 12 January, p. 6.
5. See Ralph Barker, *Against the Sea*, London, Chatto & Windus, 1972, p. 109.
6. *The New York Times*, 15 January, p. 29.
7. *Ibid.*, 18 January, p. 1.
8. Barnaby, p. 147.
9. *Lloyd's List*, 25 September 1957.
10. Otto Mielke, *Disaster at Sea*, New York, Fleet Publishing Company, 1958, p. 248–9.
11. *Marine Transportation Safety Board Report*, Washington, D.C., 12 February 1983, p. 15.
12. *Ibid.*, p. 17
13. *Ibid.*, p.19
14. *Ibid.*
15. *Ibid.*
16. *Ibid.*, p. 17.
17. *Ibid.*, p. 2.
18. *Ibid.*, p. 5.
19. *Ibid.*
20. *Ibid.*, p. 8.
21. *Ibid.*, p. 7.
22. *Ibid.*, p. 30.
23. See Carl Cahill, 'Sunken Ship's Poor Condition Cited at Hearing', *Journal of Commerce*, New York, 22 March 1983, and 'ABS Inspection of *Marine Electric* Scrutinized', 24 March 1983, p. 1.

4: Fire

1. See Thomas Gallagher, *Fire at Sea*, London, Frederick Muller Ltd., 1959, pp. 242–3; also Gordon Thomas and Max Morgan-Witts, *The Strange Fate of the Morro Castle*, London, Collins, 1973, chapter 20. Quotation of dialogue is taken from these works.
2. See Thomas, pp. 22–3.
3. *Ibid.*, pp. 72–4.
4. Gallagher, p. 18.
5. *Ibid.*, p. 14–15.
6. *Ibid.*, p. 23.
7. American Maritime Cases, 1937, p. 535.
8. *Ibid.*, 1940, p. 380.
9. Gallagher, p. 42, and see also p. 44. Cf. also *The New York Times*, 18 September 1934, p. 16.

10. Gallagher, p. 147.
11. *Ibid.*, p. 198.
12. P. J. Abraham, *Last Hours on Dara*, London, Peter Davies, 1963, p. 2. The account of the official investigation given in this book has been used as the basis for much of the account given here. It has been checked against the report of court. All of the dialogue quoted here has been taken from that source.
13. *Ibid.*, p. 128; cf. also *Report of Court 8024*, pp. 9–10.
14. *Ibid.*, p. 6.
15. Abraham, pp. 142–5.
16. *Ibid.*, p. 131.
17. *Ibid.*, pp. 116–17.
18. Details of passenger comments and observations are taken from David Marchbanks, *The Painted Ship*, London, Secker & Warburg, 1964.
19. *Ibid.*, p. 18.
20. *Ibid.*, p. 22.
21. See Geoffrey Bond, *Lakonia*, London, Oldbourne Book Company, 1966, p. 30.
22. See *Lakonia Investigation*, Greek Court of inquiry, p. 14. The crew consisted of 205 Greeks, 171 Germans and the balance were of various nationalities (p. 17).
23. Marchbanks, p. 29. Captain Kempton, of the *Montcalm*, one of the rescue ships which arrived later, estimated that the reported position was some 27 miles north of the actual position.
24. *Ibid.*, p. 37. The Greek report claimed only about 100 passengers went below, p. 26.
25. *Ibid.*, p. 28.
26. *Ibid.*
27. Marchbanks, p. 56; see also *Lakonia Investigation*, p. 34.
28. Marchbanks, p. 74.
29. *Ibid.*, p. 77.
30. Captain Kempton, of the *Montcalm*, who played such a notable part in the rescue, told the author that his initial reaction on arrival at the scene was that everyone had left the burning liner by the time he arrived. He recalled the abandonment of the *Empire Windrush*, under similar circumstances, and somewhat naively (his term) assumed that what the crew of that vessel had accomplished with such ease, those on *Lakonia* should be able to duplicate.
31. Marchbanks, p. 116.
32. *Ibid.*, p. 96.
33. *Ibid.*, p. 99.
34. *Ibid.*
35. *The Times*, London, 21 March 1969.
36. Attempts by the British government to get the Greek court of inquiry to consider the fault of the owners were resented as interference, and rejected by the court (*The Times*, London, 12 July 1966).

5: Explosion

1. *Report of the Marine Board of Investigation in the Matter of the Explosion and Sinking of the M/S Berge Istra on 30 December 1975*, p. 15.
2. *Ibid.*, p. 16.
3. *Ibid.*, p. 21.
4. *Ibid.*, p. 22.
5. *Ibid.*, pp. 28–9.
6. *Report of the Marine Board of Investigation in the Matter of the Sinking of the Oil/Ore Carrier Berge Vanga with the Loss of All Hands on or about 29 October 1979*, p. 6.
7. *Ibid.*, p. 8. Attention is also directed to the excellent technical memorandum prepared by Mr Gordon Victory on 'Possible Causes of Explosion' at the end of the report, pp. 32–4.

8. *Ibid.*, p. 6.
9. *Ibid.*, p. 12, para. 29.
10. *Ibid.*, p. 24.
11. *Ibid.*, p. 26.
12. *Report of the Formal Investigation in the Matter of the Explosions, Breaking in Two and Sinking of the VLCC Mycene on a Voyage from Genoa, Italy to Ras Tanura on 3 April 1980*, pp. 8–9.
13. D. B. Foy and Captain Peter Nind, 'The *Mycene* Inquiry', *Seaways*, January 1981.
14. *Report of Formal Investigation*, p. 10.
15. *Ibid.*, p. 14.
16. *Ibid.*, pp. 42–6.
17. *Ibid.*, p. 35.
18. 'The Tragedy of *Betelgeuse*', *Safety at Sea International*, November 1980, p. 31.
19. *Report on the Disaster at Whiddy Island, Bantry Bay, Co. Cork on 8 January 1979: Report of the Tribunal of Inquiry*, Dublin, p. 233; also pp. 21, 23.
20. *Ibid.*, p. 278,
21. *Ibid.*, p. 284.
22. *Ibid.*, p. 193; cf. also p. 311.
23. *Ibid.*, pp. 38, 283.
24. *Ibid.*, p. 284.
25. *Ibid.*, pp. 288–90, 302.
26. *Ibid.*, p. 44.
27. *Ibid.*, p. 322.
28. *Ibid.*, p. 73.
29. *Ibid.*, p. 17.
30. *Ibid.*, but see pp. 72–3.
31. *Ibid.*, see chapter 8.
32. *Ibid.*, p. 99.

6: Collision

1. In two previous books, *Collisions and their Causes*, London, Fairplay Publications, 1983, and *Strandings and their Causes*, I have dealt in detail with such casualties. Those books were written primarily for a professional audience.
2. See Cockcroft, Norman, and Lameijer, J. N. F., *A Guide to the Collision Avoidance Rules*, London, Stanford Maritime, 1982, pp. 14–16; and Griffin, J. W., *The American Law of Collision*, New York, Arnold W. Knauth, 1961, pp. 5–10.
3. See Cahill, *Collisions*, chapter 1.
4. *Report of the Marine Board of Investigation (Republic of Liberia) in the Matter of the Collision Between* Venoil *and* Venpet *off the Coast of South Africa on 16 December 1977*, p. 11.
5. *Ibid.*, p. 4.
6. *Ibid.*, p. 10.
7. *Ibid.*, p. 17.
8. *Ibid.*, p. 20.
9. *Ibid.*
10. *Decision of the Commissioner of Maritime Affairs, R. L. and Report of the Marine Board of Investigation into the Collision of the Liberian Flag VLCC* Aegean Captain *(O. N. 5816) and the Greek Flag VLCC* Atlantic Empress *off Tobago, West Indies on 19 July 1979*, 24 July 1981, Monrovia, Liberia, p. ii.
11. The board concluded that the collision occurred at 1858 (p. 21) and that the vessel had been in rain for about twenty-five minutes before (p. 42).
12. *Report*, p. 26.
13. *Ibid.*, p. 30.
14. *Ibid.*, p. 31.
15. *Ibid.*, p. 32.

16. *Ibid.*, p. 29.
17. *Ibid.*, p. 54.
18. *Ibid.*, p. 59a–59b.
19. *Ibid.*, p. 66.
20. *Ibid.*, p. 80.

7: Stranding

1. The officers and crew were recruited by the Cosulich Company in Genoa, who acted as agents for Union Oil.
2. Crispin Gill et al. *The Wreck of the Torrey Canyon*, Newton Abbot, David & Charles, 1967, p. 87.
3. *Ibid.*, p. 122.
4. See van Poelgeest, pp. 42–4.
5. A detailed examination of this point is given in my *Strandings and their Causes*. p. 13.
6. The Liberian board of investigation questioned whether even this aid was used properly. The ship was equipped with two functioning radars but only the newer one, a three-centimetre Decca, was used. The other, a ten-centimetre Raytheon, was ignored. Ten-centimetre sets are actually better able to pick up targets at a distance.
7. *Decision of the Commissioner of Maritime Affairs, R. L. and Final and Interim Reports of the Formal Investigation by the Marine Board of Investigation in the Matter of the Loss by Grounding of the VLCC* Amoco Cadiz, p. 5.
8. David Fairhall & Philip Jordan, *The Wreck of the Amoco Cadiz*, New York, Stein & Day, 1980, p. 82.
9. See Fairhall for a detailed account of this, pp. 82–6
10. *Ibid.*, p. 86.
11. edited by Wilmot N. Hess, *The Amoco Cadiz Oilspill*, p. 85.
12. Valdez had been a tiny fishing village until it was levelled by the Good Friday earthquake of 1964. The earthquake registered 8.6 on the Richter scale, and its epicentre was only a few miles from Valdez. The storage tanks, therefore, had to be heavily reinforced.
13. *Proposed probable cause, findings and recommendations of the state of Alaska.* In the Matter of the Investigation of the Accident Involving the Grounding of the Tankership *Exxon Valdez* in Prince William Sound, Alaska, on March 24, 1989. *Before the national transportation safety board Washington, D.C.* (July 17, 1989) p. 11. This report displays some bias and should be treated with caution. Unfortunately the NTSB report was not yet available at the time of writing.
14. *Ibid.*, p. 11–12.
15. Most states in the US regulate the pilotage in their waters. They issue licences for their waters after examination by a state pilotage authority. The USCG also issues Federal Pilotage licences, which enable holders of such licences (US citizens) to pilot US ships, engaged in domestic trade, in state waters. This enables masters of US ships engaged in domestic trade holding federal licences to pilot their own ships. The state of Alaska, perhaps because it has only recently acquired statehood, has not elected to set up its own pilotage service. For an excellent treatment of this subject see the article 'Pilotage – State or Federal', by Captain James Drahos, in *Seaways*, February 1990.
16. Alaska Report to the NTSB, p. 27.
17. *Ibid.*, pp. 12–13.
18. Kagan testified at an interview before the NTSB 'that he used counter rudder to slow the swing of the ship and to steady up on a course of 235° or 245°.' *Ibid.*, p. 34.
19. *Ibid.*, p. 20.
20. *Seaways*, July 1985.
21. For analysis of this problem see N. M. Shashikumar, 'US Shipping Act of 1984', *Seaways*, 1988.

22. One of the most encouraging developments is the training of officers in a dual capacity whereby they can be used as all-purpose (deck or engine) officers as operational needs require. The Dutch have just graduated their first Maroff (marine officer) trainees (see Captain S. J. Cross, 'Nautical Training in the Netherlands: Present and Future', *Seaways*, January 1990). In the UK training of dual-purpose officers began in 1987 at the Plymouth Polytechnic, see J. E. Forshaw, 'Case for the Dual-Purpose Officer,' *Seaways*., December 1987. The French embarked upon a dual licensing programme in the 1960s at about the same time a similar programme was instituted at the US Merchant Marine Academy. The French programme was developed as a means of improving the career possibilities for officers. The US programme was sadly downgraded last year due to union restrictions and other pressures. Also see my *Strandings*, p. 102.
23. Cf. Captain A. Crombie's thoughtful article 'Marine Safety Procedures and Responsibilities', *Seaways*, July 1988.
24. Quoted in *Strandings*, p. 123.
25. To quote: 'In the long term I would like the classification societies to arrange a system under which owners are certified. The classification society shall not only survey the ship, they shall also certify that the owner is an operator of acceptable standards for the ship and the trade.' *Seaways*, July 1985. p. 17. I assume that this certification would be reflected in the insurance premiums paid by a certified owner.

Conclusion

1. Whether justice will be served by prosecution of vessel personnel is questionable. The lives of the seafarers involved have been devastated. The mistakes that led to the casualty seemed to stem more from operating pressures than negligence. J. M. Noble, who has much experience in casualty investigations, in a letter published in *Seaways*, *August 1989*, suggest that this prosecution could well hinder future investigations. He questions whether the prosecution is 'really in the best interests of public safety or is it yet another means of satisfying the public appetite for retribution?'
2. A notable exception is the example of American President Lines. After several of their vessels were involved in collisions with fishing vessels in the South China Sea they rerouted their ships to the east of Taiwan to avoid the heavy concentration of fishing vessels found in the waters to the west. Some 80 miles was thereby added to the route. In the summer of 1989 they held a series of three safety conferences for their masters and operating shore staff at a cost of almost $1 million to explore the effectiveness of current safety procedures and the possible need for others. The chairman of the board, Bruce Seaton, and the president of APL, Tim Rhein, both attended these conferences and impressed upon the masters that maintenance of schedule was never to take precedence over safety. Three APL masters were assigned as 'safety at sea masters,' to ride company vessels between Far Eastern ports to advise and consult with vessel masters in implementing bridge team procedures and other APL safety procedures.
3. I am ignoring those owners who view the loss of a ship as a potentially profitable enterprise, such as in the case of the VLCC *Salem* which was scuttled off the west coast of Africa several years ago. Also excluded from consideration here are those who while not actively pursuing a policy of wrecking ships for profit, operate their ships at such a low standard that they are likely to achieve a similiar result in time. The wreck of the *Argo Merchant* on Georges Bank in 1976 is one of the better known casualties of this type.
4. Cf. van Poelgeest, pp. 53, 54. For an industry view of such regulation see, 'Fleet Management Technology Research and Development Program', a feasibility study conducted in 1981 by the Office of Research and Development of the US Maritime Administration into the desirability of establishing a shipping management centre.

The question was asked by shipping executives: '"What are the major problem areas faced in the management of your company?" and almost every company ranked government regulation and lack of clear national maritime policy as one of their three major problems. . . . Government regulation was considered the single most important problem facing the US ship operator, ranking even higher than the high cost of ships; competition; labor costs; fuel quality and fuel price. . . .' (p. 4).

5. An interesting proposal that could go far towards rectifying the endemic safety problems of the shipping industry was put forth by Captain L. J. Kovats in an article entitled 'Shipping Co-operatives', in the October 1987 issue of *Seaways*.

6. Marine Board and National Research Council, Commission on Engineering and Technical Systems, Committee on Effective Manning's report, Washington, D.C., National Academy Press, 1984; R. I. S. Nijjer, *Study Tour of Japanese Maritime Establishments*, Royal Melbourne Institute of Technology, 1985; Keiji Wada, *The Progress and Future Prospect of Modernization of the Manning System in Japan*, Tokyo, JAMRI Report, Japan Maritime Institute, (published in the *Journal of Maritime Transport*, June 1985; translation by Maritime Administration, American Embassy, Tokyo).

Appendices

1. See R. A. Cahill, *Collisions and their Causes*, pp. 21, 91, 124.
2. See R. S. Doganis and B. N. Metaxis, *The Impact of Flags of Convenience*, Polytechnic of Central London, 1976, p. 10.
3. *Ibid.*, p. 109. The authors claim that they obtained evidence of this from confidential sources from within one of the classification societies. Cf. also Sub-Standard Tankers , p. 55.
4. W. A. Cleary, (in charge of the Ship Characteristics Branch, Office of Merchant Marine Safety, USCG), 'Subdivision, Stability, Liability', *Marine Technology*, July 1982, p. 228.
5. See my *Strandings*, pp. 79–86.
6. *Effective Manning of the US Merchant Fleet*, pp. 38–40.
7. In the autumn of 1981 the author chaired a ship management symposium at the ISOS Conference sponsored by the Maritime Association of the Port of New York. The managing director of Texaco Norway presented a paper on the results of their experience with decentralized ship management aboard their vessels. A senior officer of the parent company in New York afterwards commented that he had initially been one of those opposed to the scheme, but he was now [then] one of its most firm supporters. Cf. also *Effective Manning*, p. 49.
8. *Ibid.*, p. 41.

Bibliography

Books

Abraham, P. J., *Last Hours on Dara*, London, Peter Davies, 1963.

Anderson, Roy, *White Star*, Prescot, Lancashire, T. Stephenson & Sons, 1964.

Ballard, Robert D., *The Discovery of the* Titanic, Toronto, Madison Press Books, 1987.

Barker, Ralph, *Against the Sea*, London, Chatto & Windus, 1972.

Barnaby, K. C. *Some Ship Disasters and their Causes*, London, Hutchinson, 1968.

Bond, Geoffrey, *Lakonia*, London, Oldbourne Book Company, 1966.

Cahill, Richard A., *Strandings and their Causes*, London, Fairplay Publications, 1985; and *Collisions and their Causes*, London, Fairplay Publications, 1983.

Cockcroft, Norman and Lameijer, J. N. F., *A Guide to the Collision Avoidance Rules*, third edition, London, Stanford Maritime, 1982.

Conrad, Joseph, *Some Aspects of the Admirable Inquiry into the Loss of the* Titanic, London, privately printed, 1919; and *Some Reflections Seamanlike and Otherwise on the Loss of the* Titanic, published by *The English Review II*, 1912.

Davie, Michael, *The* Titanic: *The Full Story of a Tragedy*, London, The Bodley Head, 1986.

Doganis, R. S. and Metaxis, B. N., *The Impact of Flags of Convenience*, London, a special study, sponsored by the Social Science Research Council, carried out at the Polytechnic of Central London, 1976.

Eaton, John P. and Haas, Charles A., Titanic: *Destination Disaster – the Legends and the Reality*, Wellingborough, Northamptonshire, Patrick Stevens, 1987.

Fairhall, David and Jordan, Philip, *The Wreck of the* Amoco Cadiz, New York, Stein & Day, 1980.

Gallagher, Thomas, *Fire at Sea*, London, Frederick Muller Ltd., 1959.

Gill, Crispin et al, *The Wreck of the* Torrey Canyon, Newton Abbot, David & Charles, 1967.

Griffin, J. W., *The American Law of Collision*, New York, Arnold W. Knauth, 1961.

Hess, Wilmot N., ed., *The* Amoco Cadiz *Oilspill*, Washington, D.C., a preliminary scientific report, US Oceanic Atmospheric Administration.

Hodgson, Godfrey, *Lloyd's of London*, Penguin, Harmondsworth, 1986.

Holubowicz, R. P., ed., *Progress in Marine Cargo Handling*, Cornell Maritime Press, 1963.

Lane, Tony, *Grey Dawn Breaking*, Manchester, Manchester University Press, 1986.

Lightoller, Charles Herbert, Titanic *and Other Ships*, London, Ivor Nicholson & Watson, 1935.

Lord, Walter, *A Night to Remember*, Harmondsworth, Penguin, 1976.

Marchbanks, David, *The Painted Ship*, London, Secker & Warburg, 1964.

Marcus, Geoffrey, *The Maiden Voyage*, London, George Allen and Unwin, 1969.

Mielke, Otto, *Disaster at Sea*, New York, Fleet Publishing Company, 1958.

Ocean Liners of the Past: The White Star Triple Screw Liners Olympic *and* Titanic, a facsimile of the *Shipbuilder's* 1911 midsummer edition published by Patrick Stevens, London, 1970.

Oldham, Wilton J., *The Ismay Line*, Liverpool, published by *The Journal of Commerce*, 1961.

Padfield, Peter, *The* Titanic *and the Californian*, London, Hodder and Stoughton, 1965.

Rushbrook, Frank, *Fire Aboard*, The Technical Press Ltd., 1961.

Sauerbier, C. L., *Marine Cargo Operations*, New York, Chapman and Hall, 1964.

Thomas, Gordon and Morgan-Witts, Max, *The Strange Fate of the* Morro Castle, London, Collins, 1973.

Wade, Wyn Craig, *The* Titanic, *End of a Dream*, London, George Weidenfeld and Nicolson, 1986.

Documents

US Congress, Senate, *Hearings of a Subcommittee of the Senate Commerce Committee, pursuant to Sen. Res. 283, to Investigate the Causes leading to the Wreck of the White Star Liner* Titanic, Washington, D.C., US Government Printing Office, 1912, 62nd Cong., 2nd sess., Senate document 463 (#6179).

Papers

'A Shipbuilder's View of Safety', M. Meek, W. R. Brown and K. G. Fulford, paper given at the Marine Safety Conference, University of Glasgow, Department of Naval Architecture and Ocean Engineering, 1983.

Effective Manning of the US Merchant Fleet, Committee on Effective Manning, Marine Board, Commission on Engineering and Technical Systems, National Research Council, Washington, D.C., National Academy Press, 1984.

'Fleet Management Technology Research and Development Program', prepared by Marine Management Systems, Inc., for the Office of Research and Development of the US Maritime Administration, January 1982.

Report of the Marine and Offshore Safety Conference 1983, Amsterdam, Folserier Science Publishers, 1984. Edited by P. A. Friere, R. C. McGregor & I. E. Winkle.

Oil Transportation by Tankers: An Analysis of Marine Pollution and Safety Measures. Published by the Congress of the United States Office of Technology Assessment, July 1975.

Report of the Ro-Ro 76 Proceedings International Conference on Marine Transport Using Roll-on, Roll-off Methods, London, 1976.

R. I. S. Nijjer, *Study Tour of Japanese Maritime Establishments*, Royal Melbourne Institute of Technology, 1985.

W. A. Cleary, 'Subdivision, Stability, Liability', *Marine Technology*, July 1982.

F. M. van Poelgeest, 'Sub-Standard Tankers', Rotterdam, Netherlands Maritime Institute, 1978.

J. R. Spouge, 'The Technical Investigation of the Sinking of the Ro-Ro Ferry *European Gateway*'. Royal Institute of Naval Architects, 17 April 1985, London.

Keiji Wada, *The Progress and Future Prospect of Modernization of the Manning System in Japan*, Tokyo, JAMRI Report, Japan Maritime Institute. Published in the *Journal of Maritime Transport*, June 1985. Translation by Maritime Administration, American Embassy, Tokyo.

Articles

R. A. Cahill, 'The Use of VHF Radio to Reduce Uncertainty in Marine Encounters', published in *The Journal of Navigation*, the Royal Institute of Navigation, May 1979.

Brian Elliot, 'Where Exactly Did *Titanic* Sink?', *Safety at Sea International*, June 1980

Casualty Reports

Wreck Commissioner's Court. Formal Investigation into the Loss of the SS Titanic, Evidence, Appendixes, and Index, London, HMSO, 1912. Referred to as *British Inquiry*.
Reports of Court, London, HMSO.
Report of the Ministry of Transport Inquiry into the Loss of the Motorship Princess Victoria *and Findings of the Court*, Liverpool, Charles Birchall & Sons Ltd., 1953.
Report on the Disaster at Whiddy Island. Bantry Bay, Co. Cork on 8 January 1979: Report of the Tribunal of Inquiry, Dublin.
Lakonia Investigation, Greek Court of Inquiry.
Liberian Reports.
Marine Transportation Safety Board Reports, Washington, D.C.
American Maritime Cases.
Marine Accident Report, *Foundering loss of the Ro-Ro Passenger Ship* Zenobia *at the Roads of Larnaca, Cyprus on 7 June 1980.*
Proposed Probable Cause, Findings and Recommendations of the State of Alaska In the Matter of the Investigation of the Accident Involving the Grounding of the Tankership Exxon Valdez in Prince William Sound, Alaska, on March 24, 1989, before the National Transportation Board, Washington D.C., July 17, 1989.

Periodicals

Safety at Sea International, London.
Fairplay International, London.
Seaways, the journal of the Nautical Institute, London.
The Journal of Navigation, the Royal Institute of Navigation, London.

Newspapers

Lloyd's List, London.
The Journal of Commerce, New York.
The New York Times, New York.
The Times, London.

Index

Index